Law and Language in the European Union

Europa Law Publishing, Groningen 2005

Law and Language in the European Union

The Paradox of a Babel "United in Diversity"

Richard L. Creech

Europa Law Publishing is a publishing company
specializing in European Union Law and public
international law.
For further information please contact Europa Law
Publishing via email: info@europalawpublishing.com
or visit our website at: www.europalawpublishing.com.

Typeset in Scala and Scala Sans, Graphic design by
G2K Designers, Groningen/Amsterdam

NUR 828; ISBN 90-76871-43-4

British Library Cataloguing-in-Publication Data
A catalogue record for this book is available from the
British Library

Acknowledgement

I would like to thank Deirdre Curtin and Ronald van Ooik of the Faculty of Law at the University of Utrecht, who served as my advisers for the masters thesis upon which this book was based, and Sacha Prechal and Jacqueline Lensink, who took an interest in this book and provided the catalyst for its publication. I would also like to express my fond appreciation for Rex A. Sprouse, who has encouraged my study of the interaction of legal and linguistic systems ever since I was an undergraduate at Harvard University. My parents Lawrence and Elizabeth Creech and my friend Billy have provided, in countless ways, love and support that have enabled me to research and write this book, and to them I am eternally grateful. Finally, I dedicate this book to all people who speak a European language, wherever in the world they may find themselves to be.

Richard L. Creech
Washington, DC
December 2004

Contents

Introduction

Introduction

On 29 October 2004 the heads of state or government of the twenty-five Member States of the European Union gathered in Rome to sign a Constitution for Europe which proclaimed an organization whose motto is "united in diversity."[1] In no way is the EU more diverse than in terms of language. The twenty-five Member States have twenty-two national or official languages among them, and all of these have some sort of official status within the EU's internal institutional structure.[2] In addition, there are well over one hundred regional or minority languages spoken in various parts of the EU.[3] The EU's linguistic profile has grown considerably more complex as a result of the other major EU development of 2004: the accession on 1 May of ten new Member States, which extended the EU's territory deep into the linguistically complicated topography of eastern Europe. Many of these new Member States have had long histories of acrimonious conflict between warring ethno-linguistic groups. This discord has, however, been by and largely publicly ignored by EU officials in their excitement to celebrate their new Union.

The entry of the ten new Member States was the result of a treaty which was signed in Athens in April 2003.[4] A declaration issued by the European Council on this occasion made no mention of language differences in the EU.[5] While the statement understandably highlighted themes of unity and commonality (*e.g.*, "This Union represents our common determination to put an end to centuries of conflict and to transcend former divisions on our continent"), the lack of any mention of language differences was nevertheless striking. The statement stressed that the EU was "committed to furthering respect for human dignity, liberty and human rights" and was "devoted to the practice of tolerance, justice

1 Const. for Eur. Art. I-8.

2 Advocate General Cosmas explained that the difference between these two terms is that a "national language" is "the language spoken in the whole of the territory of a Member State" and an "official language" is "the language recognised as such by a law, whether it be at the same time a national language or is spoken in part of the territory of a Member State." Opinion of Advocate General Cosmas in Case C-385/96, *Goerres*, 1998 ECR I-4431, 4456 n. 42. There are more Member States than there are national or official languages because some languages (*e.g.*, Dutch, English, French) are used in more than one country.

3 Report of the European Parliament of 14 July 2003 with Recommendations to the Commission on European Regional and Lesser Used Languages – the Languages of Minorities in the EU – in the Context of Enlargement and Cultural Diversity (2003/2057(INI)).

4 Treaty Concerning the Accession of the Czech Republic, the Republic of Estonia, the Republic of Cyprus, the Republic of Latvia, the Republic of Lithuania, the Republic of Hungary, the Republic of Malta, the Republic of Poland, the Republic of Slovenia and the Slovak Republic to the European Union.

5 European Council Declaration of 16 Apr. 2003, available on-line at http://www.eu2003.gr/en/articles/2003/4/16/2531.

and solidarity." The declaration went on to specify several aspects of diversity and types of discrimination that were anathema within the EU: "We will continue to uphold and defend fundamental human rights ... including the fight against all types of discrimination on the basis of gender, race, ethnic origin, religion or convictions, disability, age or sexual orientation." The non-inclusion of language in this list appears to evince a desire, whether consciously held or not, to minimize a form of division that has presented serious difficulties for the EU.[6]

Less than a year and a half earlier, the European Council had announced at its summit outside Brussels that the Union had come to a "crossroads."[7] This was true in multiple senses. First, the geographic scope of the EU was expanding and Europe was closer to becoming "one big family." Second, there was a need to "increase the democratic legitimacy and transparency" of the EU in light of its broad mandate over policy matters that extend beyond economics into such fields as social policy, employment, asylum and immigration, police and justice matters, and foreign and security policy. The EU institutions, the Laeken Declaration said, "must be brought closer to its citizens" and subject to "better democratic scrutiny." The Laeken Declaration, issued near the officially bilingual capital of a problematically multilingual country, made subtle reference to the polyglot nature of the Union, but made no mention of the problems raised by linguistic diversity, let alone possible solutions to them. In expounding on the centrality of democratic values in the Union, the declaration stated that the multilingual nature of the Union must be borne in mind: "Europe [is] the continent of humane values, the Magna Carta, the Bill of Rights, the French Revolution and the fall of the Berlin Wall; the continent of liberty, solidarity and above all diversity, meaning respect for others' languages, cultures and traditions."[8] Moreover, subscribing to such sentiments was identified as a *sine qua non* for

---

6 Article II-81(1) of the Constitution for Europe includes "language" among the grounds on which discrimination shall be prohibited. Speeches were also given in Athens by the President of the European Council (Greek Prime Minister Costas), the President of the European Commission (Romano Prodi), and the President of the European Parliament (Pat Cox), but none of them mentioned language issues either. The texts of these addresses are available, respectively, at the following web sites: http://www.eu2003.gr/en/articles/2003/4/16/2534, http://europa.eu.int/comm/commissioners/prodi/speeches/treaty_en.htm, and http://www.europarl.eu.int/president/speeches/en/sp0052.htm. The speech by Prime Minister Costas will be discussed again at the beginning of Chapter I.

7 European Council Declaration of 15 Dec. 2001, available on-line at http://europa.eu.int/futurum/documents/offtext/doc151201_en.htm.

8 This sentence provides merely one example of the EU's Orwellian use of language about language. "Diversity" has been defined by the declaration as meaning "respect" for differences, as opposed to simply referring to the existence of differences. Diversity, therefore, under the declaration's usage of the term, necessarily entails respect, as opposed to simply describing a state of non-uniformity that may either be respected or not.

membership in the EU: "The European Union's one boundary is democracy and human rights. The Union is open only to countries which uphold basic values such as free elections, respect for minorities and respect for the rule of law."[9]

Absent from the declaration was any glimmer of recognition that the multilingual nature of the EU may actually be an obstacle to increased democratization. The use of a particular language is very much a key factor, if not the crucial one, in constituting the identity of a people, and a "democratic" system, as the word itself indicates, is one that is connected to, and whose legitimacy stems, from that people – the *demos*.[10] Dieter Grimm has written that the lack of a common language in Europe "is the biggest obstacle to Europeanisation of the political substructure," as language is the basis upon which "the functioning of a democratic system and the performance of a parliament depends."[11] Clearly, however, multilingualism is not an automatic block to democratic formation. Within the EU itself, there are, in addition to Belgium, several states that have managed, some more easily than others, to find ways to make multilingualism and democracy co-exist.[12] But multilingualism does present a challenge, and this challenge is compounded in the EU setting, which is obviously more linguistically varied than any single Member State and where the fundamental democratic credentials of the organization have long been open to attack.[13]

This book, which is based on a thesis that I submitted in fulfillment of the degree requirements for an LLM in International and European Law at the University of Utrecht in 2002, considers the Union's approach to language differences in light of the two major transformations which it has undergone: the EU's territorial growth, with the concomitant rise in the level of its linguistic and cultural diversity (the so-called "widening" of the EU), and its evolution from something that was little more than an engine of economic integration into an organization that embodies a serious commitment to human rights principles (the so-called "deepening"). Chapter I begins with an examination of the linguistic arrangements of the EU organs themselves, where different languages are accorded different status. Particular attention is paid to the language regime in the EU's trademark office, which survived a significant legal challenge in

---

9 The Constitution for Europe restricts membership to "European states." Const. for Eur. Art. I-1(2).

10 As Weiler has argued, groups of peoples may form a larger, overarching group in a system of "coexisting multiple demoi." J.H.H. Weiler, "Bread and Circus: The State of the European Union," 4 *Colum. J. Eur. L.* (1998), 223, 244. The EU has attempted to create a pan-Union sense of people-hood by, for example, creating the concept of EU citizenship. EC Treaty Art. 17; Const. for Eur. Art. I-10.

11 Dieter Grimm, "Does Europe Need a Constitution?" 1 *Eur. L. J.* 282 (1995), 295.

12 For an interesting discussion of possible societal responses to linguistic diversity ranging from assimilation to separation to integration, and a particular discussion of the language situation in Canada, *see* Ruth Sullivan, "The Challenges of Multilingual, Multijural Legislation," 29 *Brooklyn J. of Int'l Law* 3 (2004), 986.

13 The new Constitution was designed in large part to allay these concerns.

2003.[14] Chapter II considers the EU's professed commitment to "linguistic diversity" and analyzes various programs it has adopted to foster it, such as the Lingua educational program and its proclamation of 2001 as the European Year of Languages. This is considered against the backdrop of a dispute between the European Parliament and the Council over the legal basis of the Union's authority in this area, a dispute which is of significance because it demonstrates the clash of interests in matters of language policy between the citizens of Europe (who are directly represented in the Parliament) and the Member States themselves (who are represented in the Council).[15]

Chapters III and IV examine how language regulation within the Member States has been affected by the economic provisions of the EC Treaty.[16] The EC Treaty does not, with the narrow exception of a provision allowing EU citizens to write to the EU institutions in one of the Treaty languages (and to receive an answer in that language)[17] recognize any linguistic right of its citizens, and it is silent on the power of the Member States in this field. As a result, the Member States have in principle been fairly free to regulate language use within their borders, and the European Court of Justice has not considered the right of a citizen to use a particular language, nor the right of a state to regulate language use, in any comprehensive manner. The ECJ has, however, scrutinized state language policies when they raise issues concerning the economic rights protected by the EC Treaty. Chapter III looks at cases concerning language and the free movement of goods, and Chapter IV considers the effect of linguistic rules on the free movement of people and argues that the more recent cases have reflected a growing awareness of human rights concerns. Chapter V will formally analyze the growing body of international human rights law in the field of language rights. Apart from the human rights rhetoric evinced in the declarations in Laeken and Athens, a commitment to human rights is legally enshrined in Article 6 of the EU Treaty and is at the core of the new Constitution for Europe.[18] Several recent human rights instruments from such international organizations as the Council of Europe – whose Convention for the Protection of Human Rights and Fundamental Freedoms is explicitly embraced in both the EU Treaty and the new Constitution[19] – have fleshed out the nature and content of linguistic rights, and the import of such documents for the EU is considered. In particular, I will close by suggesting the adoption of a linguistic system for

---

[14] Case C-361/01, *Estate of Christina Kik v. Office for Harmonisation in the Internal Market*, 2003 ECR I-8283, *dismissing appeal from* Case T-120/99, *Kik v. Office for Harmonisation in the Internal Market*, 2001 ECR II-2235.

[15] Case C-42/97, *Parliament v. Council*, 1999 ECR I-869.

[16] That is, the Treaty establishing the European Community (as amended by the Treaty of Amsterdam).

[17] EC Treaty Art. 21; Const. for Eur. Arts. I-10(2)(d) and II-101(4).

[18] A Charter of Fundamental Rights forms Part II of the Constitution.

[19] Treaty on European Union Art. 6(2); Const. for Eur. Art. I-9.

use within the EU that balances economic feasibility with contemporary human rights norms.

CHAPTER I

Language Regulation in EU Institutions and Bodies

On 1 May 2004, ten new Member States officially joined the European Union,[1] bringing the total number of Member States to twenty-five. A year earlier, EU leaders had gathered in Athens to celebrate the signing of the treaty that would pave the way for the accession of these new states.[2] On this occasion Greek Prime Minister Costas Simitis, who was also at the time President of the European Council, connected the increasingly multinational character of the EU to the cosmopolitanism of his capital's illustrious past:

> Here, in this place, the Agora of Athens, two and a half thousand years ago, people from different races and countries, people with different convictions, came into contact. They met one another with a feeling that they were in one of the centres of the civilised world. Here we can realise that there is no end to history. Life will continue after today. It is up to us whether this continuation will be a history of peace, creation, cooperation and solidarity. This is what we want from the European Union.[3]

Mr. Simitis drew attention to the racial and national diversity of the classical era, but made no mention of the interaction of different language groups. While the Greeks of Antiquity have unquestionably endowed western civilization with innumerable gifts,[4] tolerance of linguistic differences is not one of them. To the Greeks of Antiquity, non-Greek-speaking peoples uttered strange noises mock-

---

1 The European Union was established by the Treaty on European Union (the Treaty of Maastricht) in 1992 to be an umbrella entity for the European Community and two other "pillars" concerning non-economic matters. The European Community was itself previously known as the European Economic Community. The new Constitution for Europe which was signed on 29 October 2004 (and which will not go into effect unless and until it is ratified in each of the Member States pursuant to their respective domestic legal procedures) proclaims a new European Union which is to be the successor of both the European Community as well as the original European Union established by the Treaty of Maastricht. *See* Const. for Eur. Art. IV-438. Because of all this restructuring, it is often nearly impossible to write an accurate sentence concerning these organizations over a long period of time without awkward qualifications that confusingly call attention to these institutional changes. Accordingly, for the sake of simplicity, when these changes are not immediately relevant, I will use the terms "European Union" and "EU" to refer not only to the EU in its strict legal sense (*i.e.*, from its inception under the Treaty of Maastricht until its future replacement by a new EU pursuant to the Constitution for Europe), but also to the entire range of EEC-EC-EU-New-EU entities. I will, however, use the terms "EC" and "Community" when referring strictly to that organization (and, where appropriate, to its EEC predecessor).

2 Treaty Concerning the Accession of the Czech Republic, the Republic of Estonia, the Republic of Cyprus, the Republic of Latvia, the Republic of Lithuania, the Republic of Hungary, the Republic of Malta, the Republic of Poland, the Republic of Slovenia and the Slovak Republic to the European Union.

3 Text of this speech is available on the web at http://www.eu2003.gr/en/articles/2003/4/16/2534.

4 For an excellent and pleasantly readable recent discussion of this legacy, *see* Thomas Cahill, *Sailing the Wine-Dark Sea: Why the Greeks Matter* (2003).

ingly described as "bar-bar," and were accordingly derided as "barbarians."[5] The connection between language and group identity is thus firmly rooted in the European consciousness, as indeed it is elsewhere. Language has been viewed as a crucial, if not the most crucial, marker of group identity, be it as a tribe, village, country, or modern state.[6] Peoples who speak a different language from one's own have been regarded as something separate and apart, as the proverbial "Other." As one renowned language scholar has put it, languages demarcate "zones of silence to other men and razor-edges of division."[7]

With the Christianization of Europe language differences were attributed to the biblical story of the Tower of Babel, which explained that an angry God confounded the speech of "one people with a single language" who had dared to build a structure up into the heavens.[8] The audacious tower-builders were dispersed over the entire earth, and became different peoples (now multiple) who babbled to one another in mutually unintelligible tongues. Martin Luther, himself the instigator of significant discord, saw linguistic differences as the root cause of European conflict. In explaining the import of the story of the Tower of Babel, he wrote:

> The Frenchman has only hatred and scorn for the German, the Italians have only hatred and scorn for all others. So we can see that this division of languages has led to divisions of habits, ways of thought and priorities that have put barriers between the very essence of peoples; it can justly be called the source of all misfortunes.[9]

Four centuries after Luther penned these words, in the aftermath of two wars that brought more misfortunes to the continent than the reformist theologian could have possibly imagined, Europeans began to search for ways to overcome the destructive potential of their differences, linguistic and otherwise. The European Economic Community ("EEC") Treaty of 1957, like the European Coal and Steel Community ("ECSC") Treaty of 1951 and the Atomic Energy Community ("Euratom") Treaty of 1957,[10] aimed to link European economies together,

---

5 *Greek Civilization: An Introduction* (Brian A. Sparkes ed., 1998), 65.

6 *See, e.g.*, Robert Dunbar, "Minority Language Rights in International Law," 50 *International & Comp. L. Q.* 90, 93; Andrée Tabouret-Keller, "De L'Identité Européenne Comme Carrefour et Comme Réseau : La Place des Langues, in *Les Langues Dans L'Europe de Demain* (F. Carton & J.M. Odéric Delefosse eds., 1994) 129, 131.

7 George Steiner, *After Babel: Aspects of Language & Translation* (3d. ed. 1998), 58.

8 Genesis 11:6 (The New English Version).

9 Quoted in John Hale, "The Renaissance Idea of Europe," in *European Identity and the Search for Legitimacy* (Soledad García ed., 1993), 55.

10 These three communities are often collectively referred to in the singular as "the Community," as they share an institutional and legal framework by virtue of the Treaty of Merger of 1965 and Treaty on European Union of 1992. I will follow this usage.

especially those of France and Germany (whose antagonism was particularly noted by Luther) to such an extent that war would no longer be a conceivable policy option.[11]

A. The Legal Foundation of the EU's Language Regime

The EEC immediately needed to face the fact of language differences among its members. In addition to France and Germany, four other states – Italy, Belgium, Luxembourg and the Netherlands – became charter members of the EEC, and these six states had four official languages among them – French, German, Italian and Dutch. The EEC Treaty (or EC Treaty, as it will subsequently be called to reflect the name change effected by the Treaty on European Union) was drawn up in a single original in each of these languages. Article 248 of the Treaty (now, after the renumbering occasioned by the Treaty of Amsterdam, Article 314)[12] stated that all four texts were to be "equally authentic."[13] Article 217 (now Article 290) provided that the Council, acting unanimously, was to determine "[t]he rules governing the languages of the institutions of the Community," with the exception of the Court of Justice, which was to issue its own linguistic rules.[14]

Highlighting the importance of having an established linguistic regime, the Council addressed this issue in its very first legislative act, in the appropriately named Regulation No. 1 of 15 April 1958.[15] Regulation No. 1 followed the example of the EC Treaty in its equal treatment of the four languages, providing in Article 1 that "[t]he official languages and the working languages

---

[11] Paul Craig and Gráinne de Búrca, *EU Law: Text, Cases and Materials* (2d ed. 1998), 7-9.

[12] A discussion of the EC's treaty provisions invariably suffers from numerological complication owing to the Treaty of Amsterdam. Unfortunately, this confusion has become more pronounced, as the new Constitution for Europe has introduced yet another numbering system for the treaty's substantive provisions. Article 314 has been re-cast (and modified to reflect later linguistic additions) as Article IV-448 of the Constitution.

[13] The original drafting language was generally French, and only the French and German versions of the Treaty actually existed in final form at the time it was signed. *See*, Geert van Calster, "The EU's Tower of Babel – The Interpretation by the European Court of Justice of Equally Authentic Texts Drafted in more than one Official Language," 17 *Yearbook of European Law* (1997), 363, 369. Article 33 of the Vienna Convention on the Law of Treaties, which was opened for signature in 1969, would later provide that "[w]hen a treaty has been authenticated in two or more languages, the text is equally authoritative in each language, unless the treaty provides or the parties agree that, in case of divergence, a particular text shall prevail."

[14] Const. for Eur. Art. III-433. The Council may amend the ECJ's rules pursuant to Article 245 of the EU Treaty. (Const. for Eur. Art. III-381).

[15] [1958] O.J. 017/385; English Special Edition (I) p. 59.

of the institutions of the Community shall be Dutch, French, German and Italian." More specifically, it indicated that "regulations and other documents of general application" were to be drafted in each language (Art. 4) and that the Official Journal was to be published in each one. (Art. 5). Persons subject to the jurisdiction of a Member State were entitled to choose which of the official and working languages they wished to use in corresponding with Community institutions. (Art. 2).[16] A Member State was likewise entitled to choose any of these languages when it sent documents to a Community institution, and it was entitled to a reply in that language. (Art. 2). If the Community initiated contact, it was to use the language of the Member State (Art. 3), or, if the state had more than one, the language governed by the general rules of the state's law. (Art. 8). Finally, and significantly, Article 6 provided that "[t]he institutions of the Community may stipulate in their rules of procedure which of the languages are to be used in specific cases."[17]

The regulation is silent as to the reason four languages were to be used in the new Community. However, one commentator has explained that there were two motivations:

> There was a requirement for the political equality of the states, and moreover ... for the texts that were to receive direct application in each of the Member States, it was imperative that the governments responsible for their application and the persons to whom they were to be applied could read them in their native language.[18]

A principle of general linguistic equality is not explicit in Regulation No. 1, although one might see it as an implicit component of the regulation, as the author of the preceding comment apparently did. The institutions of the EU have also traditionally taken such a view. The Council, in 2001, stated in reply to a question from the Parliament: "The Council remains attached to

---

16 The right to use any of the Treaty languages in corresponding with Community institutions and certain specified bodies obtained treaty status with the Treaty of Amsterdam, and is now to be found in Article 21 of the EC Treaty and, in somewhat modified form, in the Constitution for Europe, Arts. I-10(2)(d) and II-101(4).

17 Rather oddly, Article 7 confers the same power upon the Court of Justice. This article would seem redundant in light of the general reference to Community institutions in Article 6 (the Court is defined as an "institution" of the Community in Article 7 of the EC Treaty). The Council likely inserted a separate provision for the ECJ because Article 217 of the EC Treaty (the only stated legal basis for the regulation) did not apply to the ECJ. The Council has the power under Article 188 of the Treaty (now Art. 245) to approve the ECJ's procedural rules, however, and this may have been a form of pre-approval of whatever language rules the ECJ chose to devise.

18 Jean-Pierre Puissochet, *L'Élargissement des Communautés Européennes : Présentation et Commentaire du Traité et des Actes Relatifs à L'Adhésion du Royaume-Uni, du Danemark et de L'Irlande* (1974), 58 (trans. by R.L. Creech).

the fundamental principle of equality of the official languages of the EU as enshrined in Council Regulation No. 1."[19] The Commission's Translation Service has explained that it "exists to meet a basic requirement of democracy itself, identified by the founding fathers of Europe as early as 1958. All the official languages, they said, were equal and must be given equal equipment."[20]

It should be stressed, however, that despite the common usage of the term, neither the EU nor the EC, as such, has any "official" languages.[21] Regulation No. 1 does not apply to the EU or EC generally, but only to the more limited set of "institutions" of the Community, a distinction whose significance became clear in the watershed *Kik* case,[22] which will be discussed below. Because *Kik* makes it clear that Regulation No. 1 does not in fact represent a legally-binding norm of linguistic equality, I submit that one should be circumspect about the terminology used to describe the languages therein, and will accordingly use the term "Regulation language" in this book when referring to their status in the larger EU context.

B. Linguistic Expansion

The ultimate outcome of the *Kik* case notwithstanding, a principle of formal linguistic equality of the official and national languages of the Member States governed, with some exceptions, the Community's approach to the languages of Member States which joined the original members of the Community in the enlargements which followed its founding.

1. First Enlargement

The United Kingdom, Ireland and Denmark joined the EC in the first enlargement in 1973, and English and Danish were added as Treaty languages and to Regulation No. 1. The addition of Danish did not significantly affect the EC's linguistic system (and it has been rumored that Copenhagen lobbied against its inclusion as part of a plan to limit the EU's languages to English and French)[23] but the advent of English, which was the language not only of the

---

19 Reply to Written Question E4099/00, [2001] C23E/68.

20 European Commission, "The Translation Service of the European Commission" (2001).

21 *See, e.g.*, the Commission's reference to "the EU's official languages" on the EU's website, http://europa.eu.int/comm/dgs/translation/index_en.htm; the Council's mention of the "eleven official working languages of the Community" in its Reply to Written Question E-0063/02.

22 Case C-361/01, *Estate of Christina Kik v. Office for Harmonisation in the Internal Market*, 2003 ECR I-8283, *dismissing appeal from* Case T-120/99, *Kik v. Office for Harmonisation in the Internal Market*, 2001 ECR II-2235.

23 Peter Hans Nelde, "Contact or Conflict? Observations on the Dynamics and Vitality of European Languages," in *Language Conflict and Language Planning* (E. Jahr ed., 1993), 165, 166.

UK and Ireland but also of the United States – the western world's political, military, and economic "superpower" – was to have profound consequences.

Irish, which has constitutional status as the "national language" and "first official language" of the Republic of Ireland,[24] obtained a unique and murky position in the EC's language framework, becoming a Treaty language but not a Regulation language. Under this quasi-official status, the EC Treaty and various other Treaties, along with some resolutions and decisions of the Council, exist in authentic Irish versions. Irish may be used in the European Parliament, although special arrangements must be made, and in theory it may be used as the language of a case in the Court of Justice, although it appears that it never has been.[25] By virtue of being a Treaty language, Irish is one of the languages that EU citizens have the right to use (and get a reply in) when corresponding with EU institutions and certain specified bodies.[26] However, this right to use Irish appears to be limited to correspondence through traditional paper-based means (now called "snail mail"), and does not include the right to send e-mail in this language, whereas the Regulation languages may be used electronically.[27] The Official Journal, the Commission has explained "is not normally published in Irish," although "occasional issues of the Official Journal are published in Irish because the subject matter either contains additions or modifications to the Treaty texts already in Irish or is of wide importance and interest to all citizens (*e.g.*, the Joint Institutions' Declaration on Human Rights)."[28] It is unclear, however, precisely who, and pursuant to what criteria, decides what matters are "of wide importance and interest to all citizens." In addition, the Commission produces documents, films, posters and the like for the general public in Irish, and maintains an office in Dublin with staff members who can speak the language.

The exact reasons for this semi-official status are obscure. Some believe that the Irish government itself wanted the Celtic language to play only a limited role,[29] a fact that could not have been publicized for domestic political reasons,

[24] Ireland Const. Art. 8. This article also provides that English is "a second official language."

[25] The ECJ's Translation Department does not even maintain an Irish language division. *See* its organizational chart posted on-line at http://curia.eu.int/en/instit/presentationfr/index_cje.htm. *See also*, European Court of Justice, "Report on Translation at the Court of Justice" (1999), 3 n.3.

[26] EC Treaty Art. 21; Irish is one of the "Constitution's languages" to which this right applies. Const. for Eur. Arts. I-10(2)(d) and II-101(4).

[27] Answer to Written Question No. P-0909/03, [2003] O.J. C280E/112. This was an answer from Mr. Prodi to a question posed by the only native speaker of Irish in the European Parliament. The Constitution for Europe does not seem to differentiate between written and electronic documents, however, and allows citizens of the Union the right to access documents "whatever their medium." Const. for Eur. Art. II-102.

[28] Answer to Written Question No. 896/86, [1987] O.J. C82/11.

[29] Anders Ahlqvist, "Language Conflict and Language Planning in Ireland," in *Language Conflict and Language Planning*, 7, 12.

but would be consistent with the general ambivalence that characterizes Ireland's attitude towards its indigenous tongue. I shall return to this topic in Chapter IV, where Ireland's paradoxical attitudes towards this language will be considered in connection with one of the ECJ's most significant decisions on the interaction of a state's language policy and the provisions of the EC Treaty.[30]

2. The Greek Enlargement

Greek became a Treaty language and Regulation language when Greece joined the EC in 1981, and this addition required the EC to adjust to a language written in an alphabet that could not be reproduced on most contemporary typewriters or word processors designed for the Roman script.[31] As will be discussed in Chapter IV, western Europeans' general lack of familiarity with the Greek alphabet has caused problems for some Greek nationals in their dealings with other Member States.[32] The launch of the euro in paper form, however, has meant that citizens of the EU now carry pieces of paper in their pockets that symbolically put the Roman and Greek alphabets on an equal footing.[33]

3. The Iberian Enlargement

Portugal and Spain acceded to the EC in 1986 and Portuguese and Spanish (more properly known, as it is in Spain, as *el castellano*) were consequently added as both Treaty and Regulation languages. No provision was made for any of Spain's other languages that have constitutionally-protected status in various autonomous regions, namely Catalan, Galician, and the non-Romance Euskera (Basque).[34]

---

30 Case C-379/87, *Groener v. Minister for Education*, 1989 ECR 3987.

31 Kristina Cunningham, "Translating for a Larger Union – Can We Cope with More than 11 Languages?" *Terminologie et Traduction* 2 (2001), 22, 30. With the accession of Cyprus in 2004, the Greek language is now spoken in two EU Member States.

32 *See*, Case C-168/91, *Konstantinidis*, 1993 ECR I-1191.

33 This is required by the Decision of the European Central Bank of 20 March 2003 on the denominations, specifications, reproduction, exchange and withdrawal of euro banknotes, Art. 1(2), [2003] O.J. L078/0016.

34 Per Article 3 of the Spanish Constitution, castellano is the "official Spanish language of the State," and "all Spaniards have the obligation to know it and the right to use it" and "the other Spanish languages will also be official in the respective Autonomous Communities in accordance with their Statutes." (trans. by R.L. Creech). *See also generally*, Generalitat de Catalunya Institut d'Esutdis Autonòmics, *Estudios Jurídicos Sobre la Ley de Política Lingüística* (1999).

4. Luxembourg's Language Switch

At the time that Luxembourg became a founding member of the EC, its official language was French, with German having a "working language" status. The predominant spoken language, however, was Luxembourgish (Lëtzebuergesch), the indigenous Germanic language of this small state. Following a wave of nationalism that picked up steam in the 1960's and 70's, Luxembourg modified its language law in 1984. Pursuant to the Act of 24 February 1984, Luxembourgish became the national language, French the legislative language, and both of these, along with German, became administrative and judicial languages.[35] The Grand Duchy has made no request for its national language to be added as a language of the EU, with the ironic result that the citizens of Luxembourg are the only citizens of the EU who do not enjoy the right to use their national language in the ECJ, which is located in their capital city.[36]

5. The 1995 Enlargement

Three historically neutral and relatively prosperous countries – Austria, Finland and Sweden – joined the EU (as it was by then called) in 1995 after the demise of the Soviet Union had led to the dissipation of Cold War tensions across the continent.[37] Finish and Swedish were consequently added as Treaty and Regulation languages, with Finnish becoming the first non-Indo-European language used in the EU.[38] Finnish has presented challenges to translators and interpreters working between it and the other languages of the EU (and *vice versa*), as the structure and vocabulary of this Ural-Altaic language differ substantially from the other languages used in the EU.[39] There is a general impression among many Finns that the EU has fared poorly with these challenges and that the quality of translations into Finnish has at times been atrocious.[40] The Commission has acknowledged that there have been problems in this area and conceded that its Finnish translations "occasionally have left something to be desired in the past."[41]

---

[35] Jul Christophory, "Lëtzebuergesch and the Overall Language Situation in Luxembourg," *Terminologie et Traduction* 3 (1998), 116, 124.

[36] Luxembourgish is included in some of the EU's "linguistic diversity" programs, however, which will be discussed in Chapter II.

[37] *See*, David P. Calleo, *Rethinking Europe's Future* (2001), 146-47.

[38] Following the 2004 accessions, three other non-Indo-European languages (Estonian, Hungarian and Maltese) are part of the EU's language mix.

[39] Rune Ingo, "Translating from Finnish into French, German, or English," *Terminologie et Traduction* 2 (1998), 199.

[40] A Finnish colleague told me that she and other Finns do not even refer to the EU's Finnish materials, and use the English language ones instead.

[41] Commission Answer to Written Question No. 1983/97, [1998] O.J. C060/74.

Austria's entry complicated the use of German in the EU, as the German that is spoken and written in that country is not the same as the German that is standard in the other German-speaking countries of the EU (*i.e.*, Germany, Belgium and Luxembourg). The distinctions extend beyond pronunciation and include lexical differences. In acknowledgment of this situation, Austria's Treaty of Accession included a protocol that provided for the use of twenty-three distinctly Austrian terms, all of them relating to food.[42] These Austrian terms were given the "same status" and were to "be used with the same legal effect as the corresponding terms used in Germany."[43] As a result, the German word for "potato" in the EU is no longer simply *Kartoffeln*, but also *Erdäpfel*, and this side dish is served not only with *Roastbeef*, but also with *Beirtied*. Some have complained that the EU has not taken note of Austria's non-culinary vocabulary, particularly its legal terminology, and contend that users of Austrian-German are disfavored in competitions for translation and interpretation positions, a charge that the Commission has denied.[44]

6. The Mega Enlargement of 2004: Eastern Europe and Mediterranean Islands

On 1 May 2004, eight eastern European states that had spent the Cold War under Communist control – the Czech Republic, Estonia, Hungary, Latvia, Lithuania, Poland, the Slovak Republic and Slovenia – and two Mediterranean island states – Cyprus and Malta – acceded to the EU. The admission of these ten new members has, in theory at least, brought ten new languages into the EU. The Act of Accession provides for nine of these:

> The texts of the acts of the institutions, and of the European Central Bank, adopted before accession and drawn up by the Council, the Commission or the European Central Bank in the Czech, Estonian, Hungarian, Latvian, Lithuanian, Maltese, Polish, Slovak and Slovenian languages shall, from the date of accession, be authentic under the same conditions as the texts drawn up in the present eleven languages.[45]

---

42 Protocol No. 10 to the Act Concerning the Conditions of Accession of the Kingdom of Norway, the Republic of Austria, the Republic of Finland and the Kingdom of Sweden and the Adjustments to the Treaties on which the European Union is Founded. [1994] O.J. C241/370.

43 *Id.*, Art. 1.

44 Commission Answer to Written Question No. 1146/98, [1998] O.J. C354/70.

45 Act Concerning the Conditions of Accession of the Czech Republic, the Republic of Estonia, the Republic of Cyprus, the Republic of Latvia, the Republic of Lithuania, the Republic of Hungary, the Republic of Malta, the Republic of Poland, the Republic of Slovenia and the Slovak Republic and the Adjustments to the Treaties on which the European Union is Founded, Art. 58, [2003] O.J. L236/33. In addition, Article 61 provides that the new language versions of the EU Treaty and other central treaties are to be "authentic under the same conditions" as the ones in the pre-accession treaty languages.

Pursuant to this Act, Regulation No. 1 has been amended to proclaim the status of the score of languages that may now be used in the EU's institutional structure:

> The official languages and the working languages of the institutions of the Union shall be Czech, Danish, Dutch, English, Estonian, Finnish, French, German, Greek, Hungarian, Italian, Latvian, Lithuanian, Maltese, Polish, Portuguese, Slovak, Slovenian, Spanish and Swedish.[46]

Conspicuously absent from the Act of Accession is one of the two co-official languages of Cyprus: Turkish.[47] Nonetheless, the EU has indicated that Turkish shall be accorded the same status as the languages specified in the Act of Accession "upon fulfillment of the necessary personnel and technical requirements."[48] It is difficult to believe that the absence of Turkish from the Act of Accession is really due to the translation and labor difficulties that the EU has suggested, however. Its exclusion rather needs to be understood as a by-product of the *de facto* division of Cyprus into two states, one predominantly Greek in ethnicity and the other mostly Turkish. The latter community, located on the northern third of the island and under the protection of the armed forces of Turkey since that country's invasion in 1974, considers itself to constitute the "Turkish Republic of Northern Cyprus," which no country in the world, with the notable exception of Turkey, has recognized as a legitimate state.[49] With UN-sponsored talks aimed at peaceful re-unification in progress, the EU admitted the "Republic of Cyprus," with its Hellenistic seat of government in Nicosia, as a Member State of the EU with theoretical sovereignty over the entire island.[50] Until a political resolution of the country's division is reached, however, the EU has indicated that it will not purport to exert authority in the disputed area.[51]

---

46 [1958] O.J. 017/385, Art. 1, as amended by the 2003 Act of Accession, Art. 58.

47 Republic of Cyprus Const. Art. 3(1). The Turkish language additionally already has a significant presence in the EU, as over three million Turkish nationals live in the various Member States. In fact, Turkey has a larger number of its citizens living in the EU than any other non-EU state. *See*, Communication of 6 Oct. 2004 from the Commission to the Council and the European Parliament: Recommendation of the European Commission on Turkey's Progress Towards Accession COM (2004) 656.

48 Act of 7 Apr. 2004 on the Adaptation of the Terms of Accession of the United Cyprus Republic to the European Union, COM(2004), Art. 8.

49 Turkish is the sole official language of the TRNC per Article 2(2) of its constitution.

50 Act of 7 Apr. 2004 on the Adaptation of the Terms of Accession of the United Cyprus Republic to the European Union, COM(2004). *See also* the website of the Delegation of the European Commission to Cyprus at http://www.delcyp.cec.eu.int/en/qa/cyprus_influence.htm

51 In 2003, the European Commission stated on the website of its delegation to Cyprus that "[t]he European Council has decided that, in the absence of a settlement, the application of the acquis to the northern part of the island shall be suspended, until the Council decides unanimously otherwise, on the basis of a proposal by the Commission."

Turkish of course is not unique in necessitating "personnel and technical requirements." All of the new languages that entered the EU in 2004 came with such requirements. The EU's language authorities were hardly caught off guard by Cypriot bilingualism, and a full year before the 2004 accession the EU's Directorate-General for Translation indicated that "[t]he working hypothesis ... at the moment is 'Ten countries, ten languages.' ... Cyprus has two official languages: Greek is already provided for Greece, but Turkish will also be needed."[52] Any lingering doubts as to the insincerity of the EU's invocation of the "personnel and technical requirements" of Turkish should disappear when one looks at the way the EU has dealt with the language from the other island state that joined the EU in 2004: Maltese. This unusual language, which is a mixture of Semitic and Romance influences, has co-official status alongside English in Malta.[53] On the date that Malta, Cyprus and the eight other new Member States joined the EU, the Council decreed that, for a period of three years, "the institutions of the European Union shall not be bound by the obligation to draft all acts in Maltese."[54] This measure was requested by the Maltese government because of problems caused by the relative obscurity of their language: "due to the current situation regarding the recruitment of Maltese linguists and the resulting lack of qualified translators it is not possible to guarantee the drafting in Maltese of all acts adopted by the institutions."[55] Lest anyone confuse this derogation as a slight against the Maltese language, the Council's derogation emphasized that "[t]he status of Maltese as an official language and a working language of the institutions of the Union remains unaffected."[56] The EU has thus singled out both Maltese and Turkish as being administratively problematic, but with respect to the former it has legally recognized the language's theoretical equality with the other EU languages but with respect to the latter it has only made a qualified pledge to do so on some unspecified future date.

---

52 Statement viewed on the website of the EU's Directorate-General for Translation on 1 April 2003. Sometime thereafter the DG revised its understanding to one of "ten countries, nine languages" and noted frankly that "Turkish will not become an official language of the European Union when Cyprus joins, pending a settlement of the constitutional issue in that country" (statement viewed on the website on 24 November 2004). *See* http://europa.eu.int/comm/dgs/translation/enlargement/preparing_en.htm.

53 In fact, Maltese has a superior position, being the "national language," while both Maltese and English serve as "official languages." Republic of Malta Const. Art. 5.

54 Council Regulation No. 930/04 of 1 May 2004 on Temporary Derogation Measures Relating to the Drafting in Maltese of the Acts of the Institutions of the European Union, Art. 1, [2004] O.J. L169/1.

55 *Id.*, pmbl (3).

56 *Id.*, pmbl (7).

7. And the Beat Goes On?

The tap-dancing around the issue of turcophonic Cypriots has served as a prelude to the more politically sensitive and culturally profound question of whether Turkey should itself be admitted to the EU.[57] At its meeting in Brussels in December 2004, the European Council agreed to open accession negotiations with Turkey in October 2005.[58] These negotiations, which are likely to take a decade to complete, will involve intense scrutiny of Turkey's less than exemplary human rights record, which has improved in recent years in anticipation of the possibility of EU membership. One of the major hurdles that the country has faced in achieving this goal is its treatment of citizens who speak languages other that Turkish, particularly the Kurds,[59] who are the most numerous people in the world without a state of their own.[60] The EU's admonishments regarding Turkey's suppression of the Kurdish language would ring more sincerely if the EU were to make provisions for the use of Kurdish should Turkey accede to the Union.

Romania and Bulgaria are tentatively expected to join the EU in January 2007,[61] and at that time, if past precedent is any guide, Romanian and Bulgarian (with the additional complication of a Cyrillic script) will be introduced into the EU. In addition, the EU plans to begin accession negotiations with Croatia in March 2005,[62] and has indicated that other west Balkan states – where language is inextricably caught up in complex and bitter questions of national

57 The linguistic divide between Asia Minor and Europe has been central to the notion of a European identity that excluded peoples on the other side of the Bosporous since the time of Herodotus, who wrote of "the perpetual enmity of the Grecian world" towards "Asia with its various foreign-speaking peoples belonging to the Persians," which was viewed as a place "quite separate and distinct" from "Europe and the Greek states." *The Histories* (Aubrey de Sélincourt, trans., Penguin Books edition printed 1985), 42.

58 Brussels European Council Presidency Conclusions of 17 Dec. 2004 (16238/04), para. 22. The European Council agreed to open these negotiations after Ankara gave assurances that it will take steps to normalize its relations with the Republic of Cyprus.

59 *See, e.g.*, Communication of 6 Oct. 2004 from the Commission to the Council and the European Parliament: Recommendation of the European Commission on Turkey's Progress Towards Accession COM (2004) 656, 2-3 (stating that the accession negotiations were "an open-ended process whose outcome cannot be guaranteed beforehand.")

60 Estimates of the number of Kuridsh speakers, who range from Turkey into Armenia, Iran, Iraq, Syria and other countries, range from seven to twelve million. The introduction of Kurdish would also increase the number of orthographic systems in use in the Union, as this language, while generally now written (at least in Turkey) in the Roman script, has also been expressed in the Arabic, Armenian and Cyrillic alphabets. *Encyclopedia of the Languages of Europe* (Glanville Price ed., 2000), 284.

61 Brussels European Council Presidency Conclusions of 17 Dec. 2004 (16238/04), paras. 6, 10.

62 *Id.*, para. 16.

identity – "have a perspective to become candidate countries."[63] The country inelegantly known as "the Former Yugoslav Republic of Macedonia" has applied for membership. With most of the continent belonging to the EU, Norway, where two forms of the Norwegian language have official status,[64] may decide yet to join the club notwithstanding the fact that the country has twice rejected membership before (in national referenda in 1972 and 1994). The EU has not defined any geographical limit on enlargement – beyond the vague requirement that members must be "European States" – and the room for linguistic expansion is therefore also open-ended.[65]

8. A New Challenge Posed by Irish and Minority Languages

As the number of languages accorded official status in the EU has grown, advocates of Irish and speakers of several minority and regional languages have become increasingly unsatisfied with their exclusion (either partial or entire) from the EU's institutional linguistic structure. The government of Ireland has reconsidered its position on the limited use of the Irish language, and Dublin has recently requested that Irish be made an official and working language of the EU.[66] In response, the government of Spanish Prime Minister José Luis Rodríguez Zapatero has stated that it plans to seek the addition of Catalan, Gallician, and Euskera/Basque.[67] Other Member States are coming under increasing pressure to seek recognition of their various subnational languages,[68] and the demand for the recognition of such languages has

---

[63] Communication of 6 Oct. 2004 from the Commission to the Council and to the European Parliament: Strategy Paper of the European Commission on Progress in the Enlargement Process. COM (2004) 657, para. 1. The language that before the disintegration of Yugoslavia used to be called "Serbo-Croatian" is now regarded by some as two, or even three, separate languages: Serbian, Croatian, and Bosnian. *See, e.g.*, the website of the Office of the High Representative and EU Special Representative in Bosnia and Herzegovina at http://www.ohr.int.

[64] That is, Bokmål and Nynorsk, which are to be treated equally under the Law on Language Use in Public Services of 1980. Sámi (formerly known as "Lapp") also has constitutionally protected status. Norway Const. Art. 110(a). I know from personal experience that an examination of the interplay between language and politics in Norway can fill a substantial portion of a university seminar.

[65] The new Constitution for Europe, in its first article, provides that "[t]he Union shall be open to all European States which respect its values and are committed to promoting them together." Art. I-1(2).

[66] Dennis Staunton, "Government to Seek Official EU Status for Irish Language," *The Irish Times*, 24 Nov. 2004. This new request does not call for the translation of all documents, however. Judgments from the ECJ, for example, would not be translated into Irish, but all regulations adopted by the Council of Ministers and the Parliament would be.

[67] Gabriela Cañas, "España Pedirá que el Catalán Sea Oficial en la UE si se Admite el Gaélico," *El Pais*, 27 July 2004.

[68] *See, e.g.*, Press Release of 27 July 2004 issued by the Plaid Cymru (The Party of Wales), available on line at http://www.jillevans.net/press040727.html.

become caught up in the debate over the ratification of the new Constitution for Europe.[69]

C. Institutional Rules of Procedure

Pursuant to Article 6 of Regulation No. 1, the various institutions of the Community have adopted policies regarding the use of languages within their confines. Generally speaking, the institutions are more linguistically inclusive when dealing with the public and individual Member States, and more restrictive when internal matters are concerned. With regards to the public, the institutions have an obligation, under Article 21 of the EC Treaty,[70] to answer correspondence from a citizen of the EU in the Treaty language of the citizen's choice. The Commission has generally used only two languages for conducting its day-to-day business: English and French, with German occasionally added in.[71] In the Council, the practice, at least before the 2004 enlargement, has been to use all Regulation languages at ministerial-level meetings, but to limit translation services to English, French and German at conferences of the Permanent Representatives Committee, and the rank-and-file staff has generally conducted their day-to-day work in a small number of languages.[72] To what extent these patterns, which generally have not been formally prescribed by any official document but have rather been established as informal custom, will be affected by the 2004 enlargement remains to be seen. None of the new languages is widely known by people who are not native speakers, but the relative positions of French and German may be altered due to the fact that German is more well known than French in the new Member States (although English is the most well-known second language in these states taken as a group).

The European Parliament, in contrast to the Commission and the Council, conducts its affairs in all Regulation languages with robust enthusiasm. The Parliament's Rules of Procedure provide that all documents are to be drawn up in the various languages, that all members "have the right to speak in Parliament in the official language of their choice" and that their speeches "shall be simultaneously interpreted into the other official languages and into any other language [that is] necessary."[73] This commitment to multilingualism often causes substantial delays in the legislative process; it may take several months

---

69 Josep Garriga, "Convergència Rechazará la Constitución Europea si el Catalán no es Oficial en la UE," *El Pais*, 15 Sept. 2004.

70 Const. for Eur. Arts. I-10(2)(d) and II-101(4).

71 Brian McCluskey, "A Different Kettle of Fish: The Challenge of Multilingual Translation in Specialist Fields" (1998).

72 Alan Forrest, "The Challenge of Languages in Europe," *Terminologie et Traduction* 3 (1998), 101, 105-06.

73 Eur. Par. Rules of Proc. Art. 138, available at the European Parliament's website, www.europarl.eu.int.

for the Parliament to prepare all the translations of a Commission proposal that are necessary in order for it to be considered.[74]

The Court of Justice's Rules of Procedure[75] allow any of the Treaty languages to be used as the language of a particular case.[76] The language of the case is generally used in the written and oral pleadings and in the minutes and decisions of the Court, with exceptions for intervening Member States (which may use their own language) and any witness or expert who is "unable adequately to express himself in" one of the Treaty languages.[77] The applicant may generally elect the language of the case, unless the defendant is a Member State or a national of a Member State, in which case the language of the case is the language of that state, or if the state has more than one official language, the applicant's choice among them.[78] In a case that comes before the Court on a request for a preliminary ruling under Article 234 of the EC Treaty,[79] the language of the case is to be the language of the court making the request.[80] Judges may use any language they wish,[81] but they have recognized the need to have a mutual common language, as they deliberate alone without the aid of interpreters, and have chosen French for this purpose and have made it the internal working language of the Court.[82] Judgments are accordingly drafted in French and then translated into the language of the case (if it is not French) and into all of the other Treaty languages.[83] As a rule, only the version in the language of the case is authentic.[84] However, because the judgment is legally operative throughout the entire EU as soon as it is issued, the Court deems it necessary to release all versions of a given judgment simultaneously, and the lengthy translation process often causes the issuance of judgments to be

---

74 Forrest at 106.

75 The Rules of Procedure of the Court of Justice of the European Communities, [1991] O.J. L176/7, as amended, most recently by Council Decision of 19 Apr. 2004, [2004] O.J. L132/2 (Hereinafter "ECJ Rules of Proc."). The Court of First Instance's language rules are similar to the ECJ's. *See*, The Rules of Procedure of the Court of First Instance of the European Communities, [1991] O.J. L136/1, as amended, most recently by Council Decision of 19 Apr. 2004, [2004] O.J. L132/3.

76 ECJ Rules of Proc. Art. 29(1).

77 *Id.*, Art. 29(4).

78 *Id.*, Art. 29(2)(a).

79 Const. for Eur. Art. III-369.

80 ECJ Rules of Proc., Art. 29(2).

81 *Id.*, Arts. 29(5), 30(1).

82 European Court of Justice, "Report on Translation at the Court of Justice" (1999), 4; Pascale Berteloot, "Babylone à Luxembourg: Jurilinguistique à la Cour de Justice," *Vortrag vor dem Europa-Institut der Universität des Saarlandes* Nr. 136 (1988), 11.

83 ECJ Report on Translation, 7.

84 ECJ Rules of Proc. Art. 31.

significantly delayed, contributing to what the Court has described as a "crisis situation."[85]

D. Getting Lost in the Translation

The "crisis" situation that the ECJ refers to, as well as the translation backlog at the Parliament, are just two examples of the logistical pressures that are placed on a system which works with so many languages. Translation (which refers to written documents) and interpretation (which refers to speech) in the EU is a mammoth task. Each institution has its own translation department (the largest being the Commission's Directorate-General for Translation) while the interpretation functions are performed by one central body, the Joint Interpreting and Conference Service. Before the 2004 enlargement, the main EU institutions (Commission, Council and Parliament) together translated nearly three million pages of text per year,[86] at an annual cost in excess of 800 million euros.[87] The EU likes to point out, in response to critics who complain about the price of polyglot administration, that "multilingualism costs each European citizen only two euros a year,"[88] and has compared the price tag as amounting to "a little more than the price of a cup of coffee."[89] With the 2004 enlargement, these costs will obviously increase. But, despite the near doubling in the number of languages used, the price of translation and interpretation, the EU insists "will not double" because "in their internal work, the EU institutions streamline the use of languages, and enlargement has brought more cost-cutting devices."[90]

Upon further scrutiny, however, the "two euro per person" claim regarding the cost of linguistic pluralism is revealed to be misleading, even if it is technically accurate from an accounting standpoint. This is true for several reasons. First, it ignores the fact that multilingualism results in institutional inefficiencies that are not reflected in the public relations-friendly "two euros a year" figure. The delays that result from inadequate translation resources in the Parliament and the ECJ have already been mentioned. One Dutch diplomat in the United Nations, where far fewer languages are used than in the EU, has

---

85 ECJ Report on Translation, 15.

86 European Commission Manuscript: "Many Tongues, One Family: Languages in the European Union," Catalogue No. NA-60-04-377-EN-C, July 2004 (hereinafter "Many Tongues Manuscript"), 18, available on-line at http://europa.eu.int/comm/publications/booklets/move/45/en.doc.

87 Commission Press Release of 17 Feb. 2004: "Commission Steps Up its Translation Capacity to Meet Demands of Enlargement." MEMO/04/34.

88 European Commission, "The Translation Service of the European Commission" (2001), 5. *See also* Many Tongues Manuscript at 18.

89 Many Tongues Manuscript at 18.

90 *Id.*

bemoaned the lost productivity occasioned by the need for interpretations.[91] Second, it glosses over the fact that translation exacts a high price in terms of the impairment of communication. The Commission has stated that "all [its] translations have to be faultless,"[92] but there simply is no such thing as a fault-free translation. Every translation represents at best a diminishment, and at worst a corruption, of the original statement's communicative value to a greater or lesser extent. Geert van Calster has explained why differences in translated texts are inevitable:

> One cannot expect different language versions of the same act or treaty always to say the same. Indeed, this would suppose a level of perfection difficult, probably even impossible to reach and/or to maintain. Words do not have a meaning as such, they only receive their meaning within their context at a certain moment. Further, each language possesses its own genius, which influences the choice of words and the arrangement of the sentence. The differences in language versions do not only appear because of this intrinsic semantic reason, they also exist because of slovenliness or, as in the case of old texts, because of semantic evolution. Another reason is time pressure.[93]

Many EU documents undergo two translations in their journey from the original document to the version in another language because so-called "pivot" or "relay" languages are used to lessen the number of language-pair translators that are required.[94] To provide direct translation from each of twenty Regulation languages into all the others would require an astounding 380 people.[95] The use of pivots simplifies the logistics of translation, but it greatly compounds the problem of textual corruption.

---

91 Statement made to R.L. Creech by Jennes de Mol of the Permanent Mission of the Kingdom of the Netherlands to the United Nations, Geneva, 8 May 2002.

92 European Commission, "The Translation Service of the European Commission" (2001), 1.

93 Van Calster at 369. Dante Alighieri expressed this notion poetically in a passage that itself resists translation: "*nulla cosa per legame musaico armonizzata si può de la sua loquela in altra transmutare, senza rompere tutta sua dolcezza e armonia.*" (Quoted in Steiner at 253).

94 For example, a recent EU report has stated that "[t]he European Parliament, which often needs to produce documents rapidly in all official languages, has developed a system of six 'pivot' languages. The six are English, French, German, Italian, Polish and Spanish. A document presented in, say, Slovak or Swedish will not be translated directly into all other 19 languages. Instead it will be translated into the pivot languages and then retranslated from one of them into the others." Many Tongues Manuscript at 18.

95 To determine the number of language pairs for X number of languages, multiply X by (X-1), so for twenty languages, we have 20 x 19 = 380. The direction of the language pairs matters, so languages P and Q involve two pairs (P to Q and Q to P), as translators and interpreters generally are only allowed to translate or interpret into, and not out of, their native languages.

Another difficulty facing the translator of a legal document is that languages are very much intertwined with the legal systems associated with them, and, as the former chief of the terminological service at the ECJ has explained, a good legal translator must therefore also be an expert in comparative law:

> Generally speaking, the translation problems which are present in a legal context not only concern the transposition of one language into another, but also the transposition of one legal order into another. It is therefore possible to say that the transposition may concern two different languages, for example the translation of a German legal text into French, but it is necessary to be equally aware of the fact that legal French such that it exists in Belgium, in Switzerland or in Canada is not necessarily the same, and that the same terms will not always correspond to the same concepts. An important risk also inheres in the existence of closely related languages such as the Romance ones – French and Portuguese, for example – in so far as the French and Portuguese legal systems are not particularly similar in all ways: in several respects the Portuguese civil code is closer to German law than to French law, and although Dutch is a language closely related to German, the former Dutch civil code was closer to the French civil code than that of the German Federal Republic.[96]

Discrepancies between multiple versions of a text, all of which are deemed to be equally authentic, themselves impose other costs: the intangible costs of uncertainty as to the "real" meaning of the text, and the concrete costs of litigation that may be necessary to determine it. In a case involving the interpretation of treaty provisions in the early, quadrilingual days of the EC, Advocate General LaGrange observed that "all four languages are authentic, which means that no single one of them is authentic."[97] In *Stauder v. Ulm*, the Court, being called upon to construe a piece of Community legislation, stated that "the necessity for uniform application and accordingly for uniform interpretation makes it impossible to consider one version of the text in isolation but requires that it be interpreted on the basis of both the real intention of its author and the aim he seeks to achieve, in light in particular of the versions in all four languages."[98] Time and time again, the ECJ has been called upon to wade through the linguis-

---

[96] Berteloot at 16-17. Berteloot is nonetheless rather sanguine about the performance of translators at the ECJ, and has likened that institution not to the Biblical tower of Babel with its attendant confusion, but rather to the post-Babel Babylon, where translators and interpreters of various ancient Near-Eastern languages such as Sumerian, Akkadian and Babylonian facilitated the orderly administration of justice under Hammurabi. *Id.* at 4, 31.

[97] Opinion of Advocate General La Grange in Case 13/61, *Bosch v. Van Rijn*, 1962 ECR 45, 70.

[98] Case 29/69, 1969 ECR 419, para. 3.

tic inconsistencies in various pieces of Community legislation and even the EC Treaty itself.[99] In these cases,

> [t]he Court has consistently kept the implications of the authenticity of all language versions in mind. The characterization of all language versions of Treaty Articles and of secondary legislation as being 'equally authentic' places them in a relationship of interdependence. Rather than each bearing the authentic content of the text in question, they form that content together.[100]

As a result, a citizen of a Member State cannot simply rely on the text of a piece of Community legislation in his own language; in theory he must also, if he is to have an accurate understanding of its meaning, consult each and every other language version. Of course, it can probably be stated as an absolute that no single person is as polyglot as the EU has become. Nonetheless, ignorance of the law is no excuse, and neither is ignorance of a particular Regulation language, even though, in the words of van Calster, the ancient maximum "*nemo ius ignorare censetur* at least supposes that the '*ius*' is drafted in a language which the persons involved can reasonably be presumed to understand."[101]

Even more problems arise with the interpretation of spoken speech. The cultural dynamics which lie in the background whenever someone speaks in a particular language are often impenetrable to those who do not speak it. Jokes, which can be an important component of any meeting, are particularly subject to butchering in interpretation. When the UK joined the EC after the first enlargement, members of the European Parliament and their interpreters were suddenly confronted with the quite foreign linguistic culture that British MP's imported from Westminster, where shouting and grumbling is an accepted practice.[102] A person listening to an interpreter is not listening to the speaker, and is therefore disconnected from him, and his ability to assess meaning-critical factors such as the speaker's mood, tone and veracity is severely compromised. The listener relies on the interpreter's ability to relate these qualities, but the interpreter is himself handicapped in his ability to observe the speaker; the interpreter is often sitting in a glass booth on the edge of a room looking at the speaker's back.[103] Moreover, the interpreter may himself be listening to an

---

99 *See, e.g.*, Case C-257/00, *Givane v. Secretary of State for the Home Department*, 2003 ECR I-345; Case C-219/95P, *Ferriere Nord SpA v. Commission*, 1997 ECR I-4411; Case 80/76, *North Kerry Milk Products Ltd. v. Minister for Agriculture and Fisheries*, 1977 ECR 425; Case 19/67, *Bestuur der Sociale Verzekeringsban v. Van der Vecht*, 1967 ECR 345. *See also*, Jan Engberg, "Statutory Texts as Instances of Language(s): Consequences and Limitations on Interpretation," 29 *Brooklyn J. of Int'l Law* 3 (2004), 1135.

100 Van Calster at 375.

101 *Id.* at 392.

102 Karlheinz Neunreither, "The European Parliament and Enlargement, 1973-2000," in *The Expanding European Union: Past, Present, Future* (J. Redmond & G. Rosenthal eds., 1998), 65, 68.

103 Eugeniusz Wyzner, "Languages in International Organizations: The Case of the United Nations," in *Language as Barrier and Bridge* (Kurt Müller ed., 1992), 7.

interpreter if a pivot or relay is being used as an intermediary, leading to a final output that has been likened to a song played on the piano with a blanket over the keyboard.[104] For the ultimate listener, there is an added delay as a second interpretation is produced. If a joke survives at all after two translations, he may get it after everyone else has stopped laughing. The interpreter is also faced with the dilemma that what is not said may be more meaningful than what is said, and the ultimate listener, unfamiliar with the dynamics of the language of the speaker, may be unable to fully apprehend this.[105]

Finally, the supposed "two euros a year" bargain touted by the EU is achieved by the decision to leave large volumes of material un-translated. Documents used internally are likely to appear only in the internal working languages of the institution (*i.e.*, English, French, and less frequently, German).[106] The Commission sometimes only prepares summaries in the various languages, or even only some of them, when it receives lengthy reports or other documents from Member States and others.[107] While such cost-saving measures may be justifiable on economic grounds, they sit uneasily with the current notion that the EU should be brought closer to the citizens of Europe and its workings made more transparent, which includes allowing access to more documents.[108] The right to obtain institutional documents now has Treaty status since the Treaty of Amsterdam (it is now in Article 255 of the EC Treaty),[109] but this right is of

---

[104] Stephen B. Pearl, "Modified Babel: The Keepers of the Tower, A Guided Tour to Interpretation at the United Nations," in Müller at 24.

[105] Steiner at 240.

[106] Brian McCluskey, "Respecting Multilingualism in the Enlargement of the European Union – the Organizational Challenge," *Terminologie et Traduction* 2 (2001), 7, 11.

[107] For example, the Commission in 2002 received an external study regarding undeclared labor in Europe. The report was written in English, and the Commission posted it in its entirety on the europa web site, along with brief summaries in French and German. In response to a complaint about the limited translation of this document, the Commission explained that "it is not possible to translate reports of external studies such as the report in question." Answer to Written Question E-1418/02, [2003] O.J. C092E/0053. Of course, what the Commission really meant was that it was not practical or feasible to translate it; it surely was "possible" to do so. *See also*, Brian McCluskey, "A Different Kettle of Fish: The Challenge of Multilingual Translation in Specialist Fields" (1998).

[108] The Constitution for Europe proclaims, in its preamble, the EU's wish "to deepen the democratic and transparent nature of its public life." The Commission's 2001 White Paper on European Governance, which calls for *inter alia*, increased openness, participation and accountability, and includes the following statement: "Democracy depends on people being able to take part in public debate. To do this, they must have access to reliable information on European issues and be able to scrutinise the policy process in its various stages. Major progress has been made in 2001 with the adoption of new rules giving citizens greater access to Community documents." [2001] O.J. 287/1, 8. *See also*, Deirdre Curtin & Herman Meijers, "Access to European Union Information: An Element of Citizenship and a Neglected Constitutional Right," in *The European Union and Human Rights* (N. Neuwahl & A. Rosas eds., 1995), 77.

[109] Const. for Eur. Art. II-102.

limited value if it does not include a right to obtain documents in a language that is comprehensible to the person exercising it.[110] Moreover, if the EU institutions are being influenced by documents that only appear in certain languages, the speakers of those languages will be able to hold the EU institutions accountable, whereas speakers of other languages will be severely hampered in their ability to do so, and Article 255 will essentially be transformed into a measure that subjects the citizens of the EU to a variable geometry of rights based on their language. A policy under which an EU citizen could request the translation, at his own expense, of a document which would otherwise go un-translated, such as that adopted by the European Economic and Social Committee in 2003,[111] is problematic for two reasons. First, it effectively amounts to a tax on speakers of some languages but not on others, as the EU languages are not equally represented in the EU's documents. Second, a person can only request the translation of a document if he knows that it exists, and the non-occurrence of the document in his native language may preclude such knowledge. Even if he is somehow made aware of the existence of a particular document in another language, his ability to assess its significance will be limited, and thus a decision as to whether he should request a translation, assuming he can afford one, may not be well-informed.

The recent mega-enlargement of the EU will aggravate the problems associated with translation and interpretation. This will necessitate increased use of pivots in interpretation.[112] The languages of eastern Europe are not widely known in the West, and difficulties in finding qualified interpreters and translators can be expected to be an ongoing concern. To counterbalance this situation somewhat, the EU has relaxed its long-standing policy that has barred translators and interpreters from rendering translations and interpretations into languages that are not their native tongues,[113] but this may result in an increased frequency of output with anomalous lexical or syntactic properties.

There is also likely to be increased use of computerized translation tools and efforts to develop more reliable ones.[114] The technology in this area has made advances, but it still tends to produce literal word-for-word translations,[115] and

---

110 Cunningham at 24.

111 Decision of the European Economic and Social Committee of 1 July 2003, Art. 16, [2003] O.J. L205/19.

112 Interestingly, the Commission has looked into the possibility of using the artificial (and therefore supposedly neutral) language Esperanto, which has a relatively strong following in eastern Europe, as a new relay language. Answer to Written Question E-0188/00, [2000] O.J. C303E/156. On the strength of Esperanto in this region, *see* Humphrey Tonkin, "Esperanto in Eastern Europe: An Insurmountable Opportunity?" in Müller, 59.

113 Many Tongues Manuscript at 19.

114 For a review of the EU's use of computerized translation tools, see Commission Report: "Translation Tools and Workflow," May 2004, available on-line at http://europa.eu.int/comm/dgs/translation/bookshelf/tools_and_workflow_en.pdf.

115 Enrique Jiménez Ríos, "Pasado, Presente y Futuro de la Traducción Automática," *Terminologie et Traduction* 1 (2001), 138.

one of the most important components of a translator's skill is knowing when such an approach would be inappropriate.[116] Still, translation machines may be relied upon to provide rough translations for internal use, or to allow a translator to see if a particular phrase or passage has been translated before, thus obviating the need for him to reinvent the wheel.[117]

E. OHIM Gives a Kik to the Illusion of Linguistic Equality

The multiplicity of languages used in the EU has long spurred calls for reduction. As was stated earlier, the Danes, a rumor has it, sought to reduce the EC's languages to only English and French at the time of the first enlargement.[118] In 1979, when the EC was contemplating the Greco-Iberian enlargements, the so-called "Three Wise Men" cautiously wrote that in a Community with nine languages it would be "essential that pragmatic arrangements [be] found allowing the number of interpreters to be reduced according to the nature of each meeting."[119] However, they hastened to add that "any attempt to limit systematically and by compulsion the use of any official language would be unjust as well as politically impractical." While Denmark may have secretly proposed using only English and French in the EU, others, including the government of the Netherlands[120] and former ECJ judge Pierre Pescatore[121] have openly made this suggestion.

The Council took a serious step towards reducing the number of languages spoken within an EU setting in 1993 when it established the language policy for the new Office for Harmonisation in the Internal Market (Trade Marks and Designs) ("OHIM"). [122] The Commission originally proposed that only one language be used, although it did not specify which one. France, also without specification, stated that two should be used, although there could be little doubt that Paris was suggesting English and French. Germany felt left out and insisted that German be included, noting the importance of German as a language of trademark applications. Italy and Spain also wanted their languages included,

---

[116] Helen Titchen Beeth & Bill Fraser, "The Hidden Life of Translators," *Terminologie et Traduction* 2 (1999), 76, 85.

[117] McCluskey, *Terminologie et Traduction* 2 (2001), 7, 18.

[118] Other international organizations such as the League of Nations and the Council of Europe provide precedent for the exclusive use of these two languages.

[119] *European Commission Bulletin* 11/1979, 27.

[120] Statement made to R.L. Creech by Jennes de Mol of the Permanent Mission of the Kingdom of the Netherlands to the United Nations, Geneva, 8 May 2002.

[121] Referenced in Forrest at 110.

[122] For background on the linguistic diplomacy surrounding the establishment of OHIM, *see* Forrest, 107-08.

although the latter was primarily concerned with having the new organization located on its territory.[123] What finally emerged from the Council was Regulation No. 40/94 of 20 December 1993,[124] which established a byzantine linguistic regime for use in OHIM business. Five languages –English, French, German, Italian and Spanish – were given "official" status in the Office.[125] The use of other languages was not categorically prohibited, however, as applicants would be allowed to submit trademark applications in any of "the official languages of the European Community." The applicant would be required to designate one of the five official languages of OHIM as a "second language" on his application, which would be the language of any proceedings that might arise in connection with the application, unless the application was itself in one of the five specified languages, and unless the parties agreed otherwise.[126]

Christina Kik, an intellectual property attorney and trade mark agent in the Netherlands, decided to challenge OHIM's exclusion of Dutch as one of these "second languages." She filed an application in Dutch that sought to trademark her own name, and she indicated Dutch as the "second language" on the application. OHIM dismissed her application on the grounds that she had not designated one of its five official languages as the "second language." Ms. Kik appealed to OHIM's Board of Appeal, and after that body upheld the dismissal, she filed an action against both OHIM and the Council with the Court of First Instance.[127]

---

[123] It ultimately was established in the Spanish city of Alicante.

[124] [1994] O.J. L11/1.

[125] Reg. 40/94, Art. 115(2). It has been reported that almost all of the total population (97 per cent) of the fifteen Member States that then comprised the EU spoke at least one of these languages as either a mother tongue or a foreign language. Victor Ginsburgh & Shlomo Weber, "Language Disenfranchisement in the European Union," Manuscript (2003), 16.

[126] If both the language of the application and the "second language" are official languages of OHIM, the regulation has a complicated set of rules to determine which language is to be used, based largely on the language used by a party opposing the application, who would be required to file papers in either the language of the application or the applicant's "second language." *See*, Reg. 40/94, arts. 115(3-7). The CFI has recently indicated that questions regarding the interpretation and application of the language rules constitute substantive legal questions and that a confused party can therefore not rely on OHIM to provide it with assistance in this regard. Case T-107/02, *GE Betz, Inc. v. OHIM* (2004) (upholding rejection of opposition where opposing party failed to provide translation of evidence), para. 70. *See also*, Case T-235/02, *Strongline A/S v. OHIM* (2003) (same), para. 39.

[127] Case T-120/99, *Kik v. Office for Harmonisation in the Internal Market*, 2001 ECR II-2235. This was Ms. Kik's second challenge to OHIM's language policy. Her previous action, in which she had not filed a trademark application but had merely contended that she had been adversely affected by the policy in her capacity as a trademark agent, was dismissed for lack of standing by the Court of First Instance. Case T-107/94, *Kik* 1995 ECR II-1717, *appeal dismissed*, Case C-270/95P, *Kik* 1996 ECR I-1987.

Ms. Kik claimed that OHIM's language regime amounted to discrimination based on nationality in violation of Article 6 of the EC Treaty (now Art. 12).[128] She argued that trademark agents in Member States where one of OHIM's languages was not spoken had a competitive disadvantage compared with agents in Member States where one of those languages was spoken, in so far as hiring an agent in one of the former states would be more costly because it would require the use of translators. Furthermore, she was of the view that OHIM's restrictive language policy impermissibly departed from the principle of linguistic equality that she contended was enshrined in Regulation No. 1. The government of Greece intervened on Ms. Kik's behalf (Greece apparently was displeased with the exclusion of Greek from OHIM's official language list, notwithstanding the fact that the original adoption of the language scheme required the unanimous consent of the Member States) and advanced even more forcefully a view that the EC Treaty's prohibition of discrimination on the grounds of nationality included a prohibition based on language. Greece cited Regulation No. 1, the equal authenticity of the various language versions of the EC Treaty, and in an apparent reference to the case law involving the interpretation of different language versions of Community legislation, the Court of Justice's repeated recognition of the equivalence of the Community's official languages.[129] Ms. Kik also contended that OHIM's policy was contrary to Article 21 of the EC Treaty,[130] which allows EU citizens the right to write to any Community institution and certain bodies in any of the Treaty languages and to receive a reply in the same language.

The Council, supported by the intervention of Spain, defended the regime it had crafted for OHIM and asserted baldly that "there is no Community law principle of absolute equality between the official languages."[131] Such a concept, the Council reasoned, could not be reconciled with Article 217 of the EC Treaty (now Art. 290),[132] which grants the Council power to prescribe the rules for the Community's languages. Spain and the Council argued that OHIM's language policy was a reasonable one, noting that applicants could file their applications in any of the Community's eleven languages, that proceedings could be conducted in any of those languages if the parties so agreed, and the office's preferred languages consisted of the five most commonly spoken languages of the Community. In addition, the Council stressed the practical constraints of using translators and the cost of an unlimited language policy, which it claimed would require it to provide OHIM with an additional budget of several tens of millions of euros per year.[133]

---

[128] Const. for Eur. Art. I-4(2).

[129] Case T-120/99, *Kik*, paras. 35-45.

[130] Const. for Eur. Arts. I-10(2)(d) and II-101(4).

[131] Case T-120/99, *Kik*, para. 52.

[132] Const. for Eur. Art. III-433.

[133] Case T-120/99, *Kik*, paras. 50-54.

The CFI was thus faced with a conflict between economic efficiency and egalitarian values, between exclusive practicality and cumbersome pluralism. Greece pointedly maintained that "if a choice is to be made between the goal of facilitating the work of the Office on the one hand, and the interests of all applicants in being able to communicate in their own official Community language on the other, it is the latter that ought always to prevail."[134] The CFI, however, disagreed with Athens, and sided with the Council. Regulation No. 1 was, in the court's view, "merely an act of secondary law," and as such could be altered by the Council. "The rules governing languages laid down by Regulation No. 1," the CFI exclaimed, "cannot be deemed to amount to a principle of Community law."[135] The CFI viewed the Council's decision regarding the languages used at OHIM, which permitted the use of "the most widely known languages" of the EU, as "an appropriate and proportionate choice, even if the official languages of the Community were treated differently."[136] The CFI did not directly address the Greek argument that linguistic discrimination amounted to nationality discrimination, although it did state that this case "does not involve an infringement of the principle of non-discrimination."[137] Immediately after making this statement the court proceeded to speak of what it viewed as the limited effect of the measure, the legitimacy of the reasons that led to its adoption, and its proportional nature,[138] none of which has anything to do with the issue of whether discrimination has occurred and is only relevant to the separate issue of whether such discrimination can be justified. The CFI flatly rejected Ms. Kik's attempt to derive rights from the linguistic inclusiveness of Article 21 of the EC Treaty (regarding writing to the Community's "institutions" and certain specified bodies), pointing out that OHIM was not an "institution" as that term was defined in the EC Treaty nor one of the specified bodies.[139] In the same vein, the Council had argued that Regulation No. 1 was inapplicable to OHIM, as

---

[134] *Id.*, para. 46.

[135] *Id.*, para. 58.

[136] *Id.*, para. 63.

[137] *Id.*, para. 60.

[138] *Id.*, paras. 61-63.

[139] *Id.*, para. 64. Article 21 of the EC Treaty specifies the Parliament and the Ombudsman, and refers to the institutions and bodies of Article 7, in which the "institutions" are identified as the Parliament, the Council, the Commission, the Court of Justice, and the Court of Auditors. Article 7 mentions two bodies: the Economic and Social Committee and the Committee of the Regions. The new Constitution for Europe, as foreseen by Curtin and Van Ooik, likewise fails to provide citizens a right to write to non-institutional entities such as OHIM in the language of their choice. Deirdre Curtin & Ronald van Ooik, "The Sting is Always in the Tail: The Personal Scope of Application of the EU Charter of Fundamental Rights," 8 *Maastricht J. of European and Comparative Law* 1 (2001), 102, 107-08. The CFI in *Kik* left aside the problem of the temporal applicability of Article 21, which only came into being with the Treaty of Amsterdam, which was signed the year after Ms. Kik filed her application in 1996.

that document likewise spoke only of the languages of the "institutions" of the Community.

The focus on a narrow definition of "institution" renders the basis of the Council's authority to determine the language policies of non-institutional bodies such as OHIM uncertain. Article 217 of the EC Treaty (now Art. 290) only grants the Council power to determine the languages of the Community's "institutions," and there is therefore a linguistic lacuna with regards to non-institutions.[140] The Council based its argument in *Kik* in part on the theory that the existence of Article 217 indicated that there was no principle of linguistic equality in the EU, as otherwise there would be no reason to give the Council power to regulate in this area, but Article 217 does not fully address the establishment of language policy in all EU settings. One could argue that Article 217 allows the Council to make linguistically discriminatory decisions with regards to the Community's institutions, but that it cannot do so when dealing with non-institutions, although it seems highly unlikely that the drafters of the Treaty could have intended such a nonsensical distinction. Nonetheless, the Court's conclusion calls out for consideration of this issue and its failure to do so renders the basis of the Council's authority over language use at OHIM uncertain.[141]

Ms. Kik appealed the CFI's decision to the European Court of Justice, and her heirs continued the case following her death shortly thereafter. The ECJ, pursuant to the recommendation of Advocate General Jacobs, upheld the CFI's ruling in September 2003.[142] The ECJ stated that the various references to language in the EC Treaty "cannot be regarded as evidencing a general principle of Community law that confers a right on every citizen to have a version of anything that might affect his interests drawn up in his language in all circumstances."[143] The Court agreed with the CFI that OHIM was not an institution

---

[140] This power is similarly limited to "institutions" in the Constitution for Europe, Art. III-433.

[141] One arguable source of the Council's power might be the same Treaty provision that was the basis for establishing OHIM in the first place, that is Article 308 (then Art. 235), which provides:
If action by the Community should prove necessary to attain, in the course of the operation of the common market, one of the objectives of the Community and this Treaty has not provided the necessary powers, the Council shall, acting unanimously on a proposal from the Commission and after consulting the European Parliament, take the appropriate measures.
In light of the statements made by the CFI, it seems likely that it would have concluded that the establishment of OHIM's language policy could be justified under Article 308. However, the ECJ has also indicated, in an advisory opinion in which human rights were concerned, that Article 308 "cannot be used as a basis for the adoption of provisions whose effect would, in substance, be to amend the Treaty without following the procedure which it provides for that purpose." *Opinion 2/94 on Accession by the Community to the ECHR*, 1996 ECR I-1759, para. 30 (ruling that the Community lacked competence to accede to the Convention).

[142] Case C-361/01, *Estate of Christina Kik v. Office for Harmonisation in the Internal Market*, 2003 ECR I-8283.

[143] *Id.*, para. 82.

or body with which citizens of the EU had a right to use any EU language,[144] but did not provide an explanation for the Council's asserted authority to regulate the language rules of non-institutional entities. The Court suggested that linguistic inequality was inherent in Regulation No. 1, pointing out that the "official languages and working languages of the Community institutions" designated therein "are not, it will be observed, exactly the same" as the languages in which the EC Treaty are to be considered equally authentic.[145] In addition, the Court noted that while Regulation No. 1 required that regulations and other documents of *general* application must be drafted and published in all eleven Regulation languages, there was no such requirement for an individual decision, "even though it may affect the rights of a citizen of the Union other than the person to whom it is addressed, for example a competing economic operator."[146] The ECJ also entertained an argument which had been raised by Greece before the CFI but which had gone unaddressed in that earlier opinion, namely that the equal authenticity of the various Treaty versions, along with the Court's case law construing different language versions of Community legislation, reflected a basic principle of the equality of languages in the EU. The Court rejected this position, stating that "[a]lthough equal account must be taken of all the authentic versions of a text when interpreting that text, that holds good only in so far as such versions exist and are authentic."[147]

The ECJ's ruling in *Kik* marked a clear retreat from the views which it had expressed in its 1999 report on language and translation at the Court, when it offered the following comment:

> [The] language regime which allows the national courts and the parties to *express themselves in their own language*, constitutes a *fundamental right* in the Community system, and is consistent with the general language regime of the Communities, which is founded on the principle of *the equality of the official languages of the Member States* of the Union laid down in Regulation No 1 of the Council.[148]

Perhaps because it was uneasy with the disconnect between its previous rhetoric and its resolution of *Kik*, the Court sought to minimize the import of its decision by stressing the commercial and voluntary nature of OHIM's mission: "Account

[144] *Id.*, para. 83.

[145] *Id.*, para. 84. The Advocate General specifically pointed out that Irish was a Treaty language but not a Regulation No. 1 language. Opinion of Advocate General Jacobs in *Estate of Kik*, para. 44.

[146] *Estate of Kik*, para. 85.

[147] *Id.*, para. 87. The Court noted by way of example that although an individual decision may be published in the Official Journal in all EU languages, only the language used in the relevant procedure will be authentic.

[148] European Court of Justice, "Report on Translation at the Court of Justice" (1999), 4 (emphasis in original).

must also be taken of the fact that the Community trade mark was created for the benefit not of all citizens, but of economic operators, and that economic operators are not under any obligation to make use of it."[149] Having thus placed the situation in a relatively narrow context, the Court easily concluded that OHIM's limited linguistic services were justifiable:

> [T]he language regime of a body such as [OHIM] is the result of a difficult process which seeks to achieve the necessary balance between the interests of economic operators and the public interest in terms of the cost of proceedings, but also between the interests of applicants for Community trade marks and those of other economic operators in regard to access to translations of documents which confer rights, or proceedings involving more than one economic operator, such as opposition, revocation and invalidity proceedings. The Court of First Instance was therefore right to find ... that, in determining the official languages of the Community which may be used [in such multi-party] proceedings, where the parties cannot agree on which language to use, the Council was pursuing the legitimate aim of seeking an appropriate linguistic solution to the difficulties arising from such a failure to agree. Similarly, the Court of First Instance was right to hold ... that, even if the Council did treat official languages of the Community differently, its choice to limit the languages to those which are most widely known in the European Community is appropriate and proportionate.[150]

Ms. Kik's estate advanced the interesting and ironic argument that OHIM's language system was unjustifiable because the body's stated goals could be achieved through a less discriminatory language policy, namely the designation of a single language, such as English, as the official language of the office. The ECJ appeared to heed the Advocate General's opinion that this position, having been raised for the first time on appeal, need not be addressed by the Court.[151] Nonetheless, the Court stated in passing that such a theory was "not apposite;"[152] the Advocate General went so far as to call it "perverse" and maintained that "it is hard to see how favouring one language could be regarded as less discriminatory than favouring five."[153] But is this really so hard to see? As will be evidenced below, English is by far the most widely-known language in the EU, and it may plausibly be contended that requiring the use of English in multi-party proceedings where the parties cannot agree on the use of another language would

149 *Estate of Kik*, para. 88. This statement ignores the fact that an economic operator's right to use a mark in connection with his trade may be extinguished by a competitor's decision to avail himself of OHIM's protective machinery.

150 *Id.*, paras. 92-94.

151 Opinion of Advocate General Jacobs in *Estate of Kik*, para. 66.

152 *Estate of Kik*, para. 95.

153 Opinion of Advocate General Jacobs in *Estate of Kik*, para. 66.

be more likely to result in situations in which neither party had a significant language advantage over another.[154] While such an anglo-centric system would obviously favor citizens of the UK and Ireland over all other EU citizens, it would reduce the inequalities between citizens who speak French, Italian, Spanish and German on the one hand and speakers of all other languages on the other hand.[155] It would certainly more effectively reduce costs at OHIM than the quintilingual system currently in place.

F. Towards a Lingua Franca? : *"Si tu veux chanter aujourd'hui, chante en anglais et tu seras compris."*[156]

The unexpected call by Ms. Kik's estate for monolingualism at OHIM should be viewed against the backdrop of the increasing use of English in EU affairs. French was traditionally the dominant language in the EC, and retained this status long after English became a Regulation language with the accession of the UK and Ireland in 1973. French documents outnumbered English ones on the desks of Commission translators until the balance shifted after the 1995 enlargement brought in three countries more comfortable with English than French.[157] In 1992, nearly 47 per cent of documents translated at the Commission were originally drafted in French while only 35 per cent were in English; by 1997 that order had flipped, with 45 per cent being in English and 40 per cent in French. By 2003 nearly 59 per cent of documents were in English, and the share of French documents had been reduced to 28 per cent.

This anglo-ascendancy reflects the general European trend that has made English the most commonly spoken foreign language on the continent by far. The European Economic and Social Committee has stated that "[c]ircumstances dictate that English will probably in time become the language spoken by a majority of Europeans."[158] It is the major language in multi-national settings in commercial, academic, and diplomatic circles. It is commonly spoken by telephone operators at emergency call centers in every Member State except Germany.[159] A pre-enlargement Barometer survey indicated that of the EU

[154] Put another way, it is arguably fairer to make both sides struggle with a relatively unfamiliar language if one party must do so.

[155] Except to the extent that knowledge of English, and the difficulty of learning it, varies among the speakers of various European languages.

[156] Contemporary French song quoted in Harro Stammerjohann, "La Fascination de l'Anglais" in *Les Langues Dans L'Europe de Demain*, 87.

[157] Colette Fleisch, "Le Service de Traduction de la Commission Face au Défi du Multilinguisme dans l'Union Européenne Élargie," *Terminologie et Traduction* 1 (1999), 92, 94.

[158] Opinion of 23 Jan. 2003, [2003] O.J. C85/126.

[159] Answer to Written Question No. E-2091/02, [2003] C028E/0178.

citizens who said they could speak a European language other than their own (some 53 per cent of those surveyed), 41 per cent said they spoke English as a second language, and it was the first foreign language of 33 per cent.[160] This is over twice the percentage that said they spoke French as a second language (19 per cent), and far ahead of German (10 per cent), Spanish (7 per cent) and Italian (3 per cent).[161] Taken as a whole, however, English is less commonly known in the ten new Member States that joined the EU in 2004. A Eurobarometer survey of linguistic abilities in the then-candidate countries (which included the ten states admitted in 2004 along with Bulgaria, Romania, and Turkey) that was conducted in 2001 revealed that only 18 per cent of the population of these countries had competence in English, which was just a little bit ahead of the number who knew Russian (14 per cent), although significantly ahead of German (10 per cent) and French (4 per cent).[162] Moreover, when one looks at individual countries, one finds that in some of them English is hardly known at all; only 14 per cent of people in Hungary and 13 per cent in Slovakia report knowing the language.[163]

The dominance of English has alarmed many.[164] In addition to the fact that knowledge of English is unevenly spread throughout the EU, both in terms of geography and socio-economic structure, knowledge of a language that is useful for international business and diplomatic purposes does not particularly help EU citizens who wish to conduct the affairs of daily life while living or working in other parts of the Union. As one group of language policy scholars has stated:

> English seems to be far from capable of resolving all the problems, particularly in the short term. Currently less than half of all Europeans can hold a conversation in English, while 89 % of students have learnt it. Generalized English is thus far from

[160] Eurobarometer Report 54, "Europeans and Languages" (Executive Summary) (2001), 1.

[161] 81 per cent of the population of the EU-15 spoke English, French or German as either a mother tongue or a secondarily acquired language. After the 2004 enlargement, this figure has declined slightly, to 74 per cent. *See* Jan Fidrmuc & Victor Ginsburgh, "Languages in the European Union: The Quest for Equality and its Cost," Manuscript (2004), 15.

[162] Candidate Countries Eurobarometer 2001 (March 2002), 36. The inclusion of Turkey, which has a large population and where English is little known (only 10 per cent report competence in it), skews the results somewhat. *See also* Susan Sarcevic, "Preserving Multilingualism in an Enlarged European Union," *Terminologie et Traduction* 2 (2001), 34, 41.

[163] Candidate Countries Eurobarometer 2001, 36. Complaints were raised about the degree to which the EU used English to communicate with the candidate countries. *See, e.g.*, Answer to Written Question No. E-3800/02, [2003] O.J. 268E/49.

[164] *See, e.g.*, the recent statement from the Opinion of the Committee of the Regions that "cautions against supporting the emergence of a de facto lingua franca." Opinion of the Committee of the Regions on the "Communication from the Commission on Promoting Language Learning and Linguistic Diversity: An Action Plan 2004-2006," para. 1.6 [2004] O.J. C073/33.

> being the practical multipurpose language that it is claimed to be. Furthermore, if it serves immediate communication purposes, it cannot function as the language used when living in a country which has another language. To live in a community implies the practice of that country's language. English as a "*lingua franca*" maintains the confusion between a language necessary for a certain political (in particular that of the European institutions), economic and scientific level, and a language necessary for interaction among the citizens themselves.[165]

It is nonetheless natural for people in a multilingual setting to gravitate towards the language that is most commonly known in any group in which they find themselves.[166] Some, such as Jürgen Habermas, believe that the widespread use of English offers Europeans the possibility of realizing the goal of forming a collective identity within the EU.[167] In terms of the language policy of the EU's internal structure, a reduction in the number of languages would certainly improve its efficiency. However, as Habermas has stated, there is always a trade-off between efficiency and legitimacy, and the democratic legitimacy of the EU has long been a sore point of contention for Europe's citizens and a conundrum for its political theorists.[168] Reducing the number of languages used would create a significant communication barrier between the EU and the vast majority of EU citizens who can only express themselves effectively in their native tongue, and the EU has committed itself to strengthening, not weakening, its connections with its diverse citizenry.

In any event, the use of English in the EU has in fact become so common that a Member State's right, under Article 3 of Regulation No. 1, to receive documents in its official language when dealing with the Commission might be disregarded by anglophone Commission functionaires. This had occurred in a

---

[165] European Language Council Reference Document, Prepared at the European Year of Languages 2001 Conference on Multilingualism and New Learning Environments at the Freie Universität Berlin, 28-30 June 2001, para. 1.5. Available on-line at http://www.fu-berlin.de/elc/docs/langpolENlong.pdf. In light of the fact that Member States continue to more or less function as self-contained political-cultural units and provide the basis for a person's national identity within the larger EU framework, the various national languages do not seem to be in any imminent danger of falling out of general use in local, intra-national affairs. For a fascinating comparison of the EU language system with that of modern India, where English and Hindi serve as linguae francae on a national scale while various other languages thrive at the level of the states, *see* David D. Laitin, "The Cultural Identities of a European State" 25 *Politics and Society* 3 (1997), 277.

[166] Philippe Van Parijs has described this phenomenon as the "maximin law of communication" under which a group will elect to use the "language best known by the member [of the group] who knows it least." Philippe Van Parijs, "Europe's Three Language Problems" (Provisional Draft 2003), 3-4.

[167] Jürgen Habermas, "Remarks on Dieter Grimm's 'Does Europe Need a Constitution?'" 1 *European L. J.* 303 (1995), 307.

[168] Jürgen Habermas, "Why Europe Needs a Constitution," *New Left Review* (2001), 5, 8.

recent case in which Finland sought the annulment of a Commission decision excluding certain payments from Community financing by the European Agricultural Guidance and Guarantee Fund.[169] The Commission had sent Finland numerous documents, some in English and some in Finnish, and the issue in the case was which of those documents could constitute the notice that the Commission was required to give a Member State in connection with an exclusion of payments, which was of importance because the Commission could only bar payments that were made in a twenty-four month period preceding the date of the notice. The first document was sent in May 1997, in Finnish, but Finland claimed that it failed to meet certain requirements (among other things, it was sent by fax, which Finland claimed was not permitted). Another document, a letter in Finnish sent in September 1998, did not contain a necessary annex. That annex, however, had been sent to Finland in July 1998, but in English. Finland received a letter with a Finnish version of the annex in December 1998, and contended that it was that letter which should be considered the requisite notice.

The ECJ disagreed and ruled that the May 1997 document satisfied the requirements for the notice, and accordingly concluded it was unnecessary to consider the sufficiency of any of the subsequent documents. The Advocate General, however, while reaching the same conclusion about the May 1997 Finnish document, had also considered the later materials, and decided that the September 1998 letter, combined with the July 1998 English annex, could satisfy the notice requirement as well, reasoning that:

> The close cooperation between the Commission and the Member State is characterised, among other things, by intensive communication between the two. Because of the frequency and rapidity with which communications need to be made, the formal requirements for such communications cannot be too demanding. That applies both to the means used - fax and e-mail will often be a more efficient way of exchanging information than a letter through official channels - and to the language of the communications, particularly where only a small number of the Commission's staff can speak the language of the Member State concerned.[170]

Citing the CFI's opinion in *Kik*, the Advocate General stated that "the choice of language may - in some cases - be limited to a language which is more widely known within the European Union."[171] He nonetheless acknowledged

---

[169] Case C-170/00, *Republic of Finland v. Commission*, 2002 ECR I-1007.

[170] Opinion of Advocate General Geelhoed in *Republic of Finland v. Commission*, 2002 ECR I-1007, para. 22.

[171] *Id.* at para. 78. This is a misreading of the CFI's decision in *Kik*, as that case did not hold that it was permissible to limit the choice to a *single* language, but rather to a limited, but plural, number of languages. In fact, the Advocate General in the *Kik* case stated explicitly that it was "perverse" to contend that only one language should be used at OHIM. Opinion of Advocate General Jacobs in *Estate of Kik*, para. 66.

that a Member State did have a right to receive materials in its own language, but essentially stated that Finland had waived that right. A custom had developed between the parties, in which the Commission sent Finland documents initially in English, and then later, after a translation was available, in Finnish. The Advocate General opined that if Finland wished to deny legal effect to documents sent to it in English, it should have informed the Commission of this at the time, and should not have raised this argument for the first time in litigation, as such an approach was "not compatible with the cooperation that takes place between the Commission and a Member State."[172] The close cooperation between the Commission and Member States differs from the relationship between the Commission and private individuals, the Advocate General stressed, and the latter are "more readily able than a Member State to rely on a formal error by the Commission in order to obtain a procedural advantage."[173] However, in a later case that involved a party who had opposed an application for a Community trademark, the CFI held that the opposing party's opposition should be rejected on the grounds that it had failed to submit supporting materials in the language of the proceeding, even though this failure was arguably the result of the Commission's representations to the opposing party.[174]

Not everyone has been as tolerant of the move towards English as the Finns who apparently acquiesced in its use in that case, however. In 1997, the Dutch Commissioner, Hans van den Broek, generated complaints when he spoke in English at both a plenary session of the Commission and in Parliament. Members of Parliament, in written questions to the Commission, asked why van den Broek had not spoken in his native Dutch on these occasions. Van den Broek himself authored the Commission's strikingly unresponsive "answer" to one such question:

> The Commission fully shares the view expressed by the Honourable Members that language is an expression of a country's culture and identity. The Commission also attaches importance to clear communication of its work to the citizens of Europe. The Commission would however remind the Honourable Member that, when its Members address another Community institution, their only obligation is to use one of the official languages of the Community.[175]

There have been complaints that the growing use of English by non-native speakers in the Commission has resulted in the proliferation of texts written in a clunky style, full of legalistic "officialese" and "fuzzy noun-based" sentences

---

172 Opinion of Advocate General Geelhoed in *Republic of Finland v. Commission,* at para. 79.

173 *Id.*, para. 23.

174 Case T-107/02, *GE Betz, Inc. v. OHIM* (2004).

175 Answer to Written Question 2671/97, [1998] C102/87; *See also* Answer to Question 3955/97, [1998] C158/196.

that bear little resemblance to "real English."[176] Concerned that the use of such awkward English was impeding the EU's ability to communicate with its citizens, the English language translation unit at the Commission, during the UK presidency in 1998, launched its "Fight the FOG" program with the aim of improving the style of English-language documents drafted by non-native speakers.[177] The campaigners have their work cut out for them. Foggy language is a problem in every political organization, even monolingual ones, as a politician will frequently, if not chiefly, use language not to clarify but to disguise a position; he will cautiously utter deliberately ambiguous statements in the hopes of duping constituents with conflicting interests into believing that he is on all of their sides. As Professor Steiner has observed, "[h]uman speech conceals far more than it confides; it blurs much more than it defines; it distances more than it connects."[178] The EU's use of language, including its language about language, has been a prime example of this phenomenon, and will be examined more closely in the next chapter, where I will take up the EU's purported commitment to what is called "linguistic diversity."

G. Conclusion

Far from being equal, the languages of the EU may be ranked as follows:

1. English
2. French
3. German
4. Spanish, Italian (and Polish?)
5. Czech, Danish, Dutch, Estonian, Finnish, Greek, Hungarian, Latvian, Lithuanian, Portuguese, Slovak, Slovenian and Swedish
6. Maltese
7. Irish
8. Turkish
9. Regional and Minority languages

English is the *primus inter pares* of the EU's linguistic realm. French and German, as the second and third internal working languages, rank below it. Spanish, Italian, and probably Polish, by virtue of the comparably large numbers

---

[176] Emma Wagner & Tim Martin, "Fighting the Fog at the European Commission," *Terminologie et Traduction* 2 (1998), 131.

[177] *Id.* In a 1995 opinion, the Economic and Social Committee blamed the use of legal jargon for the hostile reaction that the Treaty of Maastricht received in some quarters. [1995] O.J. C256/8.

[178] Steiner at 240.

of speakers of these languages, are apt to receive special treatment when the EU considers language limitations.[179] The bulk of the Regulation languages occupy the center of the list. As they are spoken by only relatively small or mid-level numbers of people (abstracting away from the use of Portuguese outside of Europe) and are not generally spoken far beyond the borders of the Member States in which they have official status, they may not be given the same preferential treatment accorded to other Regulation languages. Maltese is a Regulation language whose use is largely prevented by a derogation measure. Irish is a Treaty language, but is not a Regulation language and the speakers of this language have only very limited rights. The EU has committed itself to making Turkish a Regulation language, but has not yet done so.

All of these languages enjoy more rights than the regional or minority languages that are spoken in almost every Member State, however. Many of these have official (or quasi-official) status in particular regions of Member States, including Frisian, Welsh, Basque and Catalan, and the latter is spoken by more people in the EU than many of the Treaty or Regulation languages.[180] The exclusion of such languages from the EU's language regime raises questions about the seriousness of the EU's commitment to "linguistic diversity" and whether its language system is consistent with the human rights principles that it professes to adhere to, and which now form part of the corpus of its law.

"Linguistic diversity" and human rights ideals are also in tension with the fiscal and convenience considerations that have led to the *de facto* exclusion of all languages except English, French and German as allowable internal working languages, the growing use of one of these (English), the use of pivots in interpretations, the non-translation of many documents, and the formal attempt to limit the use of languages at OHIM. The *Kik* case demonstrates that both the Council and the EU's judiciary give substantial weight to economic and operational concerns in assessing language policy. While such considerations are undeniably relevant to the formation of any organization's rules, in the context of language policy they cannot be considered in isolation from human rights law or a proper regard for linguistic diversity. Chapter V will examine the human rights aspect of language law, but this book will now turn to the role of the EU's "linguistic diversity" programs in Chapter II.

---

179 Spanish and Italian were included as official languages in OHIM's language regime; new-comer Polish has been given status as a "pivot" language in the European Parliament.

180 With approximately eight to ten million speakers, Catalan outnumbers Danish, Estonian, Finnish, Irish, Latvian, Lithuanian, Maltese, Slovak, Slovene and Swedish. Maltese, with its 375,000 speakers, is less commonly spoken than either Welsh or Basque, which have about half a million speakers each, and ranks only slightly ahead of the 300,000 speakers of Frisian.

CHAPTER II

The EU's Commitment to "Linguistic Diversity"

A. Scope of "Diversity"

The EU often speaks proudly of the "linguistic diversity" of the Union, and has undertaken a number of measures designed to promote this source of "cultural wealth."[1] "Respect" for "linguistic diversity" is one of the objectives outlined in the new Constitution for Europe.[2] The term "linguistic diversity," however, is a prime example of the sort of mushy language that the Fight the Fog campaign should endeavor to eradicate. "Linguistic diversity," in EU parlance, often refers only to the official or national languages of the Member States (*i.e.*, the Regulation languages), whereas other times the term may include various regional or minority languages as well.

After the 2004 enlargement, approximately forty-six million EU citizens – about one out of every ten – speak a language that is not the official language of their own Member State.[3] Some of them speak languages that are not official in their own Member State but are in another (usually bordering) one (Hungarian speakers in Austria, for example), but many of them speak languages that are not official in any Member State. Some of these languages are spoken by a large number of people, notably Catalan which is spoken by at least eight to ten million people, while others are spoken by very few; Tatar, for example, is spoken by only about 900 people in Finland.[4] Some of these languages are primarily associated with a particular region of a Member State (or contiguous areas of bordering states) and are often referred to as "regional" languages. Some unofficial languages such as Yiddish and the Romani tongues are not associated with a particular region as such, but rather with an historically migratory people, and are frequently called "minority" languages, although, this term is also apt to be used to describe regional languages as well.[5] Speakers of

---

1 Resolution of 31 March 1995, [1995] O.J. C207/1. *See also, e.g.*, Resolution of 25 June 2002, [2002] O.J. C162/5.

2 Art. I-3. Such "respect" is also called for by Article II-82, formerly Article 22 of the EU's Charter of Fundamental Rights.

3 Report of the European Parliament of 14 July 2003 with Recommendations to the Commission on European Regional and Lesser Used Languages – the Languages of Minorities in the EU – in the Context of Enlargement and Cultural Diversity (2003/2057(INI)). Statistics on the number of speakers of such languages vary, due in part to definitional problems concerning "speaker," "minority," "language" and the like, but also because statistics often do not come from official sources, as many states (such as Belgium and France) do not collect census data on this sensitive issue.

4 Website of the European Bureau for Lesser Used Languages, www.eblul.org.

5 The term "minority" is heavily laden with legal significance, as it is a term used in international law, and is therefore one that states with homogenizing impulses (such as France and Turkey) often wish to avoid using. Euphemisms for minority languages have been coined, as can be seen in the name of the European Bureau for Lesser Used Languages, which was established in 1982 and is primarily funded by the EU.

regional and minority languages are unable to use their native languages with EU officials, to receive EU documents in such languages, and confront barriers to employment within the EU, as job seekers often must demonstrate linguistic competence in two or more EU languages.[6]

There are languages that are given less legal protection than those that are considered "minority" or "regional" ones. The EU's language programs generally do not include the languages of immigrant communities in the EU (such as Arabic, Chinese, or Urdu), artificially created languages (such as Esperanto), or languages that are deemed to be simply "dialects" of some other language.[7] The distinction between a "language" and a "dialect" is one that is of crucial importance in both law and policy, but is rarely directly addressed by legislators or policy-makers who often seem oblivious to the problematic issues involved in the use of these terms. The term "dialect" is used in multiple ways. It is used by linguists in a neutral sense to refer to a form of a language that differs in systematic ways from other forms of that language.[8] Understood thus, it follows that *everyone speaks a dialect*. Non-linguists, on the other hand, frequently use "dialect" in a derogatory manner to describe a variety of language that deviates from some commonly accepted standard or "correct" version – invariably the form of speech used by the socially and politically dominant group. Seldom is there any recognition, however, that the standard at issue is not of the "dialect" community's own making (the community, after all, speaks in accordance with its own standards), but rather has been imposed by an outside and more powerful group, frequently in connection with an overall pattern of subjugation. Speakers of a "dialect" may be subject to extreme socio-economic persecution, and are frequently denied the right to use their language in education, employment or in government affairs. In sum, they often have particularly strong need of language rights, but they usually *ain't got none*.

Another important point to make about dialects is that it is not always easy to determine when a given speech system should be considered a "dialect" (in the value-neutral technical sense of the word) of a particular language or rather a full-fledged language in its own right. The question of whether two related speech systems should be viewed as dialects of the same language or separate languages altogether involves an assessment of the level of difference between them, which can vary from negligible to extreme, with the determinative dividing line remaining hazy. The decision with respect to any given pair of speech systems is usually the result of political, not linguistic, considerations.[9] There

---

6 In Case T-249/01, *Rivas v. European Parliament*, [2003] O.J. C171/23, the Court of First Instance dismissed the application of a Catalan-speaking Spanish national who was denied admission to an employment competition on the grounds that he did not speak an EU language besides Spanish.

7 *See* Commission website, http://europa.eu.int/comm/education/langmin.html.

8 Victoria Fromkin & Robert Rodman, *An Introduction to Language* (3d ed. 1983), 245.

9 Robert Dunbar, "Minority Language Rights in International Law," 50 *International & Comp. L. Q.* (2001), 90, 96.

is a cliché in linguistic circles that a language is simply a dialect with an army and a navy, and indeed there is much truth to that. Norwegian, for example, would likely still be considered a dialect of Danish had Norway not obtained its independence from the Danish crown in the last century.[10] The issue of dialects will be addressed again in Chapter V in connection with a discussion of human rights issues. For now, however, the reader is asked to keep this oft-ignored issue in mind when considering the EU's commitment to linguistic diversity.

B. Rationale for Promoting Diversity and the Philosophical Clash between the Parliament and the Council

The EU offers two basic reasons for its "linguistic diversity" programs, one cultural in nature, the other economic. Pronouncements on linguistic diversity are often made with lofty rhetoric about the humanistic value of Europe's multilingualism, but the programs that stem from them often seem to emphasize the economic value of learning another language, in particular the major commercial languages of English, French and German. The EU's programs do not acknowledge that economic and political integration is in fact inherently antagonistic to linguistic diversity. Much of Europe's historical linguistic diversity disappeared in the last several centuries as a result of the increased centralization of power in Europe's nation-states and the associated spread of standard languages at the expense of regional dialects and other minority languages.[11] Diversity has been further eroded by the increased interconnectedness of far-flung areas due to revolutionary advances in transportation and communication technology.

In 1997 disagreement over the relative cultural or economic nature of "linguistic diversity" programs led to a dispute between the European Parliament and the Council which ended up before the Court of Justice.[12] The case concerned a decision which the Council had taken on "the adoption of a multiannual programme to promote the linguistic diversity of the Community in the information society."[13] The measure provided incentives to industries which developed technologies to facilitate communication between speakers of different languages, and both economic and social reasons were cited for the action. The preamble of the decision stated that "the advent of the information society

---

[10] Fromkin & Rodman at 245-46.

[11] For a look at this phenomenon in two archetypal nation-states, *see* R.D. Grillo, *Dominant Languages: Language and Hierarchy in Britain and France* (1989). *See also*, Bruno de Witte, "Cultural Legitimation: Back to the Language Question," in *European Identity and the Search for Legitimacy* (Soledad García ed., 1993), 154.

[12] Case C-42/97, *Parliament v. Council*, 1999 ECR I-869.

[13] Decision 96/664, [1996] O.J. L306/40.

provides industry and in particular the language industry with new prospects for communication and trade on European and world markets which are marked by a rich linguistic and cultural diversity," and also noted that this development "could afford the citizens of Europe greater access to information and offer them an outstanding opportunity for access to the cultural and linguistic wealth and diversity of Europe."

The Parliament and the Council disagreed over the degree to which this measure was cultural in nature, and therefore disputed which article of the EC Treaty should provide the legal basis for its adoption. The Council, viewing the program as primarily economic, was of the view that this action could be taken solely on the basis of Article 130 of the EC Treaty (now Art. 157)[14], which gives the Council authority to ensure "the competitiveness of the Community's industry." The Parliament, while recognizing that Article 130 was a valid basis, contended that the measure should also be based on Article 128 (now 151)[15], which provides that the Community is to "contribute to the flowering of the cultures of the Member States" and that cultural aspects are to be taken into account in actions under other provisions of the Treaty, "in particular in order to respect and to promote the diversity of [the Community's] cultures." The choice of a particular legal rubric was not simply an academic exercise, but rather was determinative of the extent of the role that the Parliament would have in the adoption of the measure. Measures taken under Article 128 could only be adopted with Parliament's approval under the "co-decision" procedure, which is now outlined in Article 251. Measures taken solely under Article 130, however, could be taken by the Council without Parliament's approval; there was merely a requirement that the Council "consult" with Parliament.

After the Council enacted the decision exclusively on the basis of Article 130, the Parliament brought an action for annulment of the measure before the ECJ. The Court reviewed the contested decision in detail in an effort to determine whether industry or culture was the "main or predominant component,"[16] and concluded that the measure was principally economic. "Language in [the decision's] context," the Court wrote, "is seen not as an element of cultural heritage but rather as an object or instrument of economic activity."[17] The Court saw a distinction between the vaguely worded benefits for the citizenry at large compared to the clearly identified measures that were to be taken on behalf of industrial undertakings: "Citizens are seen as beneficiaries of linguistic diversity in general, in the context of the information society. In contrast, economic operators and, more particularly, small and medium-sized enterprises, are envisioned as beneficiaries of concrete actions that will be undertaken in accord-

---

14 Const. for Eur. Art. III-279(1).

15 Const. for Eur. Art. III-280.

16 Case C-42/97, *Parliament v. Council*, para. 40.

17 *Id.*, para. 53.

ance with the action lines of the programme provided for by the decision."[18] The Court therefore easily concluded that "[t]he object of the programme, namely the promotion of linguistic diversity, is seen as an element of an essentially economic nature and incidentally as a vehicle for or element of culture as such," and could accordingly be based solely on Article 130.[19]

This case should not be understood as simply a battle for legislative turf between two competing EU institutions. The result of basing linguistic diversity measures on Article 130, and the concomitant avoidance of the co-decision procedure, is the minimization of the role of the legislative actor which is most predisposed to seeing linguistic diversity as a value in and of itself.[20] As was discussed in Chapter I, Parliament regularly conducts its sessions in all Regulation languages; the Council makes do with far fewer. Moreover, there are members of the Parliament who are pushing for greater recognition of minority and regional languages, including those who have formed the Intergroup of Stateless Nations. This organization consists of members of the European Parliament who represent regional parties in their home states and, among other things, demands that the "official languages of stateless nations must be recognised as essential elements of the rich heritage of the EU [and that] [t]he same legislative rights should be given to the languages of the stateless nations as for the official languages of the Member State."[21]

C. Promotion of Linguistic Diversity in Education

The EU's efforts in promoting linguistic diversity have been most prominent in the field of education. In 1989 the Lingua program was founded on the model of the Socrates student-exchange program (which later absorbed it) in order to fund programs that provide opportunities for students, language teachers, and prospective language teachers to study languages and to travel to other Member States in connection with their studies.[22] Lingua only finances the study of certain languages, however: its original mission applied only to the Regulation languages, along with Irish and Luxembourgish. It has a mandate to give special priority to the "less widely used and less taught languages of the EU," or, to use the bureaucratic acronym, the "LWULT"s of the

---

18 *Id.*, para. 47.

19 *Id.*, paras. 61-64.

20 The new Constitution for Europe provides for the general use of the "co-decision procedure," which is now dubbed the "ordinary legislative procedure." Const. for Eur. Arts I-34, III-396.

21 Constitutional Theses of the Stateless Nations Intergroup in the European Parliament.

22 Decision No. 89/489, [1989] O.J. L239. The EU also has a similar program – the Leonardo da Vinci program – for the promotion of language learning in connection with vocational training. *See* Dec. No. 99/382, [1999] O.J. L146/33.

EU. While minority and regional languages are by and large less used and less taught than their official counterparts, they are not among the LWULT's of the EU, which, before the 2004 enlargement, generally applied this term to Danish, Dutch, Finnish, Greek, Irish, Luxembourgish, Portuguese and Swedish. By excluding unofficial languages from the Lingua program, the EU has, in the words of Bruno de Witte, revealed that "the Community's professed commitment to linguistic diversity is selective, and does not extend all along the line."[23]

"Linguistic diversity" obtained the status of a treaty concept, although it did not become a clearer one, with the advent of the Treaty of European Union, which added a new Article 126 (now Art. 149) to the EC Treaty.[24] This article provides that the Community is to have a role in promoting education, and the Community's linguistic diversity is paradoxically posited as both a reason for, and a limit to, the Community's power to act in this area. The Community is charged with "developing the European dimension in education, particularly through the teaching and dissemination of the languages of the Member States," but is to do so "while fully respecting the responsibility of the Member States for the content of teaching and the organisation of education systems and their cultural and linguistic diversity." This limitation is consistent with the principle of subsidiarity, which has been a cardinal rule of European integration that limits the EU's competence to powers specified in the EC Treaty and bars it from taking action unless the objectives of a proposed action cannot be sufficiently achieved by the Member States.[25]

Measures taken under Article 126 (now 149) have often been limited in the breadth of the "diversity" which they embody. In 1995 the Council passed a resolution that called for "improving and diversifying" language learning and teaching.[26] The "diversifying" of language teaching was needed in order to promote the study of "languages that are less widely used or less frequently taught."[27] This was not a call for people to pick up grammars of Galician or Sorbian, however. While the resolution did not specify which languages the Council had in mind, it appears that the Council was referring to the Regulation languages. The term used in the resolution is the "languages of the Union," which could at first blush be read to refer to languages spoken in the EU, including minority and regional languages, but it does not appear that this is the meaning the Council intended. The resolution reaffirmed "the principle of equal status for each of the languages of the Union," a principle that in no way applies to minority and regional languages and could only be applied to the Regulation languages.

23 De Witte, "Cultural Legitimation: Back to the Language Question" at 169.

24 Const. for Eur. Art. III-282.

25 EC Treaty Art. 5; Const. for Eur. Art. I-11(3).

26 Resolution of 31 March 1995, [1995] O.J. C207/1.

27 *Id.* at 4.

Indeed, the resolution effectively *discourages* the study of minority or regional languages. One of its major points is that every student in the EU should learn "two languages of the Union" in addition to his or her mother tongue (which of course may or may not itself be a Regulation language).[28] If students have to study two foreign languages, and these must necessarily be Regulation languages, it seems unlikely that many students would study a third one. They, after all, have limited time in their schedules, and must also study subjects like math, science and history when they are not otherwise engaged in or preoccupied with the more urgently-felt interests of young people.

Minority and regional languages have not been entirely neglected by the EU's educational initiatives. For example, within the framework of the Erasmus student-exchange program, the EU decided to provide grants for masters-level programs that "provide for the use of at least two European languages spoken in the Member States where [the participating Erasmus institutions] are situated."[29] The Commission, in disabusing a member of Parliament who had interpreted this wording to preclude the use of Catalan in the popular Erasmus destination of Barcelona, emphasized that this provision "does not refer to 'official' Union but rather 'European' languages and does not prejudge – or exclude – the use of any particular language as the language of instruction."[30]

Nonetheless, it is the Regulation languages – and only a small number of these – that are, the clear beneficiaries of the EU's educational programs. Instead of promoting a truly diverse mix of languages, Lingua primarily finances the study of those languages which are generally deemed to be the most valuable for use in international business: English above all, followed by French and German. This is despite the fact that Lingua has a special mission to promote less commonly used languages. The failure of Lingua to achieve this goal is illustrated in the following passage from the EU's 2000 Report on the Lingua program, which speaks in reference to a program that financed study trips for foreign language teachers:

> [The program] aimed to prioritise the less widely used and lesser taught languages (LWULT) but the most common target languages were firstly English with French in second position, followed by German. There were very few examples in the survey of beneficiaries who had taken courses targeting any of the LWULT. This reflects the situation in the Member States in which the less taught

---

[28] The study of two foreign languages was pushed by France in the hopes that this would result in the study of French by students who would have opted for English if they were only required to study one language. Alan Forrest, "The Challenge of Languages in Europe," *Terminologie et Traduction* 3 (1998), 101, 105-06.

[29] 2002/0165 (COD)

[30] Answer to Written Question E-1811/03, [2004] C11E/230.

> languages ... are not taught and therefore not a priority when approving requests for a grant.[31]

Instead of encouraging respect for diversity or protecting less commonly used languages, Lingua thus seems to simply reinforce the pattern of language study that would occur even without Community support.[32] EU policymakers, with their long tradition of conceptualizing matters in economic terms, have highlighted the business and commercial advantages of language study while making vague references to the cultural benefits of language study. For example, the Council decision which created the Lingua program stressed that "the establishment of the Internal Market would be facilitated by the quantitative improvement of foreign language training within the Community to enable the Community's citizens to communicate with each other and to overcome linguistic difficulties which impede the free movement of persons, goods, services, and capital."[33] Even on its own terms, however, the EU's focus on Regulation languages is difficult to justify. As Professor de Witte has pointed out, "[i]f the intention of this programme really is to enable the Community's citizens to reap the benefits of a completed internal market and to enhance understanding and solidarity between the peoples of the Community, there seems no valid reason to include languages like Irish and Letzebuergesch, which are spoken by a few hundred thousand persons, while leaving out Catalan, which is spoken by more than six million persons within the Community."[34] The exclusion of the minority and regional languages of the EU Member States has become even more glaring in recent years as Lingua has expanded its linguistic scope to allow financing of the study of certain European languages that have official status in states outside the EU.[35]

---

31 EU Socrates Evaluation Report (2000) at 266.

32 Laitin has written on the contrasting attitudes Europeans harbor towards learning English, which people will pay handsomely for, and learning other languages, which people must be bribed to do. David D. Laitin, "The Cultural Identities of a European State" 25 *Politics and Society* 3 (1997), 277.

33 Dec. 89/489, pmbl.; *see also* Council Resolution of 16 Dec. 1997 on the early teaching of European Union languages, para. 9, [1998] O.J. C 1/2.

34 De Witte, "Cultural Legitimation: Back to the Language Question" at 69.

35 Lingua's scope expanded to include the languages spoken in the European Economic Area (which added Norwegian and Icelandic), as well as languages spoken in what were at the time EU candidate countries in eastern and central Europe. EU Socrates Evaluation Report (2000), 249, available at http://europa.eu.int/comm/education/evaluation/soc11.pdf. In January 2003 the European Economic and Social Committee issued an opinion which vaguely called for the promotion of regional and minority languages within the Socrates and Leonardo da Vinci frameworks. Opinion of 23 Jan. 2003, [2003] O.J. C85/126.

D. Limited Efforts to Protect Minority Languages

The EU has taken some small measures to promote unofficial languages. The EU is the principal source of funding (eighty per cent) of the European Bureau for Lesser Used Languages, which was established in Dublin in 1982.[36] The EBLUL is an "independent" non-governmental organization whose stated mission, according to its website (ironically available only in English and French) is to safeguard Europe's regional and minority languages and to defend the rights of those who speak them.[37] It provides information and assists in the coordination of various language-related activities. While the EU provides the bulk of the EBLUL's financing, the EU's largesse has been rather limited,[38] and in the words of an EU-sponsored study conducted by the EBLUL and the European Centre for Minority Issues, "the financial importance of the EU contribution to regional and minority languages should not be overestimated."[39] In 2001 the EU threatened to cut off its meager funding to the EBLUL if the organization did not take steps to reduce expenditures on salaries and overhead, which do consume a large portion of the EBLUL's budget,[40] and in the same year the EU suppressed spending under the EU budget's Action Line for the Promotion and Safeguard of Minority and Regional Languages and Cultures, which was the EU's most important legal basis of expenditure in this area.[41] Absent solid support from the EU and the Member States themselves, regional and minority languages can easily turn into "luxury consumption items" for a small cadre of academics and ardent nationalists.[42]

The EBLUL, as one might expect, exhibits an understanding of the problem of languages that are simply viewed as "dialects." It has indicated that attempts to distinguish between languages and dialects are misguided, as they hinder

---

[36] Commission Answer to parliamentary question, [2001] O.J. C261E/228.

[37] As Dunbar points out, these two goals are not always compatible with one another. Dunbar at 97.

[38] In 1998, for example, the EU provided the EBLUL with less than 750,000 euros. Answer to Written Question 2139/98, [1999] O.J. C050/130. In 2002 (the year following the "European Year of Languages"), the EU shelled out 810,000 euros. Answer to Written Question E-1140/03, [2003] O.J. 268E/176.

[39] Final Report on "Support for Minority Languages in Europe" of 15 May 2002, at 3, available on the europa website at http://europa.eu.int/comm/education/policies/lang/langmin/support.pdf.

[40] Administrative expenses in the proposed 2001-02 budget were nearly 75 per cent of the total. Answer to Written Question E-1111/01, [2001] O.J. C261E/227.

[41] *See* Final Report of the EBLUL & European Centre for Minority Issues on "Support for Minority Languages in Europe" at 32-33. The termination of spending was the result of the ECJ's opinion in Case C-106/96, *United Kingdom v. Commission*, 1998 ECR I-2729, which concerned technical legal issues pertaining to the budgetary process and did not directly address the issue of regional and minority languages.

[42] Laitin, "The Cultural Identities of a European State" 25 *Politics and Society* 3 (1997), 277.

an understanding of the dual nature of human language as both a system of communication unique to a particular group as well as a means for cementing group identity and staking a social boundary between those inside the group and those outside of it:

> What makes the words and sounds I use actual language, i.e. a human system that relates reality and the words I use to express that reality, is an altogether different phenomenon from the phenomenon according to which the words and sounds that I use are perceived by others as being Welsh or Portuguese. The first phenomenon can be studied by linguists, who will analyze the way phonemes and words function, the system they constitute, and the way they are ordered together. The perception, or rather the identification of this system as being a colloquial or foreign system, a contemporary or ancient system, a slang or prestigious variety, has mainly to do with issues of belonging, of identity, of processes of unification or separation, and as such will be studied by sociolinguists who focus on language acts as resulting from social phenomenon of exchange and interaction in time, space and specific contexts.[43]

While the EBLUL is thus aware of what it regards as the "irrelevant" distinction between a language and a dialect, elsewhere on its website it points out the fact that the EU will not fund projects concerning "dialects."

In addition to supporting the EBLUL, the EU funds the Mercator project, which is a network of three research foundations which provides information about minority languages,[44] and the EU directly provides some modest financing for research projects concerning regional or minority languages.[45] In addition, the EU commissioned the Euromosaic study in 1992 in order "to ascertain the current situation of the various [minority] language groups by reference to their potential for production and reproduction, and the difficulties which they encounter in doing so."[46] The report, which was completed in 1996, provided a candid assessment of the state of the EU's minority and regional language and indicated that the continued survival of several of them was very much open to

---

43 EBLUL website, quoting Bertrand Menciassi.

44 The institutions are located in minority/regional language centers and each one has its own particular area of specialization. The Fryske Akademy in Leeuwarden (or Ljowert, as it is known in Frisian) studies education, the CIEMEN foundation in Barcelona is concerned with language legislation and public administration and the University of Wales at Aberystwyth deals with press and media issues. *See* Mercator's website, http://www.mercator-central.org.

45 In 2000 the Commission had a budget of 2.5 million euros for this purpose. Answer to Written Question E-465/00, [2000] O.J. C374E/81.

46 The Euromosaic report was a joint effort of the Institut de Sociolingüística Catalana in Barcelona, the Centre de Recherche sur le plurilinguisme in Brussels, and the Research Centre of Wales in Bangor. Segments of the report quoted in this paper are obtainable on the web at www.uoc.es/euromosaic.

doubt. For example, it described the position of Mirandese, which is spoken by about 10,000 people in Portugal, as follows:

> Mirandese is very clearly in a state of decline at the present time, a process that has been accelerating since the sixties. With scant support from the public authorities and a lack of interest among its own speakers, the oral tradition of the language, its prestige and its social use are visibly dwindling. Most public manifestations of Mirandese are limited to displays of folk culture. Besides, its linguistic similarity to Portuguese contributes to Mirandese being regarded in the popular mind as a dialect of Portuguese.[47]

With regards to a language that was once enchantingly sung by medieval troubadours – Occitan – the report noted that there has been "a steady decline in the social use of the language as the oral tradition is no longer passed on and, with the perception that it serves no useful purpose, the prestige of the language has sunk to rock-bottom." With respect to another language spoken in France, the report warned that "[i]t is clear that the Breton language group is approaching a state of crisis. The relatively large number of speakers is virtually disappearing over a period of two generations. This largely derives from the negative identity associated with a prolonged period not only of neglect, but of hostility on the part of a state which has been constructed on the basis of a normativity that systematically fails to accommodate any sense of bilingualism that draws upon its internal cultural diversity."

The "internal cultural diversity" of a Member State that Euromosaic referred to is a subject that the EU studiously avoids. In an answer to a parliamentary question regarding the legal status of Basque in the Spanish province of Navarre, the Commission indicated that it believed the principle of subsidiarity left the language arrangements of Member States squarely in the hands of those Member States:

> As noted by the Honourable Member, respect for cultural and linguistic diversity in the Member States is a fundamental principle of European integration. The language arrangements applicable in the Member States fall within the competence of the Member States themselves or the relevant public authorities at national level.[48]

---

47 As this excerpt suggests, there is indeed a dispute as to whether Mirandese is better viewed as a separate language or as a dialectal variation of Portuguese. *See Encyclopedia of the Languages of Europe* (Glanville Price ed., 2000), 324.

48 Answer to Written Question E-0075/01, [2001] C174E/251.

The Commission has likewise chosen to duck recent questions about minority languages in other Member States.[49]

E. 2001: A Speech Oddity

The EU proclaimed 2001 as the "European Year of Languages," during which it sponsored a series of public events and informational campaigns designed to encourage language learning and "to raise awareness of the richness of linguistic and cultural diversity within the European Union and the value in terms of civilisation and culture embodied therein."[50] The program did not seek to disrupt the control of Member States over their own language policies, however, and therefore neither minority languages in general, nor the endangered ones identified in the Euromosaic report in particular, were specifically targeted by the program.

The Year of Languages was established by Decision No. 1934/00 which pronounced that the program was to be conducted with the understanding that "[a]ll the European languages, in their spoken and written forms, are equal in value and dignity from the cultural point of view and form an integral part of European cultures and civilisation."[51] In stating that languages are equal "from the cultural point of view," the Council suggests that there is a point of view from which they are not equal. This of course is true, as they are not equal from a *legal* point of view. As if to drive home this point, the decision declares the unequal status that various languages would have in the Year of Languages: "[The program] will cover the official languages of the Community, together with Irish, Letzeburgesch, and other languages in line with those identified by the Member States for the purposes of implementing this Decision."[52]

There were mixed motives for the Year of Languages. A mixture of economic and cultural reasons was stated in Decision 1934, but the emphasis shifts in different parts of the document. The preamble briefly mentions the economic benefits of language study, but waxes eloquent about the numerous cultural advantages that ensue from language learning. For example, it states that "[a]ccess to the vast literary heritage in the languages in which it was originally produced would contribute to developing mutual understanding and giving

---

49 *See, e.g.*, Answer to Written Question E-3198/02, [2003] O.J. C110E/182 (regarding non-Flemish speakers in Belgium); Answer to Written Question E2464/01, [2002] O.J. C093E/135 (minority languages in France); Answer to Written Question E1670/01, [2002] C040E/75 and Answer to Written Question P-3090/00, [2001] O.J. C113E/239 (minority languages in Greece); Answer to Written Question 3030/98, [1999] O.J. C096/158 (use of Finnish in the Åland Islands).

50 Decision No. 1934/00, Art. 2(a), [2000] O.J. L232/1.

51 *Id.*, pmbl. (4).

52 *Id.*, Art. 1(2).

a tangible content to the concept of European citizenship."[53] Furthermore, learning languages will help "eradicate xenophobia, racism, anti-Semitism and intolerance."[54] In the operative portions of the decision, however, the economic benefits of language are stressed: "The objectives of the European Year of Languages shall be ... to bring to the notice of the widest possible public the advantages of competencies in several languages, as a key element in personal and professional development (including in finding one's first job), in intercultural understanding, in making full use of the rights conferred by citizenship of the Union and in enhancing the economic and social potential of enterprises and society as a whole."[55] To achieve all of these goals, the EU allocated only 8 million euros, or to put it in terms that the Commission likes, about two euro cents per EU citizen.[56]

F. The Language Action Plan

After the Year of Languages ended, the Council in February 2002 re-affirmed its commitment to linguistic diversity and called for the increased implementation of measures designed to promote it.[57] Interestingly, the Council appeared to adopt a broader view of the languages that should be studied, stating that "the supply of languages should be as diversified as possible, including those of neighbouring countries and/or regions."[58]

The Council invited the Member States to take concrete steps to promote linguistic diversity and language learning and directed the Commission to formulate a plan to accomplish these goals. The Commission responded by issuing an Action Plan in July 2003, which specified several language policies that the EU would undertake in the 2004-2006 timeframe.[59] Continuing the pattern of giving pre-eminence to the economic value of language-learning over its cultural benefits by mentioning the former first, the plan stated the Commis-

---

53 *Id.*, pmbl.(7).

54 *Id.*, pmbl.(8). The European languages whose study would most facilitate an eradication of racism and anti-Semitism (such as Yiddish and Romani) are not specifically included in the program, to say nothing of the languages spoken by the often socially and economically marginalized immigrants to the EU (such as Turkish, Kurdish and Urdu).

55 *Id.*, Art. 2(c).

56 *Id.*, Art. 9.

57 Resolution of 14 Feb. 2002, [2002] O.J. C50/1.

58 *Id.*, reaffirmation (1). The Council specifically referred to the languages of other countries and regions and did not mention minority or regional languages within the EU.

59 Communication of 24 July 2003 from the Commission to the Council, the European Parliament, the Economic and Social Committee and the Committee of the Regions: Promoting Language Learning and Linguistic Diversity: An Action Plan 2004-2006. COM(2003) 449.

sion's view that "[l]anguage competencies are part of the core of skills that every citizen needs for training, employment, cultural exchange and personal fulfilment."[60] The plan called for "life-long language learning" and stressed the need for educational programs for everyone from young children to adults, including learners with special needs owing to mental or physical conditions. It called for improved teacher training and more frequent cross-border exchanges for both teachers and students. It reaffirmed the principle that all EU citizens should learn two languages in addition to their mother tongue, but it interestingly did not specify that these other two languages should be Regulation languages. To the contrary, the Action Plan emphasized the need to study all sorts of languages:

> Promoting linguistic diversity means actively encouraging the teaching and learning of the widest possible range of languages in our schools, universities, adult education centres and enterprises. Taken as a whole, the range on offer should include the smaller European languages as well as all the larger ones, regional, minority and migrant languages as well as those with 'national' status, and the languages of our major trading partners throughout the world. The imminent enlargement of the European Union will bring with it a wealth of languages from several language families; it requires a special effort to ensure that the languages of the new Member States become more widely learned in other countries.[61]

The Action Plan repeatedly bemoaned the limited focus of European language learning:

> The range of foreign languages spoken by Europeans is narrow, being limited mainly to English, French, German and Spanish. Learning one lingua franca alone is not enough. Every European citizen should have meaningful communicative competence in at least two other languages in addition to his or her mother tongue.[62]

The Commission opined that the "Member States have considerable scope to take a lead in promoting the teaching and learning of a wider range of languages than at present,"[63] and indicated that Member States "bear the primary responsibility for implementing the new push for language learning."[64]

---

60 *Id.* at 7.

61 *Id.* at 9-10.

62 *Id.* at 3. Such a statement suggests that at least one of the two foreign languages in which a citizen is competent should be something other than English, French, German or Spanish, but the plan does not say so explicitly.

63 *Id.* at 10.

64 *Id.* at 5.

For its part, the Commission, despite the seemingly ambitious nature of its plan, was unwilling to devote any additional treasure or manpower to improving language education in Europe, and made the startling pronouncement that "none of [its proposals] requires additional budgetary resources to be allocated to the Commission" and their implementation "will not require any extra human resources."[65]

G. The Biodiversity Analogy

The EU's commitment to linguistic diversity, with its emphasis on the Regulation languages, particularly English, French and German, is comparable to an environmental program that seeks to promote ecological diversity by protecting the strongest and most populous species in a given ecosystem while doing next to nothing to protect the seriously endangered ones. Many scholars have analogized linguistic diversity to ecological diversity, as both are viewed (by linguists and environmental scientists, respectively) as a thing of value itself, and the specter of extinction threatens both a large number of organisms and languages alike. Indeed, linguists estimate that of the 4,000 to 6,000 languages now spoken in the world (an exact number depends largely on the extent to which one chooses to categorize various languages as "dialects"), 50 to 90 per cent of these will be extinct within a century.[66] While the vast majority of these languages are outside of Europe, the Euromosaic report demonstrated that there is a pressing danger to the continued existence of some of the languages spoken within the borders of the EU.

Not everyone believes that language extinction is something to be concerned about; Advocate General Darmon wondered aloud if this is properly a matter for the EU's concern, asking "Is it ... for the Community to decide whether or not a particular language should survive? Is the Community to set Europe's linguistic heritage in its present state for all time. Is it to fossilize it?"[67] These questions were posed before Article 128 (now 151)[68] was added to the EC Treaty,

65 *Id.* at 25-27. The Committee on the Regions greeted the Action Plan "as an extremely positive contribution to the promotion of language learning and linguistic diversity," but asserted that the resources allocated for this aim were "not sufficient." Opinion of the Committee of the Regions on the "Communication from the Commission on Promoting Language Learning and Linguistic Diversity: An Action Plan 2004-2006," para. 1.1, 1.4, [2004] O.J. C073/33.

66 It has been estimated that the world loses a language every two weeks. Tara Pepper, "The Fall of Babel," *Newsweek*, 12 Aug. 2002, 60. *See also* Dunbar at 90; Written Question No. E-0654/02, [2002] O.J. C229E/116. For a mathematical model of language decline, *see* Daniel M. Abrams & Steven H. Strogatz, "Modelling the Dynamics of Language Death," *Nature*, 21 Aug. 2003, 900.

67 Opinion of Advocate General Darmon in Case C-379/87, *Groener v. Minister for Education*, 1989 ECR 3979, 3982, para. 19.

68 Const. for Eur. Art. III-280.

which now empowers the EU, in terms that themselves link ecological and social phenomena, to "contribute to the flowering of the cultures of the Member States." Moreover, the disappearance of a language is not only a loss for the society that spoke it, but for all of humanity as well, as mankind loses the potential to learn from both that society and from its unique language system that it used to interpret the world.[69] As a result, the EU should launch a serious effort to preserve imperiled languages. In the context of biological diversity, the EC and all twenty-five Member States are parties to the UN-sponsored Convention on Biological Diversity that was promulgated at the 1992 Earth Summit in Rio de Janeiro and are thereby committed to pursuing policies aimed at the conservation of *all* species.[70] A similar policy should be pursued in the case of linguistic diversity. In addition, this commitment to biological diversity includes conservation of diversity *within* species, which should be extended by analogy to diversity within languages so as to allow the protection of dialects.

The EU could take measures to protect endangered languages. For example, financial incentives could be provided for firms which encourage their use. Moreover, a conservationist approach need not be viewed as contrary to the economic aims of the EC Treaty. One language economist, who also uses an environmental metaphor, has explained the economic value of language conservation:

> [B]y saying that in general, minority languages have no *market* value ... it does no follow that they have no *economic* value. One should not forget that, ultimately, economics is not about financial or material performance, but about *utility*, or satisfaction, and that money is merely, in sound economic theory, a means to an end.
>
> This is clearly exemplified by environmental commodities. Clean air and unspoilt landscapes, as such, have no market value, and they cannot be bought or sold like a car, a bottle of wine or an employee's time. Nevertheless, they have economic value, because the enjoyment of clean air and unspoilt landscapes generates utility. However, because there is no market for such assets, unhampered market forces are likely to induce behaviors that will result in the destruction of those

---

69 John Dunne famously captured this sentiment when he wrote that "[any] man's death diminishes me, because I am involved in Mankind; And therefore never send to know for whom the bell tolls; It tolls for thee."

70 The convention defines "biological diversity" as "the variability among living organisms from all sources including, *inter alia*, ... diversity within species, between species and of ecosystems." (Art. 2). *See* Secretariat of the Convention on Biological Diversity, *Handbook on the Convention on Biological Diversity* (2001). A commitment to environmental protection is now also enshrined in Article 6 of the EC Treaty (and in Const. for Eur. Art. I-3).

> assets (or in an inadequate supply thereof, which is analytically the same thing). This problem is known in the literature as *market failure*.[71]

The link between economics, linguistic diversity, and environmental protection has been recognized by the EU's Committee of the Regions. In a 1998 report on the future role of peripheral areas in the EU, the Committee identified challenges facing remote communities, which are often where minority languages are spoken.[72] The report explains that many peripheral areas (including islands, mountainous regions, and rural areas far removed from commercial centers) are facing grave economic and social conditions occasioned by declines in employment in the agriculture and forestry sectors and a consequential outward movement of large numbers of young people. The Committee called on the EU to support the economic development of these areas, citing the linguistic and environmental qualities of such areas as among the reasons that make them worthy of protection:

> Peripheral areas ... possess an intrinsic value that not only supplements the values that have been lost in the more urbanized, industrial areas but also compensates for these lost values. As a consequence of their remote location many peripheral areas have preserved a way of life and an environment which has been largely lost to the more cosmopolitan areas. The diversity of language, culture and heritage which exists in peripheral areas portrays an alternative lifestyle and living experience. Combined with a clean, rural environment these factors offer development opportunities that are unique to these areas. If genuine economic and social cohesion is to be achieved in the EU then an integrated policy for peripheral areas should be implemented and compensatory measures drawn up to enable them to offset the natural handicap from which they suffer.[73]

The Committee suggested a number of specific measures that the EU could take to revitalize these areas (such as improvements in transportation and energy supplies), but warned that economic development must not threaten the cultural, linguistic and environmental qualities that made these areas particularly attractive in the first place.[74]

Since the Treaty on European Union entered into force, a Member State may, in principle, provide "aid to promote culture and heritage conservation where such aid does not affect trading conditions and competition in the Community to an extent that is contrary to the common interest" without running afoul of

---

71 François Grin, "Market Forces, Language Spread and Linguistic Diversity," in *Language: A Right and a Resource* (M. Kontra *et al.* eds, 1999), 169, 180 (emphasis in original).

72 Opinion on the Future of Peripheral Areas in the European Union, [1998] O.J. C315/15.

73 *Id.*, paras. 1.4-1.5.

74 *Id.*, paras. 2.2.2, 2.3.1.

the EC Treaty free trade rules.[75] Even before that provision was added, though, the state aid provisions of the Treaty already allowed aid to economically disadvantaged regions ("areas where the standard of living is abnormally low or where there is serious underemployment"),[76] which, as the Committee of the Regions' report indicates, is often where threatened minority languages are spoken.

The Language Action Plan delivered by the Commission in July 2003 asks national and regional authorities "to give special attention to measures to assist those language communities whose number of native speakers is in decline from generation to generation."[77] However, the new Constitution for Europe, while calling for the "respect" of linguistic diversity, stops short of expressly empowering the EU to safeguard endangered languages. An interesting juxtaposition of the things that the Union should respect with those which it should protect is provided in Article I-3(3): "It shall respect its rich cultural and linguistic diversity, and shall ensure that Europe's cultural heritage is safeguarded and enhanced." Respect, under this provision, is needed for "cultural and linguistic diversity," but only the "cultural" heritage of Europe must be safeguarded and enhanced. While "cultural heritage" may be understood by many to include linguistic heritage (language being a major component of cultural identity), the drafters of Article I-3(3) used both the terms "cultural" and "linguistic" in the first clause of the article, but only used the term "cultural" in the second.[78] Whether the failure to explicitly include a linguistic component in the second clause reflects an active (if subtly expressed) desire to forestall linguistic preservation or if the lack of parallelism in the clause merely reflects sloppy thinking and careless drafting, Article I-3(3) suggests that the EU, despite its constant vague rhetoric to the contrary, still does not take the plight of endangered languages seriously.

H. Conclusion

The EU's respect for Europe's "linguistic diversity" does not shine evenly on all the languages spoken in the EU. As Ms. Kik learned for herself, certain of the Regulation languages are more respected than others. Languages which are not Regulation languages – the minority and regional languages of the Member States – are the neglected stepchildren of the EU. Most of these languages are culturally and economically marginalized, and the EU's attention to "linguistic diversity" is often motivated by a desire to increase

75 EC Treaty Art. 87(3)(d); Const. for Eur. Art. III-167(3)(d).

76 EC Treaty Art. 87(3)(a); Const. for Eur. Art. III-167(3)(a).

77 Commission's Language Action Plan of 24 July 2003 at 14.

78 In Article II-22 of the Draft Constitution the Union had been instructed to respect three types of diversity: cultural, religious and linguistic.

the economic cohesion of the Union by encouraging the importers and exporters of tomorrow to learn the main languages of commerce. Such an approach to languages is consistent with the historically and overtly economic focus of the EC Treaty, which I will examine in the next two chapters of this book, but is not completely consonant with the human rights values which I will address in the final chapter.

CHAPTER III

Language Rights and the Free Movement of Goods

A. General Principles of Free Movement under the EC Treaty

The economic function of the EC Treaty is clearly enunciated in its statement of purpose in Article 2:

> The Community shall have as its task, by establishing a common market and monetary union and by implementing common policies or activities [specified elsewhere in the Treaty] to promote throughout the Community a harmonious, balanced and sustainable development of economic activities, a high level of employment and of social protection ..., sustainable and non-inflationary growth, a high degree of competitiveness and convergence of economic performance ... the raising of the standard of living and quality of life, and economic and social cohesion and solidarity among Member States.[1]

The EC Treaty aims to promote economic integration by generally prohibiting any restrictions on the flow of goods and services from one Member State to another and by guaranteeing the right of citizens of one Member State to work or establish themselves in another Member State. Article 28 prohibits "quantitative restrictions on imports and all measures having equivalent effect" and Article 29 provides a similar protection for exports.[2] Article 49 bans Member States from imposing restrictions on the freedom of citizens of other Member States to provide services.[3] Article 39 secures the freedom of intra-Community movement for workers, and Article 43 enables citizens of the Member States to establish themselves in other Member States, which provides them with "the right to take up and pursue activities as self-employed persons and to set up and manage undertakings" there.[4]

Each of these provisions is subject to a limitation, however, as a Member State may justify a restriction on the grounds of certain recognized state interests. For example, Article 30 provides that the terms of Articles 28 and 29 "shall not preclude prohibitions or restrictions on imports, exports or goods in transit justified on grounds of public morality, public policy or public security; the protection of health and life of humans, animals or plants; the protection of national treasures possessing artistic, historic or archaeological value; or the protection of industrial and commercial property."[5] Similar provisions allowing restrictions in instances where a state's important interests are at stake apply to the freedom of movement of workers (Article 39(3)), the right of establishment

---

1 The EU has articulated a broader range of objectives in the Constitution for Europe, Art. I-3.

2 Const. for Eur. Art. III-153.

3 Const. for Eur. Art. III-144.

4 Const. for Eur. Arts. III-133, 144.

5 Const. for Eur. Art. III-154.

(Article 46), and the freedom to provide services (Article 55).[6] In addition to the Treaty-based exceptions, the ECJ has recognized that a Member State may legitimately impose measures that amount to obstacles to intra-Community trade if such measures are "necessary in order to satisfy mandatory requirements relating in particular to the effectiveness of fiscal supervision, the protection of public health, the fairness of commercial transactions and the defence of the consumer."[7]

Requirements pertaining to language use may implicate the Treaty provisions if, for example, a state mandates the use of a particular language on product labels in its territory or requires a foreign worker to have knowledge of a particular language. Indeed, language use is such an integral part of commerce that Bruno de Witte has suggested that linguistic freedom is an implicit corollary of the EC Treaty's guarantees of economic freedom:

> Because language is the medium of practically all economic activity, the EEC Treaty indirectly acts as a source of linguistic rights for the participants in transnational economic activities. The treaty, without saying so expressly, establishes the principle of *free language use in transnational economic activity*.[8]

The ECJ has considered the extent of this principle in numerous cases. States have proffered various justifications for language rules that impose obstacles on commerce – consumer protection, promotion and protection of a national language and so forth – and the ECJ has often had to consider whether there were sufficiently compelling reasons to permit an interference with the commercial rights guaranteed by the Treaty. Such cases have often also involved an application and/or interpretation of a piece of secondary Community legislation concerning language requirements. The ECJ has generally approached these cases in the spirit of the overtly economic terms of the EC Treaty and has refrained from addressing the relevance of the EU's promotion of "linguistic diversity" or the pertinence of human rights principles, as such, in their resolution. In fact, the ECJ's opinions in these cases, as is often true with its opinions generally, tend to be rather short, and are often vague or ambiguous to such an extent that the Court seems to rival the oracle at Delphi.

---

6 Const. for Eur. Arts. III-133(3), 140, 150.

7 Case No. 120/78, *Rewe-Zantral AG v. Bundesmonopolverwaltung für Branntwein* (more commonly known as the "Cassis de Dijon case"), 1979 ECR 649, para. 8.

8 Bruno de Witte, "Cultural Legitimation: Back to the Language Question," in *European Identity and the Search for Legitimacy* (Soledad García ed., 1993), 154, 157-58 (emphasis in original).

B. Diverse Labelling Directives

The Council has issued numerous directives concerning the requirements for labels on different types of products, and these directives have contained different formulations of the type of languages which Member States may (or must) require on labels on products sold within their territory.[9] Some call for use of a Member State's "official language or languages." An example of such a requirement is Directive 89/622 on the harmonization of warnings on tobacco products.[10] Other directives, such as Directive 75/726 on the approximation of laws concerning fruit juices, require the use of the "national language or languages."[11] Other directives allow Member States to require labelling in either their "national" or "official" language or languages, as does for example Directive 76/768 on the approximation of laws relating to cosmetic products.[12] Directive 96/24 on the marketing of foodstuffs for animals also originally contained such a requirement, but was subsequently modified so as to allow the Member State in which the products are sold to select a language "from among the national or official languages of the Community."[13] Finally, some directives simply, but cryptically, require the use of a "language easily understood" in the Member State where the goods are offered for sale, for example Directive 79/112 on the approximation of the laws relating to foodstuffs.[14]

There is no apparent reason why the Community has worded the language requirements in so many different ways. As Advocate General Cosmas has observed, "the policy of the Community institutions in this area is characterised by the lack of any systematic and coherent view."[15] Elaborating on this, he stated that

---

9 Advocate General Cosmas surveyed the language requirements imposed by various directives in his opinion in Case C-385/96, *Goerres*, 1998 ECR I-4433. The examples cited in this paragraph, and more, are referenced in his opinion at I-4450.

10 [1989] O.J. L 359/1. The directive provides that cigarette packages sold in multilingual countries are required to have larger labels than those sold in monolingual ones. In a state with only one official language the warnings must cover at least 4 per cent of the package, but in countries with two official languages this increases to 6 per cent, and in those with three official languages it increases to 8 per cent. This has recently become more complicated, as the space requirements now contemplate the possibility that multilingual Member States may mandate the use of photographs or other illustrations as health warnings on tobacco packages. *See* Commission Decision 2003/641 of 5 Sept. 2003, Art. 4(3), [2003] O.J. L226/24.

11 [1975] O.J. L311/40.

12 [1976] O.J. L262/169.

13 [1996] O.J. L125/33, amending [1979] O.J. L86/30.

14 [1979] O.J. L33/1.

15 Opinion of Advocate General Cosmas in Case C-385/96, *Goerres*, 1998 ECR I-4433, 4449, para. 56.

> an analysis of these directives allows no conclusion to be drawn as to the reasons which guided the Community institutions each time they opted for one or other form of words. For instance, no rule is discernable whereby 'strict' conditions (for example use of national or official language) apply to products injurious to health whereas 'less strict' conditions (for example use of easily understood language) is sufficient for other products (for example foodstuffs). In fact, if that were the case, I do not see why, for example, fruit juices have greater health risks and should be labelled in the national language of the State in which they are consumed, ... whilst not being a requirement in the case of foodstuffs. Likewise, why should animal feedstuffs be required to be labelled in one of the national or official languages of the country ... whereas foodstuffs intended for human consumption are to be subject to allegedly more flexible criteria?[16]

C. Piageme and Progeny: In Search of a "Language Easily Understood"

Of the sundry phrasings imposed by the various directives, by far the most problematic is the "language easily understood" formulation, contained in, as mentioned above, Directive 79/112 regarding foodstuff labels, or as it is more completely entitled, the directive on "the approximation of the laws of the Member States relating to the labelling, presentation and advertising of foodstuffs for sale to the ultimate customer." The ECJ has been called upon to interpret the meaning of this non-specific language requirement several times. As these cases will be discussed in some detail, this directive's more pertinent provisions should be briefly mentioned at this point.

Article 3 lists certain types of information, known as "particulars," such as the product name, its ingredients, its quantity, expiration date, storage and usage conditions and so forth. Article 14 requires Member States to prohibit the sale of foodstuffs within their territory if these particulars are not stated "in a language easily understood by purchasers, unless other measures have been taken to ensure that the purchaser is informed." The article adds that this provision "shall not prevent such particulars from being indicated in various languages" and indicates that Member States "shall refrain from laying down requirements more detailed than those already contained" in it.

In transposing Directive 79/112, Belgium enacted legislation which required that the specified particulars must appear in, at least, the language or languages of the linguistic region where the foodstuffs were to be sold. In *Piageme v. BVBA Peeters* ("*Piageme I* "),[17] a Belgian court asked the ECJ to opine on the compatibility of this law with the directive and with Article 30 of the EC Treaty (now

---

16 *Id.* at 4451.

17 Case C-369/89, 1991 ECR I-2971.

Art. 28) after a group of marketers of mineral waters initiated proceedings against a competing firm which had marketed mineral waters labelled only in French and German in the Flemish-speaking region of the country. The Court ruled that "Article 30 of the EEC Treaty [now Art. 28] and Article 14 of Directive 79/112 preclude a national law from requiring the exclusive use of a specific language for the labelling of foodstuffs, without allowing for the possibility of using another language easily understood by purchasers or of ensuring that the purchaser is informed by other measures."[18] Expanding on this position, the Advocate General explained that in light of the consumer protection aim of the directive, and bearing in mind the need of "avoiding unjustifiable obstacles to trade," "the reference to comprehensibility of the language is aimed less at linguistic comprehensibility as such than at ensuring that the actual content of the particulars on the label can be deciphered."[19] As a result, he continued, the national court, which was the one which would assess whether a language met the "easily understood" standard, must "take into account not only any possible multilingualism in the country but also, in particular, the nature of the product and consumers' familiarity therewith, as well as the existence of other packaging of the same product which may carry the required particulars in a more accessible language, thus allowing a sort of translation by approximation."[20]

The Advocate General's instruction that the court is to factor in the multilingual nature of the country came with no guidance as to how the court was to do so. In particular there was no indication as to whether the country as a whole should be considered, or the particular linguistic region, or the product market. Likewise, it was unclear whether the court should consider the language abilities of the general population or only likely purchasers of the products in question, or what level of proficiency in multiple languages these people would need to have to be considered multilingual. Similar questions attended the suggestion that the court consider consumer familiarity with the product and the existence of other packaging.

Even more problematic, however, was the fact that the Court did not provide an unambiguous answer to the question it had actually been asked. The Court had ruled that it was impermissible for a state to require the *exclusive* use of a specific language on a label. The Belgian legislation at issue did not do this, however, as it did not exclude the use of other languages, but rather permitted other languages to appear so long as the language of the region was used. Accordingly, a second reference was made to the ECJ in an effort to obtain clarification as to whether legislation that required the use of the language of a region but did not exclude the use of other languages was permissible.[21] In

---

18 *Id.* at 2985, para. 17.

19 Opinion of Advocate General Tesauro in *Piageme I*, 1991 ECR I-2976, 2978 para. 7.

20 *Id.*

21 Case C-85/94, *Groupement des Producteurs, Importateurs et Agents Généraux d'Eaux Minérales Étrangères, VZW v. Peeters NV ("Piageme II")*, 1995 ECR I-2955.

Piageme II the Court ruled that such legislation was not in accordance with the directive or Article 30 (now Art. 28), as the directive allowed states to mandate only "a language easily understood," and this, the Court stated, "is not equivalent to 'the official language of the Member State' or 'the language of the region.'"[22] Instead, the term "is designed to ensure that the consumer is provided with information rather than to impose the use of a specific language."[23] The Court offered more guidance than it had in its previous opinion as to how the Belgian court should determine whether a language other than that of the region was one which could be "easily understood" by consumers, stating that "various factors may be relevant, though not decisive in themselves; for example, the possible similarity of words in different languages [or] the widespread knowledge amongst the population concerned of more than one language." Referring to the directive's allowance of "other measures" of informing consumers, the ECJ told the Belgian court to also consider "the existence of special circumstances such as a wide-ranging advertising campaign or widespread distribution of the product."[24]

The Court was called upon once again to consider the meaning of Directive 79/112 in the *Goerres* case, which concerned Germany's transposition of this directive.[25] Germany's law provided that the product particulars were to be stated in German, and provided further that they "may also be given in another easily intelligible language, if the provision of information to the consumer is not adversely affected thereby." Goerres ran a food shop near Aachen and was fined for offering for sale various food items, including Corn Flakes and Fanta soda, that were not labelled in German, but only in various combinations of French, Italian, and English. Goerres objected to his penalty, arguing that the directive did not permit a state to prescribe the use of a particular language and that the only permissible requirement was that the label be intelligible. Moreover, Goerres contended that regard should be had for the fact that in the case of products that were sold under widely known brand names the consumer's interest in receiving information could not be adversely affected by using other languages.[26] The German court sought the guidance of the ECJ.

There was some confusion as to whether the German law provided for the use of "another easily intelligible language" as an alternative to, or as an addition to, the use of German. The ECJ believed that the German law allowed the

---

22 *Id.* at 2976, para. 15.

23 *Id.*

24 *Id.* at 2979, para. 30.

25 Case C-385/96, 1998 ECR I-4461. For a pre-*Goerres* discussion of Germany's law in the context of EC law, *see* Frank Burmeister & Gerald Miersch, "Gemeinschaftsrechtliche Sprachregelung und deutsches Lebensmittelrecht," 1995 *EuZW* No. 9, 273.

26 Marc Frangi is similarly of this view. Marc Frangi, "Le Consommateur Français Entre Loi Toubon et Droit Communautaire," *Revue Internationale de Droit Économique* 135, 137 (2003).

use of an "easily intelligible language" as an alternative, citing a statement by the German government that the law would permit labelling "in German or another easily intelligible language."[27] The German law, the Court reasoned, accordingly did not impose a stricter requirement than the directive did. It was for the national court, the ECJ said, to determine in individual cases whether information had been provided in a form that could be understood. In so doing, the Court added that the national court must take note of the fact that the directive allows the possibility that information could be conveyed by other measures such as designs, symbols, or pictograms.[28]

Advocate General Cosmas, however, did not presume that Germany's law allowed the use of another language as an alternative to German. Although he did not overtly discuss the issue, he believed that Germany's law required the label to appear "at the very least" in German.[29] He did not see this as a violation of the directive, however. He stated that the Court's pronouncement in *Piageme II* (*i.e.*, that a "language easily understood" is not necessarily the language of the state or of the region where a given set of products are sold) was applicable only to multilingual states such as Belgium and "cannot be extended to monolingual States such as, for example, the Federal Republic of Germany, the Portuguese Republic or the Hellenic Republic."[30] Instead, he believed that in a monolingual state a "language easily understood" "must be deemed to be the national language or, where it is established by law, the official language of the State or, where there are several official languages, at least one of these, at the discretion of the State concerned."[31]

It is difficult to reconcile Cosmas's views with *Piageme*, and he indeed seems to be advocating a complete departure from it. While a narrow reading of *Piageme* could render it inapplicable to monolingual states, Cosmas' pronouncement on language rules in multilingual states appears to be directly at odds with *Piageme*'s plain assertion that a "'language easily understood' is not equivalent to the official language of the Member State." Cosmas is openly critical of *Piageme*, and identifies several problems that the case raises:

> [I]f the easily understood language is neither the official language nor the language of the region, what language is it? Is it the national language? Are the Member States still authorised, or are they no longer authorised, to legislate on matters of language? Where an assessment is made by the national court on a case-by-case basis, who is the 'purchaser' to be taken into account when it

[27] Case C-385/96, *Goerres*, 1998 ECR I-4461, para. 4.

[28] *Id.*, paras. 18-20.

[29] Opinion of Advocate General Cosmas in *Goerres*, 1998 ECR I-4433, para. 50.

[30] *Id.*, para. 34. This view had been advanced by France in a submission in the case.

[31] *Id.*, para. 50. As will be indicated below, Cosmas contradicts himself later in his opinion when he shifts the power to exercise this discretion from the state to the product marketer.

> assesses whether the language is easily understood? Is it the actual purchaser, that is to say the purchaser in the region, or the average purchaser in the Member State? Is the question whether the purchaser will be informed in one or another language or by 'other measures,' at the end of the day, a matter for the discretion of traders?[32]

With regards to the last question, Cosmas displayed deep skepticism that "other measures" could adequately inform a consumer. "[O]nly language is capable of communicating complete and reliable information concerning all the ingredients and the other particulars which are mandatory under the terms of the directive," he wrote.[33] On the possible role of "other measures" he had this comment:

> [L]anguage is not the only semiological system enabling human beings to communicate with each other. There are others which, it seems, were precursors to language, such as nods, winks, gestures, pictures, etc. Depictions have evolved from the cave-drawings of Lascaux, ancient frescoes and miniature medieval manuscripts, to the graffiti of today, comic strips and various representations and symbols which convey a message. Thus, for example, it is not impossible for a talented designer to reproduce in graphic form a large number of the characteristics of the meat contained in a packet. However, it will never be possible by this means to indicate all the characteristic features that the directive requires the consumer to be informed about. Moreover, the time, skill and familiarity required to decipher such designs would give rise to difficulties.[34]

Cosmas's worries notwithstanding, national judges have demonstrated a capability to engage in a common sense approach to determining whether, in a particular situation, a language is "easily understood" or whether communication may be effected by extra-linguistic measures. In a case which pre-dates *Piageme* but which involved the same statute, a Belgian court tried the case of a merchant who had sold or offered for sale in the Flemish-speaking region of the country beverages which he had imported from Germany and whose labels were only in German. The court concluded that Belgium's language law was contrary to Directive 79/112, and examined whether the bottles at issue were labeled in a language "easily understood" as provided in that directive. The court determined that the linguistic similarity of the Dutch and German words describing the product (caffeinated lemonade) required an acquittal, as the bottles at issue left "no doubt as to the nature of the merchandise, given that the terms *1 liter koffeinhaltige Limonade* clearly means to every purchaser *1 liter kaffeïnehoudende*

32 *Id.*, para. 39.

33 *Id.*, para. 41.

34 *Id.*, paras. 43-44.

limonade."[35] Similarly, a court in Holland ruled that Dutch purchasers of apple-sauce, who were accustomed to the word *appelmoes*, would not be confused by containers that carried only the German equivalent *Apfelmus*, and acquitted a merchant who had been charged with selling such products in violation of Netherlands' language-labeling law. In addition to the linguistic similarity of the words in question, the court took account of other measures that would communicate the content of the containers at issue, noting that the German-language containers were surrounded by Dutch-language ones.[36] In the same vein, a court in Paris acquitted a vendor of food and beverages who had offered for sale products bearing English names such as "hamburger," "cheeseburger," and "coffee drink." The merchant had been charged under France's Loi Bas-Lauriol, which generally required the use of French in commercial transactions. The court, believing that the purpose of the law was to ensure that the consumer understood the product, concluded that would-be customers were perfectly informed of the nature of the products in view of the fact that each of the anglicisms was accompanied by a picture and a description of the product in French.[37]

In his opinion in *Goerres*, Cosmas was particularly concerned about the implications of allowing national courts of multilingual states to determine which language was "easily understood" in a given area. The outcome, he wrote, would be that judges in different parts of a multilingual country would inevitably rule that the language of that region was to be used, and this, he concluded, would impermissibly restrict intra-Community trade. Citing the example of Belgium with its French, Flemish and German-speaking areas, he warned that an Italian or Greek producer who wished to export products to that country would need to "label their products in three different languages or else face being barred from a whole region of the country!"[38]

Cosmas thus believed that it was impermissible for a Member State to require different languages on labels in different regions. In such a circumstance, "[w]here there are several official languages they must be presumed to be equivalent and therefore more or less well known to the citizens of the Member

[35] Decision of the Correctionele Rechtbank Mechelen of 28 Sept. 1987, Journal des Tribunaux 1988, 48 (translated by R.L. Creech).

[36] Decision of Economische Politierechter Haarlem of 20 June 1983, discussed in Louis van Bunnen, "L'emploi des languges dans l'étiquetage et le droit communautaire," *Journal des Tribunaux* 1988, 41, 42.

[37] This decision (which is discussed in van Bunnen) was reversed by the Court of Casssation in a decision of 20 Oct. 1986, Gaz. du Palais 15-16 April 1987, 5, on the grounds that consumer protection was not the only aim of the Loi Bas-Lauriol, and that the statute was also aimed at the protection of the French language itself. That notwithstanding, the decision presaged a statement propounded by the Commission in July 2002, which is discussed in Chapter IV, regarding the needlessness of French when the English words "chicken wings" are accompanied by a photo of the product. Commission Press Release IP-02-1155 of 27 July 2002.

[38] Opinion of Advocate General Cosmas in *Goerres*, 1998 ECR I-4433, para. 67.

State."[39] In such a circumstance, a Member State could only require that a label be in one of the official languages, and the trader would have the choice among them. Moreover, Cosmas is not simply advocating this rule in situations where, as in *Goerres*, there is an applicable Community directive that permits states to require labels in a "language easily understood." He would have his rule regarding multilingual states stand even in situations where no Community directive was operative; this is clear from his simultaneously issued opinion in another case, which will be discussed below.[40]

Such a rule would surely create an uproar in the multilingual states of the EU. Cosmas's crucial supposition, moreover, is empirically false, as the official languages of multilingual states are not always "more or less well known" there. Finland, for example, owing to historical shifts in sovereignty over the country, has two national languages[41] that are taxonomically unrelated to each other – Finnish and Swedish – but the latter is, according to the 2000 census, spoken by only six per cent of the population.[42] Cosmas's position would allow distributors to elect to label the products that they sold in Finland only in Swedish, a choice that would allow them to sell the same set of products in both Sweden and Finland, and obviate the need to prepare labels in Finnish at all. There may of course be countervailing business reasons that would discourage producers from taking such a move – Finnish-speakers may disfavor products not labelled in their language – but cases such as *Piageme* and *Goerres* demonstrate that merchants do in fact sell products labelled in foreign languages. The commercial success of a product is not legally relevant, in any event, particularly when the point of the measure is to protect consumers regardless of how numerous they may be.

Because the full court assumed that the German law did not require the use of German, it did not need to address the question of whether the principle of *Piageme* was to be applied to monolingual states like Germany, and its terse opinion conceals the extent to which the Advocate General's views had any support among the judges. The Court has since had another occasion to weigh-in on this issue, however, and in *Geffroy v. Casino France* it dispelled all doubts as to whether the rules in monolingual states were different from those in multilingual states.[43] That case came to the ECJ on a request from an appellate court in Lyon which sought a preliminary ruling on the compatibility with Community law of the French law which transposed Directive 79/112. The

---

39 *Id.*, para. 82.

40 Opinion of Advocate General Cosmas in *Colim NV v. Bigg's Continent Noord NV*, 1999 ECR I-3175, para. 59. Cosmas issued both this opinion and his one in *Goerres* on the same date in February 1998. The ECJ, however, issued its opinion in *Colim* nearly one year after it ruled in *Goerres* in July 1998.

41 Finland Const. of 1999 § 17.

42 Website of the European Bureau for Lesser Used Languages, www.eblul.org.

43 Case C-366/98, 2000 ECR I-6579.

French law required foodstuffs to be labelled in French, and had been invoked against a supermarket that had sold various beverages, including bottles of Coca Cola, whose labels were generally not in French. The Court, after very briefly describing its holdings in the *Piageme* cases and in *Goerres*, concluded that "[i]t follows from that case-law that Article 30 [now Art. 28] of the Treaty and Article 14 of Directive 79/112 must be interpreted as precluding a national rule, such as that at issue in the main proceedings, from requiring the use of a specific language for the labelling of foodstuffs, without allowing for the possibility of using another language easily understood by purchasers or of ensuring that the purchaser is informed by other means."[44]

Reacting, albeit slowly, to *Piageme* (which was not a particularly popular ruling), the Council amended Directive 79/112 in 1997. Directive 97/4, which was issued after the events giving rise to *Goerres* and *Geffroy* and therefore inapplicable to them, modified the directive's language requirements.[45] Directive 97/4 provided that:

> 1. Member States shall ensure that the sale is prohibited within their own territories of foodstuffs for which the [specified] particulars ... do not appear in a language easily understood by the consumer, unless the consumer is in fact informed by means of other measures ... as regards one or more labelling particulars.
>
> 2. Within its own territory, the Member State in which the product is marketed may, in accordance with the rules of the Treaty, stipulate that those labelling particulars shall be given in one or more languages which it shall determine from among the official languages of the Community.[46]

As a result of this amendment, a Member State could apparently proclaim that its national or official language was one "easily understood" within its territory and could require its use, unless consumers could be informed by means of other measures. The same provisions were contained in Directive 2000/13, which was issued to bring "clarity" to the Community's increasingly confusing foodstuff legislation.[47]

Notwithstanding Directive 2000/13 and the Court's case law, France has continued to cling to its notorious Loi Toubon, which imposes a general requirement for the use of French in a broad range of commercial situations.[48] In July

44 *Id.*, para. 28.

45 [1997] O.J. L43/21.

46 *Id.*, Art. 8.

47 Dir. 2000/13, Art. 16, [2000] O.J. L109/29

48 La Loi Toubon (Law No. 94-665 of 4 Aug. 1994). In a 1996 dissertation, written before many of the decisions discussed above were decided, Caroline ten Dam thoroughly considered whether the Loi Toubon was compatible with EC law and concluded that it generally was not. Caroline ten Dam, "La Législation Linguistique Française dans le Cadre de la Libre Circulation en Europe," Doctoral Dissertation, Europa-Institut Universiteit Utrecht, 1996.

2002 the Commission formally asked France to "bring French law into line" with Community law.[49] The Commission observed that "[a]s it stands, French law provides that any particulars on the label of foodstuffs imported into France must be written in French," and stated its opinion that "case law of the Court of Justice, the EC Treaty and Directive 2000/13/EC on the labelling and presentation of foodstuffs preclude national regulations from imposing the use of a specific language for labelling foodstuffs without allowing the use of another language that is easily understood by the consumer or allowing the consumer to be informed by other means." The Commission chastised Paris, noting that "[t]he French authorities have acknowledged that their legislation is incompatible with Community law, and have confirmed their intention to revise the contested legislation [, but] the proposed amendment has still not been adopted." The French government slyly responded to the Commission's rebuke with a decree that provided that products could be labeled in one or more languages besides French, but did not alter the requirement that French be used, which is of course precisely what prompted the Commission's action in the first place.[50]

D. Member State Language Requirements in the Absence of a Directive

When no directive authorizes a Member State to impose a language requirement for labels on a particular class of products, is the state nonetheless free to do so? This question was presented in *Colim NV v. Bigg's Continent Noord NV*, which was another case that came before the ECJ from Belgium, and involved a language law similar to the one at issue in *Piageme* in that it required the use of the language of the linguistic region where products were sold.[51] This law, however, was part of a general consumer protection statute that had not been enacted pursuant to a Community directive. The parties in the case were two competing department stores in the Dutch-speaking part of the country.[52] One of these, Colim, initiated proceedings against its competitor, Bigg's, after an investigation supposedly revealed that Bigg's was selling products covered by the law that were not labelled in Dutch, and the court where the action was filed referred questions to the ECJ on the validity of this law.[53]

---

49 Commission Press Release IP-02-1155 of 27 July 2002.

50 Décret No. 2002-1025 of 1 Aug. 2002, 179 J.O. 13161. The confrontation between France and the Commission is discussed in Frangi and will be explored further in Chapter IV.

51 Case C-33/97, 1999 ECR I-3175.

52 *Colim* refers to the "Dutch-speaking" region of Belgium, whereas *Piageme* spoke of the "Flemish-speaking" area, and I have used the language of each case when discussing it. The region is officially known, in Dutch/Flemish, as *het Nederlandse taalgebied*. Belgium Const. of 1994 Art. 4.

53 This appears to be a classic example of the pot calling the kettle black, as Bigg's in turn conducted an investigation of Colim and reportedly found that the latter was also selling products that were not labeled in Dutch. Bigg's brought a counterclaim against Colim.

The Court first considered a claim that the Belgian language requirement was a "technical regulation" and therefore subject to the requirements of Directive 83/189, which, *inter alia*, required Member States to notify the Commission of any such regulations before implementing them.[54] Because Belgium had not informed the Commission of its language law, Bigg's had contended that it was invalid under the directive. A "technical regulation" was defined as a requirement which compelled a certain "technical specification," which was itself defined to refer to a specification concerning "the characteristics required of a product such as levels of quality, performance, safety or dimensions, including the requirements applicable to the product as regards terminology, symbols, testing and test methods, packaging, marking or labelling[.]"

Despite the fact that this definition specifically refers to labelling and two components of language (terminology and symbols), the Court decided that a language requirement did not fall within the ambit of this definition:

> [I]t is necessary to distinguish between the obligation to convey certain information about a product to a consumer, which is carried out by affixing particulars to the product or adding documents to it such as instructions for use and the guarantee certificate, and the obligation to give that information in a specified language. Unlike the first obligation, which concerns the product directly, the second is intended merely to specify the language in which the first must be carried out.[55]

This ruling was of significance, as a finding that a language requirement was a "technical regulation" would have meant that all Member States would need to notify the Commission before implementing language rules that affect intra-Community commerce.

Having dispensed with the "technical regulation" issue, the Court explained that a state's ability to mandate language requirements depended on whether a Community directive addressed the matter:

> When [Community] directives fully harmonise the language requirements applicable for a given product, the Member States cannot impose additional language requirements. By contrast, where there is only partial Community harmonisation or none at all, the Member States in principle retain the power to impose additional language requirements.[56]

The Court stressed that a Member State's power to impose a language requirement was limited, however, as such requirements "constitute a barrier to

54 [1983] O.J. L109/8.

55 *Colim*, para. 28.

56 *Id.*, paras. 34-35.

intra-Community trade in so far as products coming from other Member States have to be given different labelling involving additional packaging costs."[57] Nonetheless, because a language requirement could serve the goals of consumer protection and public health, it could be justified, but only to the extent that it was proportionate to the aims pursued. This meant, among other things, that the requirement "must not exclude the possible use of other means of informing them, such as designs, symbols, or pictograms."[58] This statement is significant, as it indicates that tolerance of such "other measures" of communication, which is expressly provided for in Directive 79/112, was also a requirement of language laws like the one from Belgium at issue which neither emanated from that directive nor contained any reference to non-verbal forms of communication itself. If a state's language laws must allow for the use of pictures and symbols, it would seem to follow that the state may not require the use of a language – neither the state's language nor any other language – on product labels, if the information could be conveyed non-verbally.[59]

E. The Pitfalls of Unilateral Multilingualism

One possible way for a manufacturer to approach the labelling conundrum is to place labels in multiple languages on its products. The large number of languages spoken in the EU, and the small size of many product containers, however, can make this difficult. In a recent case the ECJ had occasion to consider a hair dye manufacturer who had nonetheless attempted to do this.[60] The manufacturer was obligated, pursuant to Council Directive 76/768 on the harmonization of laws relating to cosmetic products, to provide various warnings regarding the use of the product.[61] The warnings were to be expressed "at least in [the] national or official language or languages" of the Member State where the products were to be sold, and were to be placed on both the product container and the external packaging. An exception was made, however, for situations in which "for practical reasons" all the information required could not appear on the container and packaging, in which case the warnings could

57 *Id.*, para. 36.

58 *Id.*, para. 41. As it had done in *Goerres*, the ECJ did not consider Belgium's law as it actually stood, but rather discussed the validity of a law which, unlike Belgium's, allowed the use of *either* the language of the area or another "language readily understood by the consumer."

59 Frangi has argued that the allowance of such "other means" of communication is open to "dangerous interpretations," stating that graphic representations may inform a consumer about a product's appearance but not about its more substantial characteristics such as its composition. Frangi at 140.

60 Case C-169/99, *Hans Schwarzkopf GmbH & Co. KG v. Zentrale zur Bekämpfung unlauteren Wettbewerbs*, 2001 ECR I-5901.

61 [1976] O.J. L262/169, as amended by Directive 93/35, [1993] O.J. L151/32.

appear in abbreviated form on the container and packaging and be stated in full on a leaflet enclosed with the product.

The manufacturer, seeking to reduce the cost of distributing products in multiple countries, had produced multilingual containers and packages, each of which contained abbreviated product information in nine languages with the full warning appearing on a leaflet enclosed inside. A business group initiated proceedings against the manufacturer in a German court, alleging that its warnings were not in compliance with the directive. The manufacturer pled that his decision to use multilingual materials allowed it to invoke the "practical reasons" exception. On a request for a preliminary ruling, the ECJ disagreed and ruled that the manufacturer was not entitled to unilaterally and for his own convenience decide to use multiple languages and thereby claim that it was "impossible" for him to comply with the directive.[62] The Court was unmoved by the interesting argument advanced by the manufacturer that multilingual packaging served not only its own interests but also those of the large number of migrant workers who worked in a Member State where their mother tongue is not spoken.[63]

F. A Prohibition on Multilingualism: The Crystal Glass Directive

Even if all required information is placed on a product's package, the robustly multilingual approach of the hair dye manufacturer is unavailable to producers of low-grade crystal, which are subject to a highly unusual directive that expressly *prohibits* the use of languages other than those of the country where the product is sold. Directive 69/493 categorizes crystal into four categories based on its lead content, with category 1 having the most lead (and therefore being the most expensive) and category 4 the least.[64] The directive establishes the terms that are to be used to describe products in each category in each of the languages of the Community and declares that, with respect to category 3 and 4 products, "[o]nly the description in the language or languages of the country in which the goods are marketed may be used." In other words, the label is to appear in the language or languages of the country where the products are sold and in no other language.

62 *Hans Schwarzkopf*, para. 35.

63 *Id.*, para. 20. Others have raised similar concerns about the intelligibility of labels on medicinal products with respect to EU nationals who reside outside their home state. *See, e.g.*, Answer to Written Question E-0506/03, [2003] O.J. 280E/58. In Case C-424/97, *Haim v. Kassenzahnärztliche Vereinigung Nordrhein* ("*Haim II*"), 2000 ECR I-5123, which is discussed at length in Chapter IV, the ECJ exhibited some sensitivity to the linguistic challenges that may confront someone who seeks dental care away from home.

64 O.J. English Special Edition 1969 (II) p. 599.

The reason for this unorthodox limitation stems from differences in the crystal nomenclature adopted for each language and the potential confusion that could result from a consumer's exposure to them. The directive established the following terms for use in the marketing of crystal:[65]

Language	*Category 1*	*Category 2*	*Category 3*	*Category 4*
English	Full lead crystal	Lead crystal	Crystal glass, Crystallin	Crystal glass, Crystallin
Dutch	Volloodkristal	Loodkristal	Sonoorglass (NL), Kristallin-glass (BE)	Sonoorglass
German	Hochbleikristall	Bleikristall	Kristallglas	Kristallglas
French	Cristal supérieur	Cristal au plomb	Cristallin	Verre sonore
Italian	Cristallo superiore	Cristallo al plombo	Vetro sonoro superiore	Vetro sonoro
Spanish	Cristal superior	Cristal al plomo	Vidrio sonoro superior	Vidrio sonoro
Portuguese	Cristal de chumbo superior	Cristal de chumbo	Vidro sonoro superior	Vidro sonoro

As the chart indicates, cognates of the English word "crystal" appear in the terms used to describe products in the two high-end categories (*i.e.*, 1 and 2) in all of the languages. With regards to the products in categories 3 and 4, however, some, but not all, of the languages diverge from this pattern, to a greater or lesser extent. "Crystal" and its cognates appear in the category 3 terms in English, German, French, and the Dutch word for use in Belgium, but not in Italian, Spanish, Portuguese or the Dutch word for use in the Netherlands. The word is even less common in category 4, appearing only in English and German. The language limitation aims to prevent speakers of one language from being misled by the non-co-extensive use of the "crystal" morpheme in another language. For example, an Italian or Spanish purchaser who saw a product bearing the French description *cristallin* (notwithstanding the fact that it also had the Italian *vetro sonoro superiore* or the Spanish *vidrio sonoro superior*) might erroneously conclude that the product was one of a higher quality than it really was. The Council and Commission have explained that the danger of confusion is severe because of the substantial price differences between the categories and the fact that most consumers are unfamiliar with crystal.[66]

Unsurprisingly, this directive has been the subject of litigation. In *Meyhui NV v. Schott Zwissel Glaswerke AG*,[67] a Belgian court referred questions to the

65 The chart provides the terms in languages which are relevant to the discussion herein. The directive also provides (after amendments following the accession of new states) terms in other Regulation languages.

66 Opinion of Advocate General Gulmann in Case C-51/93, *Meyhui NV v. Schott Zwissel Glaswerke AG*, 1994 ECR I-3881, 3890 paras. 36-39.

67 Case C-51/93, 1994 ECR I-3893.

ECJ in a case which a Belgian importer of category 3 products brought against its German exporter. The exporter had furnished the products with labels in English, French and German, thus violating the directive in two ways: by labelling them in English, and not labelling them in Dutch. The exporter contended that the directive unlawfully impeded the free movement of goods and was therefore contrary to Article 30 (now 28) of the EC Treaty. The exporter argued that the directive should have allowed the possibility of using not only the language or languages of the country where the goods were to be sold, but as an alternative a language that could be easily comprehended. In this case, the designated term for category 3 products in the languages at issue all contained the "crystal" component: German *Kristallglas*, French *cristallin*, English *crystal glass* or *crystallin*, and the missing Dutch term (for use in Belgium) *kristallinglass*.

The ECJ, after noting that the Community institutions were subject to the restraints of Article 30,[68] stated that the directive's rule "constitutes a barrier to intra-Community trade in so far as products coming from other Member States have to be given different labelling causing additional packaging costs."[69] However, the Court concluded that this measure could be justified by the need for consumer protection and was proportionate to that aim, reasoning that:

> In the case of the lower two categories ... the difference in the quality of the glass used is not easily discernible to the average consumer for whom the purchase of crystal glass products is not a frequent occurrence. It is therefore necessary for him to be given the clearest information possible as to what he is buying so that he does not confuse a product in categories 3 and 4 with a product in the higher categories and consequently that he does not pay too much.[70]

The Court stated that the requirement that the language or languages of the country of marketing be used was "appropriate" and considered the argument that another language may also be easily comprehensible to be "of only marginal importance."[71] In so doing, the Court parted company with the Advocate General, who had believed that the measure was disproportionate in that it did not take into account the fact that there would be no confusion in the case of many language combinations, citing the similarity of the terms for Category 4 products in the Romance languages, *verre sonore, vetro sonoro, vidrio sonoro,* and *vidro sonoro*.[72]

---

68 *Id.* at 3898, para. 11.

69 *Id.* at 3899, para. 13.

70 *Id.* at 3900, para. 18.

71 *Id.*, para. 19.

72 Opinion of Advocate General Gulmann in *Meyhui*, 1994 ECR at 3890 paras. 36-39. It might also be added that the directive may not do much to prevent confusion in multilingual countries or in the minds of multilingual persons.

G. Definitional Barriers to Trade

In the so-called "Cassis de Dijon" case,[73] the ECJ considered a case that was referred to it by a German court after a liquor merchant was denied permission to import a consignment of "Cassis de Dijon" into Germany from France. The German authorities denied the request for the reason that German law required fruit liqueurs such as "Cassis de Dijon" to have a minimum alcohol content of 25 per cent, whereas the French product at issue only had an alcohol content of between 15 and 20 per cent. The German government intervened in the case and argued that the minimum alcohol rule was necessary as a public health measure and served the interest of consumer protection. The Court, while recognizing that barriers to intra-Community trade are permissible if they are "necessary in order to satisfy mandatory requirements relating in particular to the effectiveness of fiscal supervision, the protection of public health, the fairness of commercial transactions and the defence of the consumer,"[74] ruled that the restriction in this case was not justifiable, and accordingly in violation of the EC Treaty, because the government's goals could be served by a less restrictive measure, namely "by requiring the display of an indication of origin and of the alcohol content on the packaging of products."[75]

No claim was made in the Cassis de Dijon case that the meaning of the term "Cassis de Dijon" was, in the German mind, inextricably linked with a certain alcoholic content. This case provided the framework, however, which would guide later cases in which Member State governments sought to justify national regulatory requirements that impeded intra-Community trade on the grounds that such requirements were necessitated by semantic properties of the national language. Such a case arose in 1980, when the Commission and Italy became entangled in a row over the definitional scope of the Italian word for vinegar, *aceto,* which Italy had restricted to use in connection with wine vinegar.[76] The result of this restriction was that producers of vinegars made from other products (*e.g.*, alcohol, cider, malt) from other Member States could not market their products using the term *aceto,* and because Italian consumers were accustomed to seeing this term on vinegar products, this meant that non-wine based vinegars became virtually unsellable. The Commission contended that Italy had violated Article 30 of the EC Treaty (now Art. 28), but Italy maintained that it was entitled to limit the use of the word *aceto,* explaining that this was necessary to protect consumers who in Italy, by "time-honoured tradition" viewed all vinegars as wine vinegars and could be misled if the term *aceto* were to be

[73] Case No. 120/78, *Rewe-Zantral AG v. Bundesmonopolverwaltung für Branntwein*, 1979 ECR 649.

[74] *Id.*, para. 8.

[75] *Id.*, para. 13.

[76] Case 193/80, *Commission v. Italy*, 1981 ECR 3019. In English, the etymological connection between vinegar, vines, and wine is obvious.

unexpectedly applied to vinegars derived from other products. Lashing out at the Commission, Italy stated:

> [The Commission] does not escape the charge of seeking to create at Community level, by distorting the real situations which differ from one Member State to another, a commercial terminology for vinegar common to and exactly the same in all the Member States, in other words strictly equivalent in every language, by assigning to a judgment of the Court the thankless task of resisting the social phenomenon which is perhaps the most unyielding to any form of authoritarian imposition: the use of language.[77]

The Court, however, sided with the Commission, reasoning on the basis of the term's use in the provisions of the EC's Common Customs Tariff that "vinegar is a generic term [*aceto e una denominazione generica*] and it would not be compatible with the objectives of the Common Market and in particular with the fundamental principle of the free movement of goods for national legislation to be able to restrict a generic term to one national variety alone to the detriment of other varieties produced, in particular, in other Member States."[78] This notwithstanding, the Court recognized that Italian customers had become accustomed to the use of the term *aceto* in connection with wine vinegar alone, and said that it would be justifiable for Italy to take steps to prevent confusion, in particular by requiring the affixation of labels that indicated the type of vinegar contained in a particular bottle. Such a requirement, the Court stressed, must apply to both domestic and imported products and to all types of vinegars, including wine vinegars.[79]

Rome responded somewhat differently than the Court intended, however. Adopting a tenuous interpretation of the judgment, the Italian government concluded that it simply needed to allow the generic term for "vinegar" in the Italian language – whatever that may be – to be used on all vinegars, and proceeded therefore to coin a new generic term that it decreed for use on such products: *agro*. Under the new law, all vinegars were to be designated by *agro di* followed by the source product, for example, *agro di vino*. The term *aceto* would continue to live on, but in a non-generic sense, and its use was to be allowed (and in fact required) exclusively in connection with wine vinegar. Wine vinegar, therefore, would be labelled *agro di vino – aceto*, while all other vinegars would be labelled without the latter term. The Commission did not believe that this system was consistent with the Court's ruling, and turned once again to the ECJ, which easily concluded that Italy had failed to comply with its judgment.[80]

---

77 *Id.* at 3027-28.

78 *Id.* at 3035-36, para. 26.

79 *Id.* at 3036, para. 27.

80 Case 281/83, *Commission v. Italy*, 1985 ECR 3397.

A similar issue arose in connection with Germany's famous beer purity law, the *Reinheitsgebot*, which, *inter alia*, provides that beer produced in Germany can only be made from the four ingredients of barley, hops, yeast, and water, and that only beers so made, whether produced in Germany or abroad, may be marketed under the term *Bier.* The application of this law prevented foreign producers of beers made from other ingredients such as rice, maize and sorghum from selling their products in Germany using the word *Bier.* The Commission viewed this as a measure having an equivalent effect of a quantitative restriction in violation of Article 30 of the EC Treaty (now Art. 28) and filed suit against Germany.[81] Germany defended its restriction on consumer protection grounds, stating that German consumers associated the term *Bier* with a beverage made from only the four raw materials listed in the *Reinheitsgebot.* It maintained that its rule was not protectionist in aim, as any foreign brewer could produce beers in conformance with the law and market them in Germany. The Court rejected Germany's position. As it did in the Italian vinegar case, the Court looked to the Community's Common Customs Tariff where *Bier* and its analogues in other languages were, it concluded, used in a generic sense. The Court also found it significant that Germany's law itself used the term *Bier* in reference to beverages that did not comply with the purity requirements.[82]

Shortly after the German beer case another case came before the Court which drew comparisons to it.[83] This case, another from Italy, raised the issue of whether "pasta" had a generic meaning. Italian law required that the flour used in dry pasta sold in Italy be made solely from durum wheat. A German company that exported to Italy pasta made from common wheat, along with the owner of a store in Italy where its products were sold, were cited for violation of this pasta purity law. They contended that the pasta law imposed an impermissible barrier to trade under Article 30 (now 28) of the EC Treaty, and the court before which their action was pending referred questions on this issue to the ECJ. In defending the law before the ECJ, Italy argued that the measure was needed to protect Italian consumers, who associated pasta with durum wheat, and also contended that the law was necessary to ensure the economic vitality of farmers in southern Italy who needed to be assured that their crops would find a market. The Court was not persuaded. Proceeding along the lines of its analysis in the beer case, the Court observed that the Italian pasta law used the term "pasta" in some contexts to refer to products that were not made solely from durum wheat (*i.e.*, with reference to fresh pasta and pasta products intended for export), and concluded on this basis that "the word 'pasta' in itself is a generic term and in no way indicates that durum wheat alone was used in its production."[84]

---

81 Case 178/84, *Commission v. Germany*, 1987 ECR 1227.

82 *Id.* at 1271, para. 33.

83 Case 407/85, *3 Glocken GmbH v. USL Centro-Sud*, 1988 ECR 4233.

84 *Id.* at 4281, para. 20. The ECJ rejected the economic argument on the grounds that unilateral action by a Member State was precluded by the creation of a common market in this sector. *Id.* at 4282, para. 26.

Advocate General Mancini passionately disagreed with the Court's assessment of the semantics of his native language. Mancini stated that "pasta" meant something different in Italy than it did in the other Member States, as in Italy the word had a precise meaning and formed the lexical keystone of an elaborate pasta-related vocabulary, whereas in other states "pasta" was used more loosely, and even inter-changeably with terms such as "spaghetti" and "macaroni." Mancini saw the result as inevitable confusion for Italians who had never known pasta products that were not made from durum wheat.[85]

H. Something to Chew On: The Meaning of Trademarks

While the ECJ has thus looked askance at arguments about the meaning of words in particular languages when Member States have sought to prevent foreign producers and merchants from using the words in a sense that is derived from a foreign understanding of the same or similar words, the Court has been more indulgent of monolingual understandings of words in cases concerning the meaning of words used in Community trademarks. The meaning of the words contained in a proffered trademark is central to the question of its validity, as Article 7(1)(c) of the Council Regulation on Community trademarks[86] states that a trademark cannot generally be granted if the proposed mark, *inter alia*, "consist[s] exclusively of signs or indications which may serve, in trade, to designate the kind, quality, quantity, intended purpose, value, geographical origin or the time of production of the goods or of rendering of the service, or other characteristics of the goods or service." Words that are thus, in the parlance of intellectual property law, merely "descriptive" of the category of goods to which they are applied are thus in principle not registerable, whereas words that can be used to distinguish products of one undertaking from those of another (often called "distinctive" words) are.[87] Determining whether a given word is descriptive of a good can be difficult enough when one must consider only its meaning in a single language. The task is obviously much more challenging when multiple languages must be considered. The trademark regulation necessitates such a multilingual assessment, however, by providing in Article 7(2)

---

85 Opinion of Advocate General Mancini in *3 Glocken*, 1988 ECR 4246 generally, but especially 4268-70. The ECJ is not the only multi-national European court that has sat in judgment of a native speaker's understanding of a word in a language which is generally unknown to the judges themselves; the European Court of Human Rights recently declined to credit a Cypriot court's understanding of the semantic properties of a Greek word that was at the center of a contempt proceeding. *Kyprianou v. Cyprus*, App. No. 73797/01 (2004).

86 Council Regulation No. 40/94 of 20 Dec. 1993, [1994] O.J. L11/1.

87 *See, e.g.*, Case C-150/02, *Streamserve, Inc. v. OHIM* (2004).

that a mark may be deemed unregisterable "notwithstanding that the grounds of non-registerability obtain in only part of the Community."

In *Proctor & Gamble Co. v. OHIM*,[88] the ECJ was called upon to opine on whether the mark "Baby Dry," which was sought by an American diaper manufacturer, was registerable. The Court referred to Article 7(2) and said that this measure "implies that, if a combination of words is purely descriptive in one of the languages used in trade within the Community, that is sufficient to render it ineligible for registration as a Community trade mark."[89] Despite this seeming recognition of the need to engage in a multilingual analysis, the Court proceeded to state, rather inexplicably, that only one language would be considered: "In order to assess whether a word combination such as BABY-DRY is capable of distinctiveness, it is therefore necessary to put oneself in the shoes of an English-speaking consumer."[90] The Court proceeded to look at the meaning of these English words in the minds of English speakers, and after determining that the words were capable of distinctiveness in English, it went no further. The Court did not, despite its indication that a finding of descriptiveness in any single language would result in ineligibility, move beyond its anglocentric analysis.

In a later case that grew out of the efforts of another American company to obtain a Community trademark, Advocate General Jacobs considered the meaning of the Wrigley Company's "Doublemint" chewing gum.[91] The Advocate General stated that in light of Article 7(2) of the trademark regulation, "presumably a sign should be assessed in the light of the perception of consumers in all Member States,"[92] and he proceeded to lay out the procedure that he believed should be followed in making this assessment. First, the mark should be viewed "from the standpoint of a native speaker of the language concerned."[93] If the words were descriptive in that language the mark would be unregisterable and it would therefore be unnecessary to proceed any further. If, however, the words were not descriptive in the first language, one must consider the mark "through the eyes (or ears) of a Community consumer whose language is different."[94] Jacobs offered a few examples of how he saw this process operating:

> For example, the English word 'handy,' meaning easy to handle, might be seen as a possible word mark, or part of a mark, for a mobile phone. Since however that word is commonly used in Germany to designate a mobile phone, it could not be

[88] Case C-383/99, 2001 ECR I-6251.

[89] *Id.*, para. 41.

[90] *Id.*, para. 42.

[91] Opinion of Advocate General Jacobs in Case C-191/01, *OHIM v. William Wrigley Jr. Co.* (2003).

[92] *Id.*, para. 80.

[93] *Id.*, para. 83.

[94] *Id.*, para. 85.

> registered as a Community mark. Similarly, a term derived from one language may acquire a different meaning or connotation in another: the English word 'smoking' does not in English designate any characteristic of formal evening dress for men, whereas in French, German or Italian it designates what would in English be known as a dinner jacket or (by those who refer to nappies as 'diapers') a tuxedo.[95]

This procedure was only to be followed with regards to languages in which the words of the proffered mark would be considered as belonging to those languages (in addition to being part of the first language), and should not, he stressed, be used in connection with languages whose speakers would not regard the words as being part of their own language.

While he recognized that "speakers of one language, knowing a term to belong to another language, might misapprehend its originality in that other language by imposing on it features of their own language," he deemed it "inappropriate to take as a normal yardstick a consumer struggling with an imperfect knowledge of a foreign tongue."[96] He therefore concluded that:

> Assessment under Article 7(1)(c) should thus not be based on the question whether a term in a language used in one part of the Community might in another part of the Community be thought to designate product characteristics, so that any innovative or unusual feature in the grammatical or semantic structure of a mark must thus pass the test of innovativeness and unusualness in each of those parts.[97]

Jacobs' pronouncements in *Wrigley*, as he recognized, went beyond the jurisprudential requirements of that case because he found that the proffered mark "Doublemint" was descriptive in English and accordingly failed to qualify for registration.[98] He therefore spoke in hypothetical terms when he contemplated the impact of other languages on a mark's validity and did not make any conclusions as to whether speakers of other languages would understand "Doublemint" as a descriptive term.[99]

Jacobs' approach is problematic for several reasons. First, it is manifestly inconsistent with the ECJ's approach in the "Baby Dry" case, where the Court failed to look at the mark's meaning in any other language after determining

---

95 *Id.*, para. 86.

96 *Id.*, para. 87.

97 *Id.*, para. 90.

98 *Id.*, para. 82. The ECJ agreed with Jacobs' conclusion without elaborating on the difficulties posed by multilingualism.

99 Germany, which intervened in the case, argued that German-speaking consumers would associate "Doublemint" with the German compound *Doppelminze* and would therefore consider the term descriptive. *Id.*, para. 81.

that it had distinctive character in English. Second, one may argue that there is no legitimate reason to distinguish the situation in which a mark is viewed as containing words that "belong to" a given speaker's language from that in which a mark is viewed as containing words that do not. The trademark regulation makes no such distinction, and if the aim of the regulation is, as Jacobs himself acknowledges, to ensure that words that are merely descriptive may be freely used by all persons,[100] speakers of a language in which a word is regarded as descriptive of a product should not be denied the ability to use that word in connection with the product simply because the word is also regarded as "belonging to" a foreign language. Third, it is not always clear what it means for a word to "belong to" a given language, as languages borrow words from other languages and incorporate them into their own lexicons. Is "sushi" an English word, or merely a Japanese word widely understood by contemporary English speakers? Are "pasta" and "beer" words that "belong to" English? Fourth, Jacobs did not articulate the reason why he made the understanding of English speakers the touchstone of the case. Most likely he viewed this as the obvious choice in light of the fact that "double" and "mint" were clearly words in the English language. However, the Court of First Instance has indicated that it is not always the speakers of the language of the mark that are to be considered, however.

In *Oriental Kitchen SARL v. OHIM*,[101] a merchant which marketed pork products to Europe's Indochinese community sought to register the mark "kiap mou," which roughly translated means "crispy pork" in Laotian and Thai. The mark's registration was opposed by a company which held multiple food-related trademarks for the word "mou" in the United Kingdom. OHIM found that there was a likelihood of confusion between the proffered mark and the older mark, and accordingly denied registration of "kiap mou." The applicant appealed, arguing that to its Indochinese clientele, the term "mou" would be viewed as simply a descriptive term for pork and that the opposing party's marks were therefore invalid, whereas the term "kiap mou" was a fanciful creation to speakers of Indochinese languages that could be trademarked. The applicant contended moreover that there would be no likelihood of confusion among its Indochinese customers, as the sign "kiap mou" was sufficiently distinctive from "mou" for the two companies' goods to be differentiated.

The CFI rejected the applicant's attempt to focus on speakers of Laotian, Thai and other Indochinese languages, however, expressing doubt as to whether the goods in question were exclusively intended for such a limited customer base.[102] Because the trademark regulation proscribed registration of a mark where there was a likelihood of confusion "in the territory in which the earlier

---

[100] *Id.*, para. 17, citing Joined Cases C-108/97 and C-109/97 *Windsurfing Chiemsee*, 1999 ECR I-2779. para. 25.

[101] Case T-286/02 (2003).

[102] *Id.*, para. 32.

trade mark is protected,"[103] the court focused on the population of the United Kingdom, where the earlier marks had been registered, as a whole. The court stated that

> Such a public is in the very great majority anglophone. The words mou, kiap and kiap mou have no meaning in English and they bear no resemblance to the English words which have a meaning equivalent to that of these words in Laotian or Thai. Moreover, there is nothing in the case file or the applicant's arguments to suggest that a significant proportion of that public has a sufficient knowledge of the Laotian or Thai languages to understand the meaning of the words in question in those languages. It also follows from those considerations that, from the point of view of the relevant public, and contrary to the applicant's submission, mou is not descriptive of the goods covered by the earlier mark. It will be viewed by that public as a term which is invented and inherently distinctive.[104]

The CFI accordingly upheld the denial of the registration sought, and thereby indicated that the language of a mark will not always determine the language upon which an inquiry of consumer understanding is based.

I. Conclusion

The trademark cases and the decisions regarding governmental efforts to police the definitions of vinegar, beer, pasta and several other food and beverage products within their territories[105] indicate that the speaker of one language may have an understanding of a word's meaning that differs from the understanding that speakers of another language have of the same or similar word. The ECJ has made it clear that Member States are constrained in their ability to prevent the meaning of words in their respective national languages from being modified by contact with the languages of other Member States. As the Court stated in the *Bier* case:

> [C]onsumers' conceptions which vary from one Member State to the other are also likely to evolve in the course of time within a Member State. The establish-

[103] Council Regulation No. 40/94 of 20 Dec. 1993, Art. 8(1)(b), [1994] O.J. L11/1

[104] *Oriental Kitchen SARL v. OHIM*, paras. 41-42.

[105] *See, e.g.*, recent cases concerning attempts by Spain and Italy to prohibit the application of the words for "chocolate" to products that contain vegetable fats other than cocoa butter, Case C-12/00, *Commission v. Spain*, 2003 ECR I-459 and C-14/00, *Commission v. Italy*, 2003 ECR I-513; France's restrictions on the use of names for cheese, Case C-448/98, *Ministère Public v. Guimont*, 2000 ECR I-10663 and Case 286/86, *Ministère Public v. Deserbais*, 1988 ECR 4907; the Netherlands' restriction on the term "Jenever" to beverages with a minimum alcoholic content of 35 per cent, Case 182/84, *Miro BV*, 1985 ECR 3731.

> ment of a common market is, it should be added, one of the factors that may play a contributory role in that development. Whereas rules protecting consumers against misleading practices enable such a development to be taken into account, ... the legislation of a Member State must not 'crystallize given consumer habits so as to consolidate an advantage acquired by national industries concerned to comply with them.'[106]

However, when there is a real risk that similar words in different languages may cause confusion, an attempt to "crystallize" the meaning of a word may be permissible, as the crystal glass case, appropriately enough, reveals. Such efforts are pre-destined to fail in the long run, however, as a language is a dynamic system that resists ossification.[107] Nonetheless, at some point enough words in a state's language may be sufficiently transformed by exposure to the languages of other states that people may begin to worry that the fundamental nature of the language is being dramatically altered. Can a state take steps to protect its language from being overwhelmed by other languages in such circumstances? When the continued existence of a state's language appears to be threatened, is it legitimate to, as one Advocate General put it, "fossilize" the linguistic picture in a state?[108] This question was raised in the seminal case concerning language restrictions in the context of the free movement of people, to which I will now turn.

---

[106] *Commission v. Germany*, 1987 ECR 1227 at 1270-71, para. 32. The American Supreme Court Justice Oliver Wendell Holmes used this mineral metaphor nearly seventy years earlier when he wrote that a word's meaning could not be crystallized once and for all: "A word is not a crystal, transparent and unchanged; it is the skin of a living thought and may vary greatly in color and content according to the circumstances and the time in which it is used." *Towne v. Eisner*, 245 U.S. 418, 425 (1918).

[107] As Tarja Salmi-Tolonen has written, the meaning of a word is more a consequence of its use than an inherent property of the word itself. Tarja Salmi-Tolonen, "Legal Linguistic Knowledge and Creating and Interpreting Law in Multilingual Environments," 29 *Brooklyn J. of Int'l Law* 3 (2004) 1167, 1176. A consideration of the relationship between a word and its meaning takes us into the rarefied world of metaphysics, and this has been a major topic of ontological discourse since Aristotle's time.

[108] Opinion of Advocate General Darmon in Case C-379/87, *Groener v. Minister for Education*, 1989 ECR 3979, 3982, para. 19.

CHAPTER IV

Language Rights and the Free Movement of People

A. Member State Imposition of Language Requirements on Migrant Workers

1. The *Groener* Case and Regulation 1612/68

In *Groener v. Minister for Education*, the ECJ considered whether Ireland could require a citizen of another Member State to possess knowledge of the Irish language in order to hold a teaching position in a predominantly, if not exclusively, English-speaking institution.[1] The case was initiated by Anita Groener, a Dutch national who had sought appointment to a permanent teaching position at an art college in Dublin after having worked there in a temporary capacity for several years. The Irish Minister of Education had previously issued administrative measures which required that persons holding certain teaching positions, including the one sought by Mrs. Groener, demonstrate knowledge of the Irish language, either by producing a specified certificate or by passing an examination. Mrs. Groener did not have the certificate and, after taking a crash-course in Irish, failed the exam. She consequently was not hired, and as a result initiated legal proceedings in an Irish court, where she alleged that the Irish language requirement violated the EC Treaty's provision on the free movement of workers (then Art. 48, now Art. 39)[2] and Regulation 1612/68,[3] which specifically addresses the issue of linguistic requirements. The Irish court requested the ECJ's guidance on these issues.

The ECJ examined Regulation 1612/68, which the Council had issued in 1968 to flesh out Article 48 (now Art. 39) of the EC Treaty. Article 3 of the regulation states:

> [P]rovisions laid down by law, regulation or administrative action or administrative practices of a Member State shall not apply:
>
> -- where they limit application for an offer of employment or the right of foreign nationals to take up and pursue employment or subject these to conditions not applicable in respect of their own nationals; or
>
> -- where, though applicable irrespective of nationality, their exclusive or principal aim or effect is to keep nationals of other Member States away from the employment offered.
>
> *This provision shall not apply to conditions relating to linguistic knowledge required by reason of the nature of the post to be filled.*[4]

---

1 Case C-379/87, 1989 ECR 3987.

2 Const. for Eur. Art. III-133.

3 [1968] O.J. English Special Edition L257 (II) p. 475.

4 *Id.* (emphasis added). In the United States, the agency responsible for enforcement of federal employment discrimination laws, the Equal Employment Opportunity Commission, is of the view that a rule requiring employees to speak English may violate Title VII of the Civil Rights Act of 1964, 42 U.S.C.

Article 3 thus establishes a general rule that prevents a Member State from either engaging in direct discrimination against foreign nationals (the first indent) or from pursuing policies that result in indirect, or *de facto* discrimination (the second indent) against foreign nationals who are desirous of employment in that state, and this general rule is subject to the linguistic exception in the third indent. The Court concluded that there was no issue of direct discrimination, but opted not to rule on the question of indirect discrimination before first considering the applicability of the linguistic exception, reasoning that if it was applicable there would be no need to tackle the presumably more difficult question of indirect discrimination.[5]

Turning to the question of whether knowledge of Irish was "required by reason of the nature of the post to be filled," the Court began its analysis with the recognition that at the college in Dublin

> the teaching of art, like that of most other subjects taught in public vocational schools, is conducted essentially or indeed exclusively in the English language. It follows that ... knowledge of the Irish language is not required for the performance of the duties which teaching of the kind at issue specifically entails.[6]

One might have thought that such a statement would have definitively resolved the case in Mrs. Groener's favor, but the Court was quick to indicate that such thinking would be premature: "However, that finding is not itself sufficient to enable the national court to decide whether the linguistic requirement in question is justified 'by reason of the nature of the post to be filled.'"[7]

This statement is indeed remarkable. The Court departed from the language of the linguistic proviso of Article 3, which by its terms allows language requirements only when they are "required" by the nature of the position, and transformed the issue into whether the linguistic requirement could be "justified,"

---

§ 2000e *et seq.*, which prohibits discrimination, *inter alia*, on the basis of "national origin," "unless an employer shows it is necessary for conducting business." *See* EEOC's website at www.eeoc.gov/facts/fs-nator.html. A federal court in Dallas has agreed with the EEOC's interpretation and awarded more than $700,000 to thirteen Hispanics who had worked at a company which had prohibited the use of Spanish at all times (except when Spanish-speaking customers were present), even during lunch and other breaks. *EEOC v. Premier Operator Services, Inc.* (N.D. Tex. 2000), described in EEOC press release, available at www.eeoc.gov/press/9-19-00.html.

5 *Groener*, 1989 ECR 3987, paras. 13-14. The Advocate General, while qualifying his remarks, did not seem to think that Mrs. Groener had been subject to indirect discrimination. Opinion of Advocate General Darmon in *Groener*, 1989 ECR 3979, 3983-85, paras. 30-34.

6 *Groener*, 1989 ECR at 3992, para. 15.

7 *Id.*, para. 16.

which is a different matter altogether.[8] Because something can be justified without being required, the Court in essence broadened the scope of the linguistic proviso, despite the fact that it, as a measure that permits discrimination in contravention of the general proscription against it, is something that should be interpreted narrowly. Indeed, earlier decisions of the Court had indicated that when questions arose about the scope of provisions of the regulation or other Community measures designed to promote the ability of workers to travel throughout the Community, they were to be interpreted in such a manner as to favor the rights of workers.[9] Furthermore, in an earlier case the Advocate General had indicated that the Court could not freely interchange the terms "necessary" and "justified" when reviewing whether a restriction on the free movement of goods could be justified under the public morality exception what was then Article 36 of the EC Treaty, and is now Article 30.[10]

Having essentially re-written the linguistic proviso, the Court proceeded to consider whether there was justification for the Irish language requirement. The Court took note of "the special linguistic situation in Ireland," remarking upon the constitutional status of Irish as both the country's "national language" and "first official language" and observing that "although Irish is not spoken by the whole Irish population, the policy followed by Irish governments for many years has been designed not only to maintain but also to promote the use of Irish as a means of expressing national identity and culture."[11] The Court proclaimed that this was a legitimate policy under EC law: "The EEC Treaty does not prohibit the adoption of a policy for the protection and promotion of a language of a Member State which is both the national language and the first official language."[12] Nonetheless, the Court added that such a policy is subject to limits:

---

8 Indeed, the Court's use of quotation marks suggests that the Court was consciously aware that its reasoning was not supported by the wording of the regulation. The phrase from the proviso is "required by reason of the nature of the post to be filled." In referring to this passage, the Court cuts out the word "required," inserts the word "justified," and only then chooses to quote the passage verbatim.

9 For example, the Court has broadly interpreted the "social advantages" that workers are entitled to under the regulation. *See, e.g.*, Case 65/81, *Reina v. Landeskreditbank Baden-Württemberg*, 1982 ECR 33. Similarly, the Court has limited the circumstances under which a state may invoke the "employment in the public service" exception to justify discriminatory treatment of foreign workers under Article 48 (now 39) of the EC Treaty. Case 149/79, *Commission v. Belgium*, 1980 ECR 3881. In *Groener*, the Advocate General called for a narrow interpretation of the linguistic provision, although he concluded that such a reading would nonetheless allow the rule challenged by Mrs. Groener. Opinion of Advocate General Darmon in *Groener*, 1989 ECR at 3980, para. 10.

10 Opinion of Advocate General Warner in Case 34/79, *Regina v. Henn and Darby*, 1979 ECR 3818, 3820. The European Court of Human Rights has similarly stated that "necessary" is not synonymous with "indispensable." *Handyside v. The United Kingdom*, App. No. 5493/72, Series A, No. 24 (1976), para. 48.

11 *Groener*, 1989 ECR at 3992-93, paras. 17-18.

12 *Id.* at 3993, para. 19.

> [T]he implementation of such a policy must not encroach upon a fundamental freedom such as that of the free movement of workers. Therefore, the requirements deriving from measures intended to implement such a policy must not in any circumstances be disproportionate in relation to the aim pursued and the manner in which they are applied must not bring about discrimination against nationals of other Member States.[13]

The Court stressed "[t]he importance of education for the implementation of such a policy," explaining that

> Teachers have an essential role to play, not only through the teaching which they provide but also by their participation in the daily life of the school and the privileged relationship which they have with their pupils. In those circumstances, it is not unreasonable to require them to have some knowledge of the first national language.[14]

The Court accordingly concluded that it was permissible for Ireland to require its teachers to have an "adequate knowledge" of Irish,[15] and having effectively

---

[13] *Id.* Advocate General Darmon noted that the measure "must be strictly necessary in order to achieve that aim." Opinion of Advocate General Darmon in *Groener,* 1989 ECR at 3980, para. 11.

[14] *Groener,* 1989 ECR at 3993, para. 20. The Language Action Plan adopted by the Commission in July 2003 saw a need to protect national languages against English encroachment in educational settings, stating that "[i]n non-anglophone countries recent trends to provide teaching in English may have unforeseen consequences on the vitality of the national language [and] [u]niversity policies should therefore include explicit actions to promote the national or regional language." Communication of 24 July 2003 from the Commission to the Council, the European Parliament, the Economic and Social Committee and the Committee of the Regions: Promoting Language Learning and Linguistic Diversity: An Action Plan 2004-2006. COM(2003) 449, p. 9.

[15] The rules which may be imposed regarding how knowledge of the language must be obtained, as well as the means of evidencing it, are subject to limits. A requirement that the knowledge be acquired on the state's territory would not be valid, *Groener,* 1989 ECR at 3967, para. 23, and the Commission has stated that an employer may not require that a language be the mother tongue of an employee. Communication from the Commission of 11 Dec. 2002, COM(2002) 694. *See also,* Answer to Written Question E-1733/03, [2004] O.J. 011E/221. In a more recent case, the Court indicated that an employer may not insist that linguistic knowledge be demonstrated solely by presentation of a government-issued certificate which is only issued by one province of the state. Case C-281/98, *Angonese v. Cassa di Risparmio di Bolzano SpA*, 2000 ECR I-1. The European Court of Human Rights recently reviewed the reasonableness of the use of a particular language test in a case in which it held that Latvia's testing of members of the country's Russian-speaking minority for competence in the Latvian language in order for them to be eligible to stand for parliamentary elections was in violation of the European Convention on Human Rights. *Podkolzina v. Latvia*, App. No. 46726/99 (2002). The EU itself has been faulted for failing to ensure an adequate assessment of the linguistic capabilities of its prospective employees. In a decision that was reversed by the Court of First Instance, the Commission turned down a job applicant whose

disposed of the case, declined to consider the compatibility of the rule with Article 48 of the EC Treaty (now 39).[16]

While one may applaud the sensitivity that the Court displayed towards a struggling language, much of the opinion is open to serious questioning. One major problem with the reasoning has already been mentioned. In addition, the attention that the Court, and even more so the Advocate General, paid to Ireland's policy of promoting the Irish language would seem to be more appropriate to an analysis under Article 48 of the EC Treaty (now Art. 39) regarding the free movement of workers, which expressly provides for a public policy exception to that freedom.[17] The Court declined to consider the EC Treaty, however, and there is no public policy component in the linguistic proviso of Regulation 1612/68. The only linguistic requirements that the regulation permits are those that are "required by nature of the post to be filled;" it says nothing about linguistic requirements that may facilitate the advancement of a state's public policy.

Groener raised more questions than it answers. While the case establishes that a state is permitted under the EC Treaty, in some circumstances, to require citizens of other Member States who wish to reside there to have some knowledge of its national (and first official) language, the Court's judgment left the contours of this power unknown. As Professor de Witte has said:

> The consequences of *Groener* appear rather ambiguous. On the one hand, the Irish regulation (and, indirectly, similar regulations elsewhere in the Community) is allowed to stand, and this somewhat corrects the impression that, from the point of view of market integration, linguistic diversity is not so much a cultural asset as an obstacle to efficient communication. On the other hand, the Court has established its jurisdiction to check whether language regulations do not impinge on the exercise of Community rights.[18]

The uncertainty of *Groener*'s impact manifested itself in the *Goerres* case concerning German labels discussed in Chapter III. In that case, Advocate General Cosmas deduced from *Groener* the conclusion that a state had the authority to determine that its national language was the "language easily

oral assessment was presided over by a panel on which none of the assessors had any real knowledge of one of the two languages in which the candidate was to be evaluated. Case T-102/01, *Pérez-Díaz v. Commission.*

16 *Groener,* 1989 ECR at 3994, paras. 24-25.

17 Art. 39(3) of the EC Treaty (and Art. III-133(3) of the Constitution for Europe) states that the freedom of movement for workers is "subject to limitations justified on grounds of public policy, public security or public health."

18 Bruno de Witte, "Surviving in Babel? Language Rights and European Integration," in *The Protection of Minorities and Human Rights* (Y. Dinstein & M. Tabory eds., 1992), 277, 295.

19 Opinion of Advocate General Cosmas in *Goerres,* 1998 ECR I-4433, 4452, paras. 59-60.

understood" within the meaning of the label directive.[19] The ECJ, however, apparently did not draw this inference, and in fact did not even cite *Groener* in its opinion.

2. Sauce for the Irish Goose is Not Sauce for the French Gander: The EU's Differing Approaches Towards Language Protection Efforts in Two Member States

Even if public policy were a relevant factor in assessing the legitimacy of Ireland's language requirement in *Groener*, one can wonder if the Court was justified in concluding that the requirement that teachers at the Dublin art college know Irish is truly proportionate to that policy, given the fact that there is no evidence that Irish was ever used there.[20] Indeed, relatively few people in Ireland have much command of the language – only fifteen per cent have good or high competence – and even if Mrs. Groener had passed the exam, she would have simply joined the twenty to thirty per cent of the Irish population with minimal knowledge of the language.[21] Irish-speakers, all of whom apparently also speak English,[22] simply do not speak Irish with people with limited Irish abilities. As one commentator on the country's language scene has explained, "if a Gaeltacht peasant, bilingual since birth, goes to an agricultural agency for help and meets an anglophone agent who studied Irish in school ten years ago, it would be totally unnatural for them to speak Irish."[23] The theoretical, and remote, possibility that one day an Irish-speaking aspiring artist would wish to speak to Mrs. Groener in Irish does not seem sufficient to justify the infringement of Mrs. Groener's present and concrete Treaty-based right to work in the Emerald Isle. Indeed, in an earlier case the Court was somewhat dismissive of arguments regarding the "possibility" of communication difficulties in multilingual settings.[24]

---

20 Interestingly, the Court did not consider (and it apparently was not argued) that the language requirement might be necessary to ensure an art teacher's aesthetic appreciation of the art scene in Ireland.

21 The European Parliament provides the following information on its website at http://www.europarl.eu.int/language/apprendrega_en.htm: "Taking the population of the State as a whole, the evidence from a variety of social surveys is that about 5% of the population has a high active competence in Irish (this figure includes the traditional Irish-speaking communities of the *Gaeltacht*), a further 10% or so has a good competence and regularly makes some use of the language, and another 20-30% are on a declining scale towards low passive competence."

22 Christina B. Paulston, *Linguistic Minorities in Multilingual Settings* (1994), 81.

23 *Id.* at 89.

24 In Case 247/81, *Commission v. Germany*, 1984 ECR 1111, the Court considered a German law which required marketers of pharmaceutical products in Germany to have their headquarters in Germany. The Court rejected the argument that this was necessary, *inter alia*, to avoid the linguistic difficulties that German officials had encountered when they had contacted firms in other states while performing their

Moreover, the Court takes the asserted public policy of Ireland at face value, despite the fact that Ireland's commitment to the promotion and protection of Irish has been pursued with what can only be viewed as pronounced ambivalence. Although one might have expected Mrs. Groener to highlight this point, there is no indication that she ever even suggested that Ireland's public policy was not as straight-forward as the Irish government would have the Court (and segments of its domestic constituency) believe. As a result, the Court may perhaps be forgiven if it gave Ireland's stated public policy more credit than it deserves. Nonetheless, a discussion of *Groener* would seem incomplete if it did not consider whether Ireland is truly committed to promoting and protecting Irish.

The organ which the government has charged with the task of promoting the use of Irish, the *Bord na Gaeilge*, has identified two goals of the country's language policy. One is the encouragement of the use of Irish as a vernacular language leading to the ultimate establishment of an "effectively bilingual society," and the other is the promotion of Irish as a symbol of cultural and national identity.[25] The most concrete action that Ireland has taken in the pursuit of both aims is, as noted by the Court, to require Irish as a subject of study for primary school students and to offer it as an optional course for secondary school students.[26] The vast majority of these students are native English-speakers who do not approach the language as a living means of communication, but rather as a cultural relic akin to Latin or classical Greek. This policy may be effective in promoting a cultural identity, but it does not further the goal of achieving an "effectively bilingual society." Anglophone children are given little, if any, encouragement to use their Irish skills outside the classroom, and there are doubts over the extent to which serious competence in the language is acquired. English is by far the most commonly spoken language in the country, and is the language associated with economic opportunity, both in Ireland and abroad.[27]

If Ireland truly wished to promote the use of Irish as a widely spoken language, it would need to implement measures that gave people a true incentive to use it, that is to say a reason to choose it over English, and very few Irish citizens wish to shift from English to Irish. The Irish population may support small measures designed to promote the symbolic presence of Irish, but there is little enthusiasm for actually using it, and the government has acted accordingly.

---

supervisory functions. Germany was not very specific in describing the impact of the claimed language problem, which may have led the Court to downgrade it to a mere "possibility" rather than an actuality. In any event, the Court stated that "these difficulties can be resolved by the undertakings and by the administrations in the same way as in every other field of trade," without specifying what that was. *Id.* at para. 13.

[25] Paulston at 82.

[26] *Groener*, 1989 ECR at 3993, para. 18.

[27] Paulston at 84-85.

Indeed, many believe that it was the Irish government that originally sought to minimize the role of Irish in the EU.[28] One author has pointed to a telling example of the attitude of the political establishment towards the Irish language, noting that "at the time of the recent presidential election [he was writing in 1993], none of the three candidates for the highest office of the country was able to muster up much competence in its first official language."[29] One does have to wonder why Mrs. Groener, who is a Dutch woman seeking employment in an environment where Irish is unlikely to ever be used, should be required to be proficient in a language which the president of Ireland, who is an Irish national and who symbolically represents the entire country, himself cannot effectively use.

With regards to the promotion of Irish as a symbol of national identity, or as the *Bord na Gaeilge* referred to it "a symbol of Irish identity and of the separateness of its people,"[30] such a policy sits rather uneasily with the integrationist aim of the EC Treaty. In a case which did not directly involve language issues, the ECJ ruled in 1982 that the Irish government had violated the free movement of goods provision of the EC Treaty with a "Buy Irish" campaign which encouraged Irish citizens to purchase goods manufactured in Ireland but which did not involve any measures that directly penalized foreign goods.[31] It is difficult to understand why a rhetorical and non-binding exhortation to "Buy Irish" is invalid while a legal requirement to "Speak Irish" is acceptable. It is also unclear to what extent measures designed to protect Irish will be viewed as acceptably proportionate in light of their resulting infringement on intra-Community economic movements. What, for example, would the Court make of a rule, such as that adopted by the Galway County Council in late 2002, which required persons buying new homes in the scenic areas of the Gaeltacht to be fluent in Irish?[32] Such a measure would greatly limit the ability of most non-Irish citizens (and indeed most Irish ones as well) to work in and establish themselves in western Ireland, but the need to protect the vibrancy of Irish in the one area of the country where the besieged language actually has some currency would seem to be rather compelling if one views the protection of the language as a valid endeavor at all.

In sum, there should be serious doubts as to whether requiring a foreign national who is functional in a language that is both an official language of her

---

[28] Anders Ahlqvist, "Language Conflict and Language Planning in Ireland," in *Language Conflict and Language Planning* (E. Jahr ed., 1993), 7, 12. As mentioned in Chapter I, the government apparently changed its mind in 2004 after several new and relatively unknown languages became part of the EU's linguistic makeup.

[29] *Id.* at 13.

[30] Paulston at 83.

[31] Case 249/81, *Commission v. Ireland*, 1982 ECR 4005.

[32] Brian Lavery, "Ireland: Speak Gaelic or Hit the High Road," *New York Times*, 19 Dec. 2002.

host state and the medium of communication in her place of employment to demonstrate minimal competence in another language which is spoken by a fraction of the country and which serves primarily as a symbol of the "separateness" of its people from the rest of Europe should be considered "strictly necessary" to achieving Ireland's public policy, such that it is. These points aside, the uniqueness of Ireland's situation makes it uncertain what applicability *Groener* might have in states where different linguistic dynamics are at work. Indeed, one may wonder whether if Mrs. Groener had sought a teaching position at a school in Paris where English (or Dutch, or any other language besides French) was to be used the Court would have upheld a rule requiring her to *parler français*. The Court's opinion was based on "the special linguistic situation in Ireland," where one official language needed protection from another official language, and its reasoning may therefore not be applicable in states without dueling official languages. Indeed, the operative portions of the Court's ruling are carefully worded: "the EEC Treaty does not prohibit the adoption of a policy for the protection and promotion of a language of a Member State which is both the national language and the first official language." Read narrowly, *Groener* only applies to situations where a Member State is seeking to protect and promote a language which is both its national and first official language, which implies (if it does not logically necessitate) that there be another language with secondary official status. Such a reading would rule out *Groener*'s applicability to an officially monolingual state such as France,[33] whose language protection measures, in contrast to Ireland's, have generally received hostile treatment from EU organs.

Indeed, there is a long history of linguistic antagonism between the Commission and France, where authorities have been on guard against perceived threats to the beauty and majesty of their language since Cardinal Richelieu founded the *Academie Française* in 1635.[34] The confrontation in July 2002 over the foodstuffs directive was discussed in Chapter III, but a similar episode, with another cagey legal response from France, occurred twenty years earlier. In 1982 the Commission commenced proceedings against France following that country's expansion of its Loi Bas-Lauriol so as to require the use of French on all goods imported into France.[35] The government subsequently issued an administrative decision which stated that the law would not be applied

[33] Article 2 of the Constitution of 1958 provides that French is the language of the Republic. Caroline ten Dam, however, has argued that *Groener* would apply in a French educational context. Caroline ten Dam, "La Législation Linguistique Française dans le Cadre de la Libre Circulation en Europe," Doctoral Dissertation, Europa-Institut Universiteit Utrecht, 1996, pp. 88-89.

[34] In 2003 the government banned the use of the English term "e-mail" in its ministries and mandated that the francophilic "courriel" be used in its stead. *See*, "You've Got Courriel," *International Herald Tribune*, 29 July 2003.

[35] The 1982 affair is discussed in ten Dam's dissertation at p. 8.

to goods coming from other Community members. Although the law remained on the books, the administrative action was sufficient to prevent the matter from reaching the ECJ. In fact, neither the Loi Bas-Lauriol nor the later Loi Toubon has, surprisingly, ever found its way before the Court.

The Commission has contended that the mandatory use of French on products sold in France is not always necessary for consumer protection. For example, in the 2002 instance, the Commission stated that French could not be required if a consumer could be informed by other means, and provided as an example that it would be unnecessary to require French in a fast-food restaurant where the English words "chicken wings" were accompanied by a photograph of the product.[36] The Commission's focus on *consumer* protection in France contrasts with its emphasis on *language* protection in Ireland, which is all the more remarkable because language protection is one of the stated goals of French language legislation. Indeed, the protection of the French language is viewed by many as the primary purpose of the Loi Toubon. While French legislators posited both consumer protection and language preservation as goals, Caroline ten Dam has argued that the latter was the stronger motive:

> The most important official motive at the root of the Loi Toubon is of a cultural character. This is so because this motive is advanced first not only at the beginning of the statement of motives (where the first line describes the French language as "the cement of national unity and a fundamental element of our heritage (*patrimoine*)," but also in the law itself (where the first line of the first article provides that "the French language is a fundamental element of the personality and heritage of France.")[37]

Marc Frangi has suggested that the battles between the Commission and France are the result of the failure of the Commission to comprehend the cultural forces that underlie French legislation:

> In the linguistic realm as in most other sectors, notably public services, the European Commission undergoes an analysis which is above all economic in nature. Put another way, it approaches the linguistic question first from a consumerist angle: is the consumer of a given good or service correctly informed by the labe-

---

[36] Commission Press Release IP-02-1155 of 27 July 2002.

[37] Ten Dam at 33 (trans. by R.L. Creech). Ten Dam nonetheless does not believe that the Loi Toubon is justifiable, as "there is no causal link between the obligation to use the French language in the marketing of goods on the one hand, as manufacturers in general try to inform consumers with a minimum number of words in order to reduce labeling and documentation expenses, and the protection of the French language on the other hand, which, in our opinion, is not effected by the reading of lists of ingredients and instructions for use." *Id.* at 76 (trans. by R.L. Creech).

> ling provided by the manufacturer or supplier? In contrast, the approach of the French authorities is founded principally on the concept of the general interest, which, certainly, is not identical to consumer protection.[38]

In the French conception of the general interest, Frangi explains, language protection is a corollary of a philosophy that regards the national language as the glue of social cohesion and the guarantor of equality.[39] Frangi contends that French authorities resolve the tension between their desire to protect their language and their need to respect EU law by opting for a "superficial adaptation" of EU law which involves taking partial or ambiguous steps towards responding to the Commission's concerns. In addition to the French responses to the Commission's interventions in 1982 and 2002, Frangi cites the reaction of the French government to the ECJ's *Geffroy* decision[40], which consisted of the Ministry of Culture's issuance of a circular which, while it seemed to address the Court's concerns, was of uncertain legal status.[41]

3. Dentists in Deutschland: The *Haim* Case

The ECJ again considered the parameters of a Member State's ability to impose language requirements on citizens of other Member States in the second of two cases which came before the Court that involved Germany's decision to refuse the appointment of a certain foreign dentist to eligibility to practice under Germany's social security scheme.[42] The dentist at issue, Salomone Haim, was an Italian national who had received his dentistry diploma in Turkey in 1946, where he practiced his profession until 1980. In 1981 he obtained permission to practice dentistry in Germany, but the following year he took up his profession in Belgium, where the authorities recognized his Turkish diploma as equivalent to the Belgian dental credentials. Thereafter, in 1988, Haim applied to the German dental authorities to be enrolled on the register of dentists who could participate in the German social security plan, but his application was denied. Haim challenged this decision in the German court system, claiming that it violated both a Community directive regarding the mutual recognition of dental qualifications as well as his right of establishment under Article 52 (now 43)[43] of the EC Treaty.

---

38 Marc Frangi, "Le Consommateur Français Entre Loi Toubon et Droit Communautaire," Revue Internationale de Droit Économique 135, 137 (2003).

39 *Id.*

40 Case C-366/98, 2000 ECR I-6579, discussed in Chapter III.

41 Frangi at 141-42.

42 Case C-424/97, *Haim v. Kassenzahnärztliche Vereinigung Nordrhein* ("*Haim II*"), 2000 ECR I-5123.

43 Const. for Eur. Art. III-137.

The directive at issue, Directive 78/686 required Member States to recognize dental qualifications awarded by another Member State.[44] In the first preliminary reference from the German court, the ECJ ruled that this directive did not require Member States to give legal effect to the decision of another Member State to recognize credentials awarded in a non-Member State.[45] The Court indicated that Article 52 (now 43) would still be relevant to Haim's case, however. When Haim's case continued in the German court, the state dental authority argued, *inter alia*, that Haim was not eligible to participate in the social security scheme because he had insufficient knowledge of German. Uncertainty about the validity of such a language requirement in the face of Community law, among other things, prompted the court to seek the guidance of the ECJ once again.

The interpretation of Directive 78/686 was among the issues, as it was unclear after the Court's previous ruling in *Haim I* whether this directive was applicable in any respect to dentists whose credentials were obtained outside the Community. The directive addressed the issue of language requirements, but in uncertain terms. Article 18(3) provided that "Member States shall see to it that, where appropriate, the persons concerned acquire, in their interest and in that of their patients, the linguistic knowledge necessary for the exercise of their profession in the host Member State." Even if one were to disregard the fact of Haim's diploma from a non-Member State, this provision arguably did not apply to Haim. Article 18(3) only allowed states to impose linguistic requirements on dentists when they were "necessary for the exercise of their profession," and the exercise of Haim's profession as such was not at issue (Germany had authorized him to practice in 1981); the case was rather concerned with the more limited issue of Haim's suitability for appointment under a social security scheme. The ECJ, however, simply concluded that the directive did not have any relevance at all when the dentist at issue did not have a diploma from another Member State.[46]

The Court did nonetheless consider Germany's linguistic requirements in the context of Article 52 (now 43) of the EC Treaty. Citing its previous case law, the Court stated that "national measures which restrict the exercise of fundamental freedoms guaranteed by the Treaty can be justified only if they fulfill four conditions: they must be applied in a non-discriminatory manner; they must be justified by overriding reasons based on the general interest; they must be suitable for securing the attainment of the objective which they pursue; and they must not go beyond what is necessary in order to attain that objective."[47]

---

44 [1978] O.J. L233/1.

45 Case C-319/92, *Haim v. Kassenzahnärztliche Vereinigung Nordrhein* ("*Haim I*"), 1994 ECR I-425.

46 *Haim II*, para. 53.

47 *Id.* at para. 57, citing Case C-55/94 *Gebhard* v. *Consiglio dell'Ordine degli Avvocati e Procuratori di Milano*, 1995 ECR I-4165, para. 37.

With regards to the issue of justification, the Court agreed that language requirements could serve a legitimate public interest:

> [T]he reliability of a dental practitioner's communication with his patient and with administrative authorities and professional bodies constitutes an overriding reason of general interest such as to justify making the appointment as a dental practitioner under a social security scheme subject to language requirements. Dialogue with patients, compliance with rules of professional conduct and law specific to dentistry in the Member State of establishment and performance of administrative tasks require an appropriate knowledge of the language of that State.[48]

The Court stressed that the language requirement would be invalid if it was excessive in light of the aims justifying it: "[I]t is important that language requirements designed to ensure that the dental practitioner will be able to communicate effectively with his patients, whose mother tongue is that of the Member State concerned, and with the administrative authorities and the professional bodies of that State do not go beyond what is necessary to attain that objective."[49] The Court continued with an interesting comment which recognized that not everyone in a given Member State is a national of that state or conversant in its language, stating that in assessing the proportionality of a language requirement, regard should be had for the fact that "it is in the interest of patients whose mother tongue is not the national language that there exist a certain number of dental practitioners who are also capable of communicating with such persons in their own language."[50]

The ECJ has also considered state practices that do not directly require knowledge of the state's language, but which nonetheless may operate to the disadvantage of citizens of other Member States who do not know it. An example of such a practice is a test for a driver's license which is conducted in a particular language with which migrant workers may have limited abilities. This was addressed by the Court in *Choquet*, in which the Court held that a Member State may require a citizen of another Member State who is permanently established in its territory to obtain a driver's license from his host state in order to drive there, even if he already has a license from his state of origin.[51] The Court ruled that such a requirement is not in itself an obstacle to the freedom of movement protected by the EC Treaty, but warned that it could become such if a state failed to take appropriate account of the linguistic difficulties that non-nationals might

---

48 *Haim II*, para. 59.

49 *Id.*, para. 60.

50 *Id.*

51 Case 16/78, 1978 ECR 2293.

encounter in the testing process.[52] While the Court did not elaborate on this point, the Advocate General suggested that one appropriate approach might be for the state to conduct its examinations of foreign nationals orally.[53]

4. Future Issues: A Look at Latvia

The recent addition of ten new Member States to the EU is likely to result in situations in which EU citizens run into snags with linguistic regimes while working or traveling in this newly added territory. With the zeal of the recently liberated, several ex-Communist and former Soviet client states have taken steps to promote their own indigenous languages. The three Baltic states – Estonia, Latvia and Lithuania – have all de-established Russian as an official language, and replaced it with Estonian, Latvian, and Lithuanian respectively.[54] This has brought acute hardships to the substantial portion of these states that is ethnically Russian, particularly in Latvia, where between thirty to forty per cent of the population is of Russian heritage. The enshrinement of a new national language and resurrection of a national identity in Latvia have been accompanied by a draconian new citizenship law which has had the effect of denying Latvian citizenship to much of this Russian-speaking population.[55] The law, enacted in 1994, generally conferred citizenship only upon persons who had Latvian citizenship at the time the country came under the control of the USSR in 1940 and the descendants of such persons.[56] As a result, large numbers of Russians who settled there (often not voluntarily, it should be added)

---

[52] *Id.*, para. 8.

[53] Opinion of Advocate General Reischl in *Choquet*, 1978 ECR 2304, 2309, para. 3(c).

[54] Uldis Ozolins, "Separating Language from Ethnicity: The Paradoxes of Strict Language Policies and Increasing Social Harmony in the Baltic States," in *Language: A Right and a Resource* (M. Kontra *et al.* eds., 1999), 245, 248; Eve Conant, "Saying *Nyet* to Russian," *Newsweek*, 1 July 2002, 30-31.

[55] For a while Latvia's actions complicated Riga's efforts to gain admission to the EU. The European Commission, in its 1997 report on the progress of Latvia towards the accession requirements stated that "Latvia needs to take measures to accelerate naturalization procedures to enable the Russian speaking non-citizens to become better integrated into Latvian society. It should also pursue its efforts to ensure equality of treatment for non-citizens and minorities." Nonetheless, the Commission somewhat incongruously opined that in Latvia "there are no major problems over respect for fundamental rights." Commission Opinion on the Application for Membership of Latvia (1997), contained in Graham Avery & Fraser Cameron, The Enlargement of the European Union (1999), 69. In 2002 the EU called upon Latvia to "ensure implementation of the language law and its implementing regulations in line with the principle of proportionality [and] international standards, [and to] continue to implement further concrete measures for the integration of non-citizens." Council Decision of 28 January 2002 on the Principles, Priorities, Intermediate Objectives and Conditions Contained in the Accession Partnership with Latvia, [2002] O.J. L44/45. *See also*, Ozolins passim.

[56] Citizenship Act of 22 July 1994 (*Pilsonības likums*).

during the Soviet era, and their children and grandchildren, were generally denied citizenship. Many of these were allowed to live in Latvia as "ex-USSR citizens," but many others – particularly those who had been in the military services of the USSR or the Russian Federation and their families – were, as a result of a treaty between Russia and Latvia which aimed to, as the preamble put it, "eradicate the negative consequences of their common history," required to leave Latvia.[57]

In 2003, the European Court of Human Rights held that Latvia had committed a human rights violation when it ordered the deportation of two Russian-speaking Latvians who found themselves caught up in the transformation of the Baltic's geopolitical landscape: a 44 year-old woman who had lived in Latvia since she was one month old, and her 23 year-old daughter, who had been born there and lived there her entire life.[58] The woman was the wife of a man who had served in the Soviet and Russian armies, and whose removal, along with that of his family, was arguably required by the terms of the Russian-Latvian accord.[59] The man left Latvia and moved to Russia, but his wife and daughter stayed behind and contested the removal order in the Latvian legal system. After their legal efforts failed, they joined their husband/father in Russia.

The Court agreed with Latvia's argument that the enforcement of the treaty served a legitimate national security aim.[60] However, the Court held that Latvia must make exceptions for particular situations when the removal of a former member of the Russian military and his family would result in an interference with the right to family life (Article 8 of the European Convention on Human Rights) which was disproportionate to the aim pursued.[61] The Court accordingly balanced the rights of the woman and her daughter against those of the state, and in so doing, considered Latvia's argument that the two were never significantly integrated into Latvian society, as evidenced by, Latvia maintained, their lack of proficiency in the Latvian language. The applicants rebutted Latvia's assessment of their linguistic abilities by pointing to the mother's history of working as a secretary for a Latvian company and the daughter's obtainment of a certificate which attested to her fluency in Latvian.[62] The government derided these credentials, and in particular denigrated the daughter's certificate as

57 The Treaty between Latvia and Russia on the Conditions and Schedule for the Complete Withdrawal of Russian Federation Military Troops from the Territory of the Republic of Latvia and their Status Pending Withdrawal (signed 30 Apr. 1994, effective 27 Feb. 1995). The Russian Federation succeeded to control over the armed forces of the Union of Soviet Socialist Republics in 1992.

58 *Slivenko v. Latvia*, App. No. 48321/99 (2003).

59 The precise effect of the treaty was disputed by the parties, and the Court declined to weigh in on the debate over its interpretation. *Id.*, para. 105.

60 *Id.*, para. 112.

61 *Id.*, paras. 117-122.

62 *Id.*, para. 74.

attesting to only "the lowest degree of proficiency in the Latvian language."[63] The Court was unswayed by Latvia's position, however, and indeed seemed to suggest that language proficiency did not play a particularly significant role in determining whether someone had the right to reside in a given place, stating:

> As regards the respondent Government's argument about the level of the applicants' proficiency in Latvian, the Court observes that, insofar as this is a relevant consideration, it has not been shown that the degree of the applicants' fluency in the language - although the precise level is in dispute - was insufficient for them to pursue a normal everyday life in Latvia. In particular, there is no evidence that the level of the applicants' knowledge of Latvian was in any way different from that of other native Russian speakers living in Latvia, including those who were able to obtain the status of "ex-USSR citizens" in order to remain in Latvia on a permanent basis.[64]

The year before this decision was handed down, the Court of Human Rights had administered another language-related chastisement to Latvia. In 2002, the Court held that Latvia had acted unlawfully with respect to its implementation of a law which required parliamentary candidates to demonstrate competency in the Latvian language.[65] In that case, a Russian-speaking woman had been stricken from a list of eligible candidates on the grounds that she did not have the requisite high level of competence in Latvian. While the Court agreed with Latvia that a state could legitimately require a candidate for its national parliament to have sufficient knowledge of its official language,[66] it nonetheless concluded that the procedure which Latvia used to assess the woman's language abilities ran afoul of human rights norms. In particular, the Court noted that the would-be candidate was subjected to language testing that went beyond that which was objectively required by Latvian law, that the government deviated from its standard procedure by investing a single civil servant with full responsibility for assessing the applicant's linguistic knowledge, and that the language examination consisted largely of questions regarding the reasons for her political orientation.[67]

---

63 *Id.*, para. 88.

64 *Id.*, para. 124.

65 *Podkolzina v. Latvia*, App. No. 46726/99 (2002).

66 *Id.*, para. 34.

67 *Id.*, para. 36.

B. Rights of Migrant Workers to the Use of Their Own Language

A citizen of one Member State who speaks a particular language does not have a general right to demand that officials in another state communicate with him in that language. However, in some particular matters, principally those involving social security programs, education for children and criminal proceedings, an EU citizen will enjoy some linguistic rights outside of his state of origin.

1. Language Rights in Social Security Programs

The right of a citizen of a Member State to work in another Member State includes a right to participate in the social security programs of that state. This was established in 1971 when the Council issued Regulation No. 3 on Social Security for Migrant Workers, also known as Reg. No. 1408/71.[68] This measure grants a migrant worker the right to use his own language in documents that he submits to officials in his host state, as long as that language is an official language of another Member State. Interestingly, there is no requirement that the language be an official language of his own state of origin, which potentially means that, in this narrow area, he may have more language rights abroad than he would have had if he had stayed in his home state. As de Witte points out, it also means that a migrant worker may enjoy language rights in a host state which that state's own citizens do not have, giving as an example the fact that Belgium may require its nationals to use French in one part of the country and Dutch in another, but these restrictions could not be applied to citizens of other Member States.[69]

Another piece of Community legislation regarding social security programs, Regulation 574/72, guarantees a migrant worker the right to be notified of certain administrative decisions (concerning invalidity, old age and death benefits) "in his own language," without expressly requiring that such a language have official status somewhere in the Community.[70] In addition, without specifying exactly what it meant, the ECJ has indicated that when a Member State issues social security decisions that are not technically subject to this regulation, it "must nevertheless take care that legal certainty is not prejudiced by a failure arising from the inability of the worker to understand the language in which a decision is notified to him."[71]

---

68 [1971] O.J. English Special Edition (II) p. 416.

69 De Witte, "Surviving in Babel? Language Rights and European Integration" at 290.

70 Art. 48, [1972] O.J. English Special Edition (I) p. 159.

71 Case 66/74, *Farrauto v. Bau-Berufsgenossenschaft*, 1975 ECR 157. The case concerned an Italian national who had received by mail a notice written in German from German social security authorities. He chal-

2. Education Rights for the Children of Migrant Workers

Directive 77/486 on the education of the children of migrant workers imposes a duty on the host state to teach such children the official language (or one of them) of the host state, and calls on the host state to take "appropriate measures" to "promote the teaching of the mother language and culture of the country of origin," with an eye towards, as the preamble states, "principally to facilitating their possible reintegration into the member States of origin."[72] The directive thus appears motivated not so much by a wish to improve the educational opportunities for children as it is by the desire to prevent them from presenting difficulties for their parents should they decide to return home.[73]

3. Language Rights in Criminal Proceedings

A citizen of the EU who faces criminal charges in a Member State of which he is not a national has no general right to have those proceedings conducted in his own language, indeed he may not even have that right in his home country if his language does not have official status there.[74] The ECJ has indicated, however, that when a Member State grants its own citizens the right to use a particular language in criminal proceedings, the same right must be accorded to citizens of other states. The Court so held in *Ministère Public v. Mutsch*,[75] which involved a German-speaking (and apparently monolingual) Luxembourg national who permanently resided in the German-speaking region of Belgium, where he was employed as a roofer. Indeed, he was born in that area and there was no indication in the case that he had ever lived anywhere else. After taking part in a "pub-crawl" which ended with him coming to blows

---

lenged the decision referenced in the notice, and the case was sent to the ECJ for a preliminary ruling, where the issue was whether mail was a valid method of effecting service. The Court concluded that it was. *Id.* at 162, para. 6. The Advocate General offered a concrete view of how the worker's lack of familiarity with the language of the host state should be taken into account, stating in effect that if service of a decision set in motion the running of a time period during which the recipient was required to take some action in order to preserve his rights, the decision should not be deemed to have been given until the worker had obtained a translation. Opinion of Advocate General Trabucchi in *Farrauto*, 1975 ECR, 163, 168.

72 Directive 77/486, Pmbl., Art. 3, [1977] O.J. L199/32.

73 De Witte, "Surviving in Babel? Language Rights and European Integration" at 291.

74 The European Convention for Protection of Human Rights and Fundamental Freedoms, Art. 6(3)(e), provides that, at the very least, he has the right to a free interpreter if criminal proceedings against him, whether in his home state or elsewhere in the Member States of the Council of Europe, are conducted in a language that he does not understand or speak.

75 Case 137/84, 1985 ECR 2681.

with the police, Mutsch faced criminal charges in a local court where, under Belgian law, proceedings were to be conducted in French. The law provided an exception, however, and allowed Belgian nationals to opt for the use of German in the court. While the law was worded so as to apply only to Belgian nationals, the court nonetheless ordered the use of German in Mutsch's proceedings. The prosecutor filed an appeal with the Cour d'Appel in Liège, which having doubts about the compatibility of the Belgian nationality requirement with Community law, referred questions to the ECJ.

The main issue before the ECJ was whether the right to free movement of workers under Article 48 of the EC Treaty (now Art. 39) prohibited the sort of nationality restriction imposed by Belgian law, particularly in light of Regulation 1612/68, which, among other things, guarantees migrant workers the same "social advantages" as nationals of their host state. The Court was clear in pronouncing that language rights were closely linked to the right of free movement: "In the context of a Community based on the principles of free movement of persons and freedom of establishment the protection of the linguistic rights and privileges of individuals is of particular importance."[76] The Italian government, which was the defender of the Belgian law before the Court (the Belgian government apparently did not file a submission), argued, *inter alia*, that the use of a particular language could not be deemed a "social advantage" within the meaning of the regulation, as that regulation only applied to measures which bore a connection with an employment relationship, and the use of a language in criminal proceedings, it contended, did not. Furthermore, Italy suggested that a Member State should be allowed to enact laws designed to benefit an officially recognized minority within its territory and to limit the exercise of those rights to persons who are members of the minority and residents of the territory concerned. The Court was unpersuaded by either of these arguments, however, and concluded that "[t]he right to use his own language in proceedings before the courts of the Member State in which he resides, under the same conditions as national workers, plays an important role in the integration of a migrant worker and his family into the host country, and thus in achieving the objective of free movement for workers."[77] The Advocate General amplified this position in his opinion, pointing out that a worker's ability to use his language in a Member State of which he is not a national may be the reason that would cause him to move there in the first place.[78]

In the case of *Bickel and Franz*, the Court expanded its holding in *Mutsch* in two significant respects.[79] First, the ECJ indicated that the right to use one's language in the courts of another Member State is not limited to persons who

---

76 *Id.* at 2695, para. 11.

77 *Id.* at 2696, para. 16.

78 Opinion of Advocate General Lenz in *Mutsch*, 1985 ECR 2682, 2689.

79 Case C-274/96, 1998 ECR I-7637.

are habitually resident in that state, and second, this right is not restricted to situations where the nationals of that state themselves have a general right to use that language. Bickel and Franz were speakers of German, the former a national of Austria and the latter of Germany, who ran into legal difficulties while in Italy. Bickel was a truck driver who, while engaged in his profession, had been arrested for driving under the influence of alcohol, and Franz had been arrested for possession of an unlawful knife while in Italy as a tourist. These events, and the court which tried them, occurred in the bilingual province of Bolzano, whose residents were entitled, under national law, to select either German or Italian for use in criminal proceedings. Italian authorities believed that Bickel and Franz, as non-residents of Bolzano, were not entitled to this choice. The court was uncertain as to whether limiting the option of German-language services to residents of Bolzano was compatible with EC law, and consequently asked the ECJ to weigh-in on this issue.

The ECJ reiterated its holding in *Mutsch* and stated that "the exercise of the right to move and reside freely in another Member State is enhanced if the citizens of the Union are able to use a given language to communicate with the administrative and judicial authorities of a State on the same footing as its nationals."[80] The Court stated that while a state was generally free to adopt whatever rules of criminal procedure that it wished, including the rules governing language use in criminal cases, Community law did not allow the state to discriminate on the basis of nationality in so doing.[81] Italy argued that there had been no discrimination on such grounds, as the right to a trial in German was not based on nationality, but rather on residency in the province of Bolzano, and that non-Italian citizens were therefore treated no differently than Italians who lived outside of the province.[82] The Bolzano provision, Italy explained, would allow non-Italians who resided in Bolzano to opt to use German, and would not accord such a right to German-speaking Italian nationals in other parts of the country.

---

80 *Id.* at 7655, para. 16.

81 *Id.* at 7655-56, para. 17. The Court, and the Advocate General, relied heavily on the decision in *Cowan v. Trésor Public*, Case 186/87, 1989 ECR 195, where the Court had indicated that a British national who had been assaulted on the Paris metro while visiting the City of Lights as a tourist was entitled to receive payment under a national compensation system which had been restricted to French citizens. *Bickel and Franz*, 1989 ECR at 7655, para. 14; Opinion of Advocate General Jacobs in *Bickel and Franz*, 1998 ECR I-7639, 7643, para. 16.

82 Italy also advanced the same argument which it had previously advanced in *Mutsch* regarding the asserted right of a state to protect a national linguistic and cultural minority present in a particular region and to limit measures taken towards that aim to persons who reside in that region. The Court, as it had before, rejected this argument.

However, because most German-speaking Italian nationals lived in the province of Bolzano, the Court found that such a law amounted to indirect discrimination against nationals of other Member States. The Court explained:

> Italian nationals are at an advantage by comparison with nationals of other Member States. The majority of Italian nationals whose language is German are in a position to demand that German be used throughout the proceedings in the Province of Bolzano, because they meet the residence requirements laid down by the rules in issue; the majority of German-speaking nationals of other Member States, on the other hand, cannot avail themselves of that right because they do not satisfy that requirement.[83]

Having been held to be discriminatory, the Bolzano residency rule would be valid only if there was an objective justification for it, and the Court reasoned that there could be no such justification given that the judicial system in Bolzano was already set up to conduct trials in German and that the authorities would therefore incur no additional costs.[84] As a result, the Court concluded, the EC Treaty prohibited a national rule that conferred on the residents of one region of a state the right to use a particular language in criminal proceedings if that rule did not also confer the same right on nationals of other Member States "whose language is the same."[85]

Even after *Bickel and Franz*, a number of questions are left open regarding the scope of the right that a citizen of one Member State has to use a particular language in criminal proceedings in another Member State. While it is certain that a Member State may not treat non-nationals differently than it treats its nationals in this regard, it is not entirely clear what might be considered "different" treatment in all circumstances. The Italian law regarding Bolzano, and the Court both in that case and in *Mutsch*, speak in terms of a person being able to use "his" language, but it is not obvious what it means for a language to be ascribed to a person.[86] Does this mean that the person must be able to actually *speak* the language (as Bickel, Franz and Mutsch could), or does it suffice if he can merely *understand* it? This may be the case if the language is not his mother tongue and is known to him only as a foreign language. In such circumstances may a state require a minimum level of competence in order to invoke the right?

---

83 *Bickel and Franz*, 1998 ECR at 7659, para. 25.

84 *Id.* at 7659, para. 30. Indeed, as the Advocate General pointed out, conducting a trial in Italian would entail greater expense, as the defendants would then be entitled, under the European Convention on Human Rights, to an interpreter. Opinion of Advocate General Jacobs in *Bickel and Franz*, 1998 ECR at 7648-49, para. 40.

85 *Bickel and Franz*, 1998 ECR at 7659, para. 31.

86 What it means to "know a language" is the ultimate question with which the science of linguistics is concerned and is one that has not yet been satisfactorily answered.

If so, does this not have the potential of amounting to at least indirect discrimination against non-nationals, who will generally have a lesser degree of competence in the language concerned? To put these questions more concretely, could a Dutch-speaking citizen of the Netherlands, who knows no Italian but has a moderate ability to understand (but not speak) German, be entitled to choose to have a trial in Bolzano conducted in German? If so, could he choose this and still be entitled to the services of an interpreter under the European Convention on Human Rights?

In the operative paragraph of the judgment in *Bickel and Franz*, the Court stated that a Member State was precluded by the EC Treaty from granting language rights to its citizens without conferring the same rights on nationals of other Member States "whose language is the same." The requirement that the language be "the same" is necessary in order for Treaty rights to be implicated, as a citizen of one Member State would have no basis under the Treaty for claiming a right to a trial in a second state in a language that was not "the same" as one of the languages that could be used by citizens of the second state. What it means for two individuals to speak "the same" language is not a simple matter, however, although it was unaddressed, and likely uncontemplated by the Court. Leaving aside the point that no two people speak identically – everyone speaks his or her own idiolect – the varieties of what is called "German" that are spoken in different parts of the EU are not, in fact, "the same," as was discussed in Chapter I. Bolzano borders Austria, and until the breakup of the Hapsburg empire after the First World War was under Austrian sovereignty. Austrian-German, as was indicated above, differs in non-trivial ways from the standard German of Germany (and elsewhere in the EU), and this fact has been recognized, at treaty level, by the EU.[87] Indeed, most television and radio advertisers produce separate versions of commercials for the two countries.[88] Is Franz, a German national whose German is presumably not "the same" as that spoken in Bolzano therefore not entitled to a trial in what is deemed "German" in northern Italy? It seems unlikely that the Court meant to imply that this could legitimately occur, but a narrow reading of the case could permit just such an outcome, and Italy has not demonstrated a tendency to construe the Court's decisions in a liberal manner.[89]

---

87 Protocol No. 10 to the Act concerning the conditions of accession of the Kingdom of Norway, the Republic of Austria, the Republic of Finland and the Kingdom of Sweden and the adjustments to the Treaties on which the European Union is founded. [1994] O.J. C241/370.

88 Irmgard Rieder, "Das Österreichische Deutsch aus der Sicht des Sprachmittlers," *Terminologie et Traduction* 2 (1997), 155.

89 In addition to the restrictive reading of *Mutsch* which Italy advocated in *Bickel and Franz*, one will recall that Italy embraced an interpretation of the Court's decision in Case 193/80, *Commission v. Italy*, 1981 ECR 3019 (the first vinegar case) that was so narrow that it bordered on contempt.

If the concept of what constitutes "the same" language is given some elasticity, as it would have to be to allow Franz the right to a trial in Bolzano German, there are implications for closely-related languages, such as Swedish and Danish,[90] or Czech and Slovak,[91] which are arguably as much "the same" as the standard German of the Federal Republic of Germany and Austrian German are. Germany has designated Danish as a "regional or minority language" in the *Land* of Schleswig-Holstein under the European Charter for Regional or Minority Languages, and has guaranteed speakers of Danish there certain rights to use their language.[92] Although Germany has not provided the right to use Danish in criminal cases, if it were to do so, a Swedish national would arguably be entitled to its use (that is, of Danish) in court to the same extent that Franz would be entitled to the use of Bolzano-style German.[93]

Francesco Palermo has written that a citizen of one Member State who faces proceedings in another Member State should be entitled, regardless of his mother tongue, to elect the use of either that state's official language or another language if that other language is offered to that state's own nationals. To do otherwise, he believes, would allow a rule that "implicitly discriminates on the basis of nationality."[94] Whether a rule that discriminates on the basis of language is *ipso facto* a rule that discriminates on the basis of nationality within the meaning of the EC Treaty is unclear, however, although the rulings in the *Kik* case would seem to suggest that it was not. The broad view of indirect

---

90 *See Encyclopedia of the Languages of Europe* (Glanville Price ed., 2000), 408-09, 465.

91 In a Eurobarometer study of foreign language proficiency in the Member States admitted in the most recent enlargement, which is cited on the europa website, Czech and Slovak were treated as the same language. *See* http://europa.eu.int/comm/education/policies/lang/languages/index_en.html#Foreign%20language%20skills.

92 For example, the use of Danish in documents and evidence submitted to a court, pursuant to Article 9 of the European Charter. A list of the provisions of the Charter which Germany has designated as applicable to it may be found at the website of the Council of Europe at www.coe.int.

93 One should be wary of vesting too much importance in the labels given to particular languages. The fact that the languages spoken in Germany and Austria are both customarily called "German" (*deutsch*) whereas Swedish (*svenska*) and Danish (*dansk*) go by different names, is more a reflection of political and historical dynamics than it is of any intrinsic linguistic properties of the languages concerned. Indeed, some languages, like German, are known by many different, and etymologically unrelated, names to speakers of other languages (*e.g.*, in German as *deutsch*, in English as *German*, in French as *allemand*, and in Polish as *niemiecki*) in terms that reflect the historical interaction of the language communities involved. Other languages are known by various names *within* their own speech communities, and the name used in any particular circumstance may serve as an indicator of the national or political identity of the speaker, for example the Belgian language variously called *Nederlands* or *Vlaams*.

94 Francesco Palermo, "The Use of Minority Languages: Recent Developments in EC Law and Judgments of the ECJ," 8 *Maastricht L.J.* 3 (2001), 299, 312.

discrimination in *Bickel and Franz,* however, could be invoked to support the equation of the two concepts.[95]

4. Language Rights in Civil Proceedings

The ECJ's reasoning in *Bickel and Franz* and *Mutsch* should be equally applicable to civil proceedings, and nationals of a Member State should accordingly have the right to use their own language in civil proceedings occurring in another Member State on the same terms that citizens of the latter state may do so. Since January 2003 a citizen of a Member State who is unable to afford the costs associated with the litigation of a civil or commercial matter in another Member State may be entitled to state-sponsored assistance in overcoming the linguistic barriers that he may face.[96] Pursuant to Directive 2002/8, Member States (except Denmark, which is expressly exempted from it)[97] are obligated to bear the costs associated with interpretation and translation of necessary documents in any civil or commercial case that involves a litigant who qualifies for legal aid and who is a citizen of another Member State.[98] The documents covered by the directive are those that are "required" by the adjudicating body and which are presented by the aid recipient.[99] The translation of such documents is thus in essence for the court's benefit, and the court will presumably have the documents translated into the language in which the proceedings are to be conducted. Interpretation of speech (*e.g.*, witness testimony), however, accrues to the benefit of both the court and the aid recipient. It is unclear which of these is entitled to choose the language into which the language of the case is to be interpreted, and whether there are restrictions on what that language may be (*i.e.*, whether the right to interpretation is limited to interpretation into one of the Regulation languages or into a language that is the native tongue of the aid recipient).

---

[95] It should be borne in mind that there is no uniform relationship between languages and states. In some instances, a language is significantly connected with only one particular state (*e.g.*, Danish, Irish and Finnish, or, at least in terms of distribution within Europe, Portuguese and Spanish). Other languages, however, have vibrancy in multiple states, although they may be particularly associated, to a greater or lesser extent, with one historically and culturally dominant power (*e.g.*, English, French, Italian, German, Dutch, Greek, Hungarian and Russian).

[96] Directive 2002/8, [2003] O.J. L26/41. In 1977 the European Parliament passed a resolution which would have recognized "the right of Community citizens to use their mother tongue ... in court actions." The Council, however, did not enact this measure. *See*, De Witte, "Surviving in Babel? Language Rights and European Integration" at 290.

[97] Directive 2002/8, pmbl.(34).

[98] *Id.*, Art. 7.

[99] *Id.*

Another uncertainty in the directive pertains to the language in which applications for legal aid are to be filed. The directive allows litigants to file for legal aid in either their home country or in the country where the forum is located.[100] Under Article 13(2), such applications are to be completed in either "(a) the official language or one of the languages of the Member State of the competent receiving authority [*i.e.*, the Member State where the litigation is to occur] which corresponds to one of the languages of the Community institutions; or (b) another language which that Member State has indicated it can accept in accordance with Article 14(3)." Article 14(3) in turn provides that "Member States shall notify the Commission of the official language or languages of the Community institutions *other than their own* which is or are acceptable to the competent receiving authority for completion of the legal aid applications to be received."[101] Whether Member States are thereby obligated to select a language other than their own official language or languages, or whether they are merely given the option to do so, is likely open to debate. Strictly speaking, the requirement only relates to languages that a Member State deems "acceptable," and there is no express requirement that it view any languages other than its own as such. On the other hand, a requirement to accept applications in at least one foreign language may be viewed as implicit in the directive's wording, particularly given its overall aim of promoting access to courts in disputes of a multi-national character.[102]

C. Dealing with the Greek Alphabet: An iota of Respect

Following the admission of Greece, there were no longer simply multiple languages in the Community, but multiple alphabets as well. The case of a man named Χρήστος Κωνσταντινίδης has indicated that the EC Treaty requires the other Member States to be alert to Greek sensitivities regarding their script.[103] In that case, a Greek national resident in Germany claimed that the method adopted by the German government for the transliteration of Greek names into Roman characters resulted in a spelling of his name that was offensive to him and injurious to his business and social relations. The Greek man wished his name to be recognized as "Christos Konstantinidis," which he said was a spelling that would enable German-speakers to pronounce his name as correctly as possible. The German government, however, used an international system of transliteration that was not based solely on phonetics, but entailed

---

[100] *Id.*, Art. 13(1).

[101] Emphasis added.

[102] The second language designation is also reminiscent of the two-language scheme in OHIM's application process.

[103] Case C-168/91, *Konstantinidis*, 1993 ECR I-1191.

instead a character-for-character substitution, and the application of this system to Mr. Konstantinidis resulted in spellings for both his first and last names that differed from his preferred spelling: "Hrēstos Kōnstantindēs."[104] The German authorities entered this spelling of his name in their records after he married a German woman. Mr. Konstantinidis challenged this action in a German court, where he contended that the spelling favored by Germany amounted to a violation of his rights to free movement for purposes of work under Article 48 of the EC Treaty (now Art. 39), his right of establishment under Art. 52 (now Art. 43), and his freedom to provide services under Article 59 (now Art. 49).[105] The court sought the ECJ's guidance on these issues.

Mr. Konstantinidis' concern was that he was already known, both socially and professionally, under the name spelled "Christos Konstantinidis," and that the new spelling would cause confusion and result in a substantial loss of earnings as well as administrative difficulties. Moreover, Mr. Konstantinidis, who was born on the 25th of December, was bothered by the fact that in changing his first name from "Christos" to "Hrēstos" the German government had destroyed the religious nature of his, to use a fitting term, Christian name. Germany defended its use of its transliteration system, arguing that its system of character-for-character correspondence resulted in a transliteration which would be the same in every country, whereas phonetic transliterations of the sort preferred by Mr. Konstantinidis would result in the same Greek name being transcribed differently in different parts of the Community, as the Roman characters did not have the same phonetic value in all of the Community's languages.

The Court approached the case solely in terms of the right of establishment provision of the Treaty (Art. 52, now Art. 43), observing that Mr. Konstantinidis was self-employed as a masseur. This provision, the Court stated, "constitutes one of the fundamental legal provisions of the Community," and must be borne in mind in considering a state's right, the existence of which the Court acknowledged, to transcribe Greek names into Roman letters.[106] The Court indicated where the limits of a state's power would lie:

> [Transcription rules] are to be regarded as incompatible with Article 52 of the Treaty only in so far as their application causes a Greek national such a degree of inconvenience as in fact to interfere with his freedom to exercise the right of establishment enshrined in that article. Such interference occurs if a Greek national is obliged by the legislation of the State in which he is established to use, in the pursuit of his occupation, a spelling of his name derived from the translit-

---

[104] A further alteration was added by the German government. Because their typewriters were unable to produce letters with bars over them, they produced such letters with acute accents instead.

[105] These three rights are enshrined in the Constitution for Europe in Articles III-133, 137 and 144, respectively.

[106] *Konstantinidis*, 1993 ECR at 1218, paras. 12-14.

> eration used in the registers of civil status if that spelling is such as to modify its pronunciation and if the resulting distortion exposes him to the risk that potential clients may confuse him with other persons.[107]

The Court's statement is as noteworthy for what it does not say as for what it does say. The Court views the issue of the spelling of a name only in the connection of problems that may be encountered in the pursuit of a profession, particularly "inconvenience" and the risk that potential clients might be confused. There was no indication that the insult to Mr. Konstantinidis's religious feelings would itself require Germany to abandon its system, even though one could imagine such a conclusion being reached while still staying within the framework of an analysis solely under the right of establishment; citizens of one Member State are likely to be deterred from moving to another Member State if they expect that their religious convictions will not be respected there.

In any event, it was unclear whether Mr. Konstantinidis was in fact required to use the spelling dictated by Germany professionally or if he only had to use it when dealing with the state. Advocate General Jacobs addressed this point, but believed that it was not significant, and that even if the challenged spelling existed only "in the dusty archives of the State," Mr. Konstantinidis would still be entitled to have his official records relating to birth, marriage, and death – "the most significant and sacred evens in a person's existence" – issued with a name that was not insulting and offensive.[108] Indeed, the Advocate General saw this case in much broader terms than simply the right to be unhindered in the pursuit of work, commenting that "Community law does not regard the migrant worker (or the self-employed migrant) purely as an economic agent and a factor of production ...; it regards him as a human being who is entitled to live in [another Member State] 'in freedom and dignity.'"[109]

The Advocate General spoke at length about the human rights aspect of Mr. Konstantinidis's case, although he acknowledged that such comments were not "strictly necessary" in light of the fact that the case could be resolved on the grounds of discrimination under the Treaty.[110] The Advocate General stressed that the Court must ensure the observance of the European Convention on Human Rights "within the sphere of Community law," stating in particular that human rights were relevant to an assessment of a state's proffered justifications for abridging freedoms under the EC Treaty.[111] He noted that the ECHR contained guarantees of liberty and security (Art. 5) and respect for private and family life (Art. 8), and after examining other international human

---

[107] *Id.* at 1218-19, paras. 15-16.

[108] Opinion of Advocate General Jacobs in *Konstantinidis*, 1993 ECR I-1198, 1205, para. 26.

[109] *Id.*, para. 24.

[110] *Id.* at 1207, para. 31.

[111] *Id.*, para. 34, p. 1210, para. 43.

rights instruments and the constitutions of Germany and other Member States concluded that:

> It is possible to infer from [such instruments] the existence of a principle according to which the State must respect not only the physical well-being of the individual but also his dignity, moral integrity, and sense of personal identity. I do not think there can be any doubt that those 'moral rights' are violated if a State compels someone to abandon or modify his name, unless at any rate it does so for a very good reason.[112]

As of 2004, the Greek and Roman alphabets are not the only two writing systems in wide use in the EU. Nearly 1.5 million ethnic Russians in the new Member States in the east use the Cyrillic script. Furthermore, the Cyrillic alphabet may attain official status in the EU should the candidacy of Bulgaria for admission prove successful. The potential for future transcription battles is therefore somewhat significant.[113]

D. Conclusion

The words of Advocate General Jacobs in *Konstantinidis* indicate the potential influence of human rights principles in cases before the ECJ. The full court has yet to directly consider such principles in its opinions regarding language use in any substantive way, however, but I will now examine them in the final chapter.

---

[112] *Id.* at 1209, para. 39.

[113] The European Court of Human Rights has recently spoken about the role that the orthographic form of the Moldavian language (which has historically been written in both Latin and Cyrillic letters) has had in the ongoing battle in Moldova over the country's warring Romanian and Russian identities. See *Ilascu v. Moldova and Russia*, App. No. 48787/99 (2004), para. 28, and the elaboration on this subject by Judge Kovler in a dissenting opinion in the same case.

CHAPTER V

Language Rights as Human Rights

The EU's commitment to human rights has been a work in progress. The original EC Treaty made no mention of human rights principles (with the exception of a reference to the "equality between men and women" in Article 2), but the Court of Justice gradually came to recognize the relevance of human rights in its interpretation of the economic terms of the Treaty. The EU finally proclaimed a comprehensive Charter of Fundamental Rights at the European Council meeting in Nice in December 2000,[1] and this Charter was incorporated into the Constitution for Europe that was propounded by the European Convention in July 2003 and ultimately signed by the heads of state or government of all twenty-five Member States in Rome on 29 October 2004.

A. The Evolution of the EU's Judicial and Political Approach to Human Rights

In the very early years of the Community the Court rejected challenges to Community measures that were based on human rights principles out-of-hand.[2] In 1969, however, the Court acknowledged the relevance of such principles in *Stauder v. Ulm*, although it resolved the case in such a way that it was unnecessary to examine these concepts.[3] The following year, in a case concerning the economic liberty rights of an importer/exporter of cereals, the Court stated that Community measures could not be invalidated by claims that they ran counter to fundamental rights as embodied in the constitution of a Member State, but that there may be an "analogous guarantee inherent in Community law" that the Community must abide by.[4] In *Nold v. Commission*, in which a coal wholesaler claimed that the Commission's adoption of certain rules pertaining to the supply of coal infringed its fundamental rights, the Court identified the source of the Community's human rights norms as the "constitu-

---

1 [2000] O.J. C364/1

2 *See, e.g.*, Cases 36-38 and 40/59, *Geitling v. High Authority*, 1960 ECR 423; Case 40/64, *Sgarlata v. Commission*, 1965 ECR 215.

3 Case 29/69, 1969 ECR 419. While this case did not involve issues of language rights, it was the direct result of the multilingual nature of the Community. At issue in the case was the interpretation of a Community decision regarding the provision of discounted butter to certain categories of consumers where the wording in the different language versions differed as to whether the name of an eligible consumer must be stated on the coupon used to redeem the butter. The German and Dutch versions contained such a requirement, and a German war veteran challenged this as a violation of the right to human dignity. The Court, however, interpreted the provision in harmony with the French and Italian versions (the EC was quadrilingual at the time), which only required that the coupons be "individualized," and thus determined that the decision did not impose a name requirement.

4 Case 11/70, *Internationale Handelsgesellschaft v. Einfuhr und Vorratstelle für Getreide und Futtermittel*, 1970 ECR 1125, para. 4.

tional traditions common to the Member States" and "international treaties for the protection of human rights on which the Member States have collaborated or of which they are signatories."[5] In particular, the Court has specified the Council of Europe's Convention for the Protection of Human Rights and Fundamental Freedoms of 4 November 1950 ("ECHR") as relevant to a consideration of Community law,[6] and that, furthermore, the Member States are themselves bound to respect the protections accorded by the ECHR when they implement Community law.[7] In addition, the Court, after initially stating that it could not consider the matter, has held that Member States are limited by the ECHR when they proffer justifications for interfering with the free trade provisions of the EC Treaty.[8] Nonetheless, as the review of the language use cases in Chapters III and IV indicated, the Court often avoids addressing human rights issues which appear relevant to the resolution of the cases before it, and the Court typically words its opinions in exclusively economic terms. Indeed, some authors have claimed that when the Court does invoke human rights principles, it invariably applies them in such a way so as to further economic freedom over other types of human rights concerns. One such criticism is the following:

> [I]t is economic integration, to be achieved through the acts of Community institutions, which the Court sees as its fundamental priority. In adopting and adapting the slogan of protection of human rights the Court has seized the moral high ground. However, the high rhetoric of human rights protection can be seen as no more than a vehicle for the Court to extend the scope and impact of European law.[9]

Moreover, the Court signaled that human rights principles had a limited role in the EU when it ruled in 1996 that the Community lacked the capacity to accede to the ECHR as the EC Treaty then stood.[10]

The Community's political institutions endorsed the ECJ's attention to human rights principles in 1977 when the Commission, Council and Parliament

---

5 Case 4/73, 1974 ECR 491, para. 13.

6 *See, e.g.*, Case 36/75, *Rutili v. Minister for the Interior*, 1975 ECR 1219.

7 *See, e.g.*, Case 249/86, *Commission v. Germany*, 1989 ECR 1263; Case 222/84, *Johnston v. Chief Constable of the Royal Ulster Constabulary*, 1986 ECR 1651.

8 *See* Case C-260/89, *Ellinki Radiophonia Tileorassi AE v. Dimotiki Etairia Pliroforissis*, 1991 ECR I-2925, which marked a retreat from Cases 60-61/84, *Cinéthèque v. Fédération Nationale des Cinémas Français*, 1985 ECR 2605.

9 J. Coppel & A. O'Neill, "The European Court of Justice: Taking Rights Seriously?" 29 *CMLR* 669 (1992), 692.

10 *Opinion 2/94 on Accession by the Community to the ECHR*, 1996 ECR I-1759. The Union has legal personality under Article I-7 of the Constitution for Europe, and is expressly directed to accede to the ECHR in Article I-9(2).

issued a joint declaration that "stress[ed] the prime importance they attach to the protection of fundamental rights, as derived in particular from the constitutions of the Member States and the [ECHR]," and stated that "[i]n the exercise of their powers and in pursuance of the aims of the European Communities they respect and will continue to respect these rights."[11] Such a declaration, however, is not binding, and over the next fifteen years the Community's pronouncements on human rights were confined to similar measures of "soft" law, among which were some measures on the rights of linguistic minorities.[12] In 1992, human rights principles were expressly included in the Treaty on European Union. Article 6 of the TEU proudly proclaims that "[t]he Union is founded on the principles of liberty, democracy, respect for human rights and fundamental freedoms, and the rule of law, principles which are common to the Member States."[13] Moreover, Article 6 provided further that "[t]he Union shall respect fundamental rights, as guaranteed by the [ECHR] and as they result from the constitutional traditions common to the Member States, as general principles of Community law."[14] In addition, a beefed-up non-discrimination clause was added to the EC Treaty, allowing the EU to, within the limits of the Treaty provisions, "take appropriate action to combat discrimination based on sex, racial or ethnic origin, religion or belief, disability, age or sexual orientation."[15] Discrimination on language grounds was not contained in this provision, but it was included in the non-discrimination article of the Charter of Fundamental Rights, which, as incorporated in the Constitution for Europe provides in Article II-81(1) that "any discrimination based on any ground such as sex, race, colour, ethnic or social origin, genetic features, *language*, religion or belief, political or any other opinion, membership of a national minority, property, birth, disability, age or sexual orientation shall be prohibited."[16] In addition, Article II-82 of the Constitution calls for "respect" of the Union's "linguistic diversity."

The EC's Badinter Commission, which was set up to offer legal guidance on various issues concerning state succession raised by the break-up of Yugoslavia, stated in one of its opinions that "respect for the fundamental rights of the

---

[11] Declaration of 5 Apr. 1977, [1977] O.J. C103/1.

[12] *See, e.g.*, The Parliament's Resolution on Measures in Favour of Linguistic and Cultural Minorities of 11 Feb. 1983, [1983] O.J. C68/103; the Parliament's Resolution on the Languages and Cultures of the Regional and Ethnic Minorities in the European Community of 30 Oct. 1987, [1987] O.J. C318/160.

[13] TEU Art. 6(1). Similar sentiments are echoed throughout the Constitution for Europe, for example in Article I-2 which states that "[t]he Union is founded on the values of respect for human dignity, freedom, democracy, equality, the rule of law and respect for human rights, including the rights of persons belonging to minorities. These values are common to the Member States in a society in which pluralism, non-discrimination, tolerance, justice, solidarity and equality between women and men prevail."

[14] TEU Art. 6(2); Const. for Eur. Art. I-9(3).

[15] EC Treaty Art. 13.

[16] Emphasis added.

individual and the rights of peoples and minorities" are among "the peremptory norms of international law."[17] When the European Council established the criteria for the admission of new states in central and eastern Europe at its conference in Copenhagen in 1993, "human rights and respect for and protection of minorities" in these countries were proclaimed as a necessary condition for membership.[18] However, some scholars, such as Bruno de Witte, have accused the EU of turning a blind eye towards human rights issues in the existing Member States while focusing on the human rights records of applicant countries. Minority rights, he has said is "an export article and not one for domestic consumption."[19]

B. An Overview of the International Protection of Language Rights

The notion of "language rights" encompasses many distinct types of rights. Linguistic freedom is implicitly linked to many of the civil and political rights of classical liberal theory that are not expressly concerned with language *per se*, such as the freedom of expression, the right to privacy and family life, educational rights, and religious freedom, among others. Such rights are enjoyed by all persons under various international instruments irrespective of whether they are members of a minority language group. In addition, members of minority groups, or the groups as collective units, and even their languages themselves are explicitly given rights under several international human rights conventions. There is a robust debate among academics as to whether minorities as such should be accorded any rights, or whether rights should only attach to individual human beings, as minority groups may at times have interests that are adverse to particular members.[20] In addition, there is widespread disagreement over what should constitute a "minority" entitled to protection. There is no generally accepted definition of this term in international law,[21] and commentators have quarreled over whether there should be a minimum numerical threshold, a requirement of non-dominance, whether there

---

17 Arbitration Commission, EC Conference on Yugoslavia, Opinion No. 1 (1991), para. 1(e), 92 ILR 162.

18 *Bulletin of the European Communities*, 6 (1993).

19 Quoted in Francesco Palermo, "The Use of Minority Languages: Recent Developments in EC Law and Judgments of the ECJ," 8 *Maastricht L.J.* 3 (2001), 299, 301 n. 12.

20 *See, e.g.*, Robert Dunbar, "Minority Language Rights in International Law," 50 *International & Comp. L. Q.* (2001), 90, 94-95; Kristin Henrard, *Devising an Adequate System of Minority Protection: Individual Human Rights, Minority Rights and the Right to Self-Determination* (2000), 233-43.

21 As recently noted by the European Court of Human Rights in *Gorzelik v. Poland*, App. No. 44158/98 (2004), paras. 67-68.

must be a majority identity in the state at issue (which is relevant to states where no single group constitutes a majority), and so forth.[22]

1. Language Rights in Europe

The protection of linguistic minorities has long been a matter of international concern in Europe.[23] The modern era of international linguistic protection begins, however, with the dismantling of the multi-ethnic and polyglot Austro-Hungarian and Ottoman empires after World War I and the numerous treaties and international pledges that were made concerning minority protections in newly created states and states whose borders had shifted.[24] In reviewing one such pledge given by Albania, the Permanent Court of International Justice delivered an opinion that has served as the blueprint for contemporary systems of linguistic protection.[25] In this case, the PCIJ stated that:

> The idea underlying the treaties for the protection of minorities is to secure for certain elements incorporated in a State, that population of which differs from them in race, language or religion, the possibility of living peaceably alongside that population and co-operating amicably with it, while at the same time preserving the characteristics which distinguish them from the majority, and satisfying the ensuing special needs.[26]

Minority protection, the PCIJ stated, thus imposes a dual requirement on states:

> In order to attain this object, two things were regarded as particularly necessary, and have formed the subject of provisions in these treaties. The first is to ensure that nationals belonging to racial, religious or linguistic minorities shall be placed in every respect on a footing of perfect equality with the other nationals of the State. The second is to ensure for the minority elements suitable means for the

---

[22] *See, e.g.*, Henrard at 16-55; Malcolm N. Shaw, "The Definition of Minorities in International Law," in *The Protection of Minorities and Human Rights* (Y. Dinstein & M. Tabory eds., 1992), 1.

[23] In 1516, for example, France and the Swiss Confederation concluded a treaty providing for the protection of the non-German speaking peoples in the latter country. Fernand de Varennes, "To Speak or Not to Speak: The Rights of Persons Belonging to Linguistic Minorities," Working Paper prepared for the UN Sub-Committee on the Rights of Minorities (1997), 2.

[24] For a discussion of the internal language policies of Austria-Hungary before its demise, *see* Louis LeBorgne, "Les Droits Linguistiques à l'École et dans l'Administration de l'Autriche-Hongrie entre 1867 et 1914," in *Language and Law : Proceedings of the First Conference of the International Institute of Comparative Linguistic Law* (Montreal, 1988) (P. Pupier & J. Woehrling eds., 1989), 325.

[25] *Advisory Opinion on Minority Schools in Albania*, Series A/B, No. 64 (1935).

[26] *Id.* at 17.

> preservation of their racial peculiarities, their traditions and their national characteristics.[27]

Minority protection is therefore said to consist of both "negative" obligations of states not to discriminate against minorities or interfere with their pursuit of their identity as well as "positive" obligations to affirmatively undertake measures to allow minority identities to prosper, such as providing education or government services in a minority language.

The ECHR, to which every Member State of the EU is a signatory, does not provide any rights for minorities as such; all of the rights guaranteed under this convention are vested in individuals. The right to non-discrimination on the basis of language is included in Article 14, but that provision only applies to the right not to be discriminated against in "[t]he enjoyment of the rights and freedoms set forth in this Convention." The Court of Human Rights, which is charged with adjudicating claims under the ECHR, ruled in the so-called "Belgian Linguistics case"[28] in 1968 that Article 14 does not grant any implicit language rights, and Article 14 has thus not been a significant source of language rights in Europe, although, as will be discussed below, a ruling in 2001 suggested that the Strasbourg-based tribunal is warming to a broader view of the article.[29] The only language rights that are expressly provided for in the ECHR pertain to language use in criminal proceedings, and are rather limited even in that narrow field. Articles 5 and 6 guarantee that a person charged with a criminal offense has the right to be informed of the charges against him "in a language which he understands" and "to have the free assistance of an interpreter if he cannot understand or speak the language used in court." These provisions do not entitle the speaker of a minority language to the use of his own language, but rather only to one that he "understands" or "speaks," the result of which is that in many cases the state will not be required to do anything special since most speakers of minority languages today are also competent in their country's official or national languages.

The Council of Europe supplemented the ECHR with the European Charter for Regional or Minority Languages ("ECRML") which was opened for signature in 1992 and went into effect in 1998.[30] As the COE's Explanatory Report to the

---

[27] *Id.*

[28] More formally known as the *Case Relating to Certain Aspects of the Laws on the Use of Languages in Education in Belgium* (Merits), Series A (1968).

[29] *Cyprus v. Turkey*, App. No. 25781/94 (2001).

[30] As of December 2004, twelve of the twenty-five Member States of the EU have become parties to the ECRML, having both signed and ratified it. These are Austria, Cyprus, Denmark, Finland, Germany, Hungary, the Netherlands, the Slovak Republic, Slovenia, Spain, Sweden and the United Kingdom. In addition, six states have signed the charter but have not yet ratified it: the Czech Republic, France, Italy, Luxembourg, Malta and Poland.

ECRML states, such an instrument was considered necessary because the ECHR did not provide any measures of positive protection for minority languages and the people using them.[31] The ECRML reflects an awareness, as stated in the preamble, that some of Europe's languages "are in danger of eventual extinction" and that the protection of minority languages "contributes to the maintenance and development of Europe's cultural wealth and traditions." The ECRML is unique among international language rights conventions in that it provides rights neither for groups that speak minority languages, nor individuals who do so, but its focus is rather on the actual languages themselves. The ECRML accordingly provides no system, as the ECHR does, for individuals to file complaints alleging violations; the only enforcement mechanism is the requirement for state parties to submit periodic reports which describe the implementation of their obligations.[32] The Charter applies to "regional or minority languages" (defined as languages that are different from the official language or languages of a state and are "traditionally used within a given territory of a State by nationals of that State who form a group numerically smaller than the rest of the State's population")[33] and "non-territorial languages" (described as those which "although traditionally used within the territory of the State, cannot be identified with a particular area thereof").[34] The ECRML expressly excludes two categories of languages from its scope: "dialects of the official language(s) of the State," and "the languages of migrants."[35]

The ECRML provides two types of obligations. State parties are required to apply the provisions of Part II to all regional or minority languages within their territory, but have discretion to choose which of the more concrete obligations in Part III they will apply (although they must choose at least 35 of them), as well as which languages they will accord such protections. Part II consists of general and relatively vague commitments, such as "the recognition of the regional or minority languages as an expression of cultural wealth," and is full of wording that imparts considerable discretion to the states (*e.g.*, they shall take "appropriate measures" which are to be assessed "according to the situation of each language.")[36] Part III provides an extensive à la carte menu of approximately one hundred protections with respect to language use in various settings such as education (Art. 8), judicial authorities (Art. 9), administrative authorities and public services (Art. 10), the media (Art. 11), cultural activities and facilities (Art. 12), economic and social life (Art. 13), and trans-frontier exchanges (Art. 14). By authorizing state parties to specify which languages will receive which protec-

[31] COE's Explanatory Report on the European Charter for Regional or Minority Languages, para. 3.

[32] ECRML Arts. 15-16.

[33] ECRML Art. 1(a).

[34] ECRML Art. 1(c). The Explanatory Report gives Yiddish and Romani as examples of such languages. (para. 36).

[35] ECRML Art. 1(a).

[36] ECRML Art. 7(1).

tions, the ECRML may be seen as allowing the fox to not only guard the proverbial chicken coop, but to choose which chickens he will guard and which ones he will turn into cordon bleu. The COE's explanatory report indicates, however, that a state's discretion must be exercised "within certain limits" and should be based on the particular factual situations of each language, such as the number of speakers, the degree of linguistic fragmentation, and the state's administrative and financial capacities.[37] Invoking the concept of proportionality, some have suggested that a state party is thus obligated to undertake as many options as can be justified by the number of speakers of a given language and the degree of linguistic homogeneity of the region where it is spoken.[38]

Nonetheless, the states have non-reviewable discretion to decide for themselves what protections to provide to which languages, and as Justice William O. Douglas of the U.S. Supreme Court once said, absolute discretion "is more destructive of freedom than any of man's other inventions."[39] The ECRML explanatory report explicitly provides that states are responsible for "deciding whether the form of expression used in a particular area of their territory or by a particular group of their nationals constitutes a regional or minority language within the meaning of the charter."[40] This means that states are the arbiters of whether a given speech system is a "dialect" outside the purview of the charter. As was stated in Chapter II, the classification of speech systems as "dialects" or separate "languages" is a problematic exercise and people who speak stigmatized dialects may face real discrimination that should be remedied by the adoption of measures that affirm and promote their human dignity as well as the cultural value of their native tongue.

The issue of "dialects" versus "languages" is particularly acute in Italy, where there is considerable variance in speech forms due in large part to the relatively late consolidation of the Italian state.[41] In fact, the language that is commonly called "Italian" is not the native language of the majority of Italian citizens.[42] In Venice and its vicinity, for example, the vernacular language is Veneto, which has been recognized as a separate language by UNESCO and by the Summer Institute of Linguistics in the United States. It has not been accorded such recognition by the EBLUL, however, nor by the Italian government, which did not include Veneto among the languages which it identified when it ratified the ECRML.[43] In the United Kingdom there has been a dispute as to whether

---

37 ECRML Explanatory Report, paras. 22-23.

38 Henrard at 33, 216.

39 *United States v. Wunderlich*, 342 U.S. 98, 107 (1951).

40 ECRML Explanatory Report, para. 40.

41 *Encyclopedia of the Languages of Europe* (Glanville Price ed., 2000), 251-276.

42 *Id.* at 255.

43 The Commission, in response to a complaint about the lack of universal recognition of Veneto, stated that it did not intervene in the affairs of the EBLUL and that "[t]he recognition of regional and minority languages is a matter for the Member States." Answer to Written Question E-679/01, [2001] O.J. C235E/236.

Scots – a form of speech that like modern English is descended from the Germanic and Scandinavian languages of the Dark Ages (and which should not be confused with the Celtic language known as Scottish Gaelic) – should be considered as something more than a dialect of English.[44] Linguists generally consider Scots to be a distinct language, and the EBLUL recognized Scots as such in 1995. Nonetheless, the UK did not identify Scots as a language to be protected under the ECRML, although it did recognize Gaelic, which is spoken by far fewer people than Scots is.[45] An offshoot of Scots spoken by the descendants of Scots-speakers who migrated to Northern Ireland from the seventeenth century onwards, Ulster Scots, also known as Ullans, is now itself the subject of the "language" versus "dialect" debate.[46] It is this sort of potentially endless fragmentation of languages that leads people to argue against providing rights to speakers of "mere" dialects.[47] However, Robert Dunbar has persuasively argued that regard must be had to the particular circumstances of any given linguistic situation, and that there is no theoretical justification to deny protections to speakers of marginalized or disadvantaged dialects, nor is there any reason to exclude dialects from any conceptualization of the positive cultural value of linguistic diversity.[48] This does not mean, however, that the services that must be provided to dialect speakers are without limitation, for as Kristin Henrard has suggested, an application of the general proportionality principle would operate to preclude a state obligation to take measures with regards to a language which deviates only slightly from the language spoken by the rest of the population.[49]

---

44 Hector L. MacQueen, "Laws and Languages: Some Historical Notes from Scotland," presented at a meeting of the Ius Commune Research School in March 2002, 3.

45 Because it has not been officially recognized by the UK, and also because of substantial stigmatization within Scotland itself, there has not been a census of the number of speakers of Scots, and surveys of speakers have encountered confusion regarding distinctions between Scots, English with Scots elements, and dialects of standard English spoken in Scotland. Nonetheless, it is generally believed that a significant portion of Scotland's five million people use the language to some degree or other, compared to the 68,000 speakers of Scottish Gaelic who were counted in the 1991 census. *Encyclopedia of the Languages of Europe* at 416, 421. The Scottish Parliament, while it uses English as the exclusive language of legislation, allows for the use of both Scots and Gaelic in parliamentary proceedings. *See* "The Parliament's Use of Language," The Scottish Parliament Information Centre SPICe Briefing 03/22, 31 Mar. 2003.

46 *See* Article posted on the BBC's website at http://www.bbc.co.uk/northernireland/education/stateapart/agreement/culture/ulsterscots1.shtml.

47 Mala Tabory, "Language Rights as Minority Rights," 40 *Israel Yearbook on Human Rights* (1980), 167, 189.

48 Dunbar at 97.

49 Henrard at 52.

Complementing the ECRML is the Council of Europe's Framework Convention for the Protection of National Minorities, which was opened for signature in 1995 and went into effect in 1998.[50] The Framework Convention, which concerns minorities defined by ethnic, cultural, linguistic, or religious features, addresses similar language issues as the ECRML does, but differs in that it vests rights in persons, who under Article 3 are entitled to exercise their rights both individually and in community with others. Article 3 also guarantees that no one can be saddled with a minority identity against his will by stating that individuals belonging to a national minority have the right to choose whether to be treated as such a member or not.

The three instruments of the Council of Europe that have been discussed – the ECHR, the ECRML, and the Framework Convention – are all binding on their respective parties, and the ECJ has particularly referenced the ECHR as a source of the EU's human rights principles. I will soon consider the relevance of these instruments in the EU context. Before doing so, however, it is appropriate to consider briefly the language rights protections in the United Nations system, as the UN's approach has been quite influential in this field.[51]

2. Language Rights and the United Nations

Article 13 of the UN Charter called for "the realization of human rights and fundamental freedoms for all without distinction as to race, sex, language, or religion." In a provision analogous to Article 14 of the ECHR, the UN's Universal Declaration of Human Rights provided, in Article 2, that "[e]veryone is entitled to all the rights and freedoms set forth in this Declaration, without distinction of any kind, such as ... language." The UN fleshed out several of the general provisions of the Declaration when it prepared the International Covenant on Civil and Political Rights, which contains a similar non-discrimination provision in Article 2, and a more general non-discrimination clause in Article 26, but more significantly includes Article 27, which would go on to be the inspiration for the ECRML and the Framework Convention. Article 27 of the ICCPR provides that "[i]n those States in which ethnic, religious or linguistic minorities exist, persons belonging to such minorities shall not be denied the right, in community with the other members of their group to enjoy

---

[50] All twenty-five Member States, with the exception of France, have signed the Framework Convention. All but five of these signatories have ratified the treaty; Belgium, Greece, Latvia, Luxembourg and the Netherlands have not done so. (Information current as of December 2004).

[51] Mention should also be made of the non-binding pronouncements on language rights of another intergovernmental organization, the Conference for Security and Co-operation in Europe (which became the Organization for Security and Co-operation in Europe in 1994), which authored the 1990 Copenhagen Document of the Conference on the Human Dimension of the CSCE as well as the more recent 1998 Oslo Recommendations regarding the Linguistic Rights of National Minorities.

their own culture, to profess and practise their own religion, or to use their own language." Article 27 is a right that belongs to individuals, but it is one that they have the right to exercise in community with others. The UN's Human Rights Committee has interpreted Article 27 broadly so as to impose positive obligations on state parties.[52]

In 1992 the UN General Assembly adopted a Declaration on the Rights of Persons Belonging to National or Ethnic, Religious and Linguistic Minorities.[53] The document is of significance in that, although it is non-binding in itself, it was adopted by a broad consensus and its contents may thus be viewed as reflective of the *opinio juris* on the international law of minority protection.[54] The Declaration contains a general pronouncement regarding the right of persons belonging to minorities to use their own language[55] and it directs states to "create favorable conditions to enable persons belonging to minorities to ... develop their ... language."[56] However, it also provides that the state need not take such measures "where specific practises are in violation of national law and contrary to international standards,"[57] and contains other highly non-committal language, such as the statement that states "should" (not "shall") take "appropriate measures so that, wherever possible, persons belonging to minorities have adequate opportunities to learn their mother tongue or to have instruction in their mother tongue."[58] Furthermore, several key elements of minority language rights are left out altogether, such as the issue of the use of a minority language with state officials. Such characteristics of the Declaration led Henrard to conclude that "[o]verall, the careful, cautious formulation of minority rights in combination with the weak normative value of the Declaration entails that the effective level of minority protection after the adoption of the Declaration is mainly determined by the goodwill of the states."[59] Another commentator, however, had a more sanguine view of the Declaration, reasoning that:

---

52 Tove Skutnabb-Kangas, "Linguistic Diversity, Human Rights and the 'Free' Market," in *Language: A Right and a Resource* (M. Kontra *et al.* eds., 1999), 187, 212. Article 27 is not applicable everywhere in the EU, however. France, consistent with its view of the unity and indivisibility of the country, lodged a reservation when it ratified the ICCPR stating that "the French Government declares that article 27 is not applicable so far as the Republic is concerned." *See* ICCPR ratification and reservation status at http://www.ohchr.org/english/countries/ratification/4_1.htm.

53 G.A. Resolution 47/135 of 18 Dec. 1992.

54 Henrard at 186.

55 UN Declaration on the Rights of Minorities, Art. 2(1).

56 *Id.*, Art. 4(2).

57 *Id.*

58 *Id.*, Art. 4(3). Three cumulative levels of discretion are thus provided for: a state *should* take *appropriate* measures wherever *possible*. And this is in the context of a non-binding document to begin with.

59 Henrard at 193.

> Instead of a specific set of actions which a state must undertake, [the Declaration] gives a broad sense of direction: states have an obligation to take appropriate steps through legislation and other measures in order to protect the existence of the language of minorities as the essential component of their identity. States must also adopt legislation or take other measures to encourage an environment conducive to the promotion of minority languages. What this requires in concrete terms will depend on the specific conditions of each state, on any threat to the existence of linguistic minorities, and on any condition which stifles the promotion of their language.[60]

C. Minority Language Education

Chapter II included a discussion of the EU's linguistic diversity programs and the limited role that minority languages play in such programs, particularly in the field of education. The EU's exclusion of minority languages is inconsistent with the spirit, if not the letter, of international conventions concerning language rights in education. The right to education in a minority language is arguably the most crucial minority language right, and it is perhaps not hyperbolic to say, as some have, that to fail to teach a language is to kill it.[61] It should come as no surprise that the seminal international pronouncement on minority language rights – the PCIJ's 1935 opinion in the Albanian schools case – was in an educational context, and the centrality of education to the continued viability of a language was recognized by the ECJ in *Groener.*[62] It is noteworthy in that case, however, that the undertaking of positive efforts to promote a minority language was described by Advocate General Darmon as a "right" of states,[63] while human rights law that has evolved since then would suggest that this is not merely a right of states, but an affirmative duty as well. Indeed, whether *Groener* should be understood as implying anything about the legitimacy of state powers with respect to the promotion of minority languages that lack official status is unclear. Bruno de Witte has suggested that the minority status of Irish may not have been nearly as important to the Court as its official status, and that the ECJ may have looked less kindly upon the infringement of the free movement rights of Mrs. Groener if Ireland had sought to merely promote a minority, but unofficial, language.[64]

---

60 De Varennes at 15.

61 *Id.* at 13, quoting Claude Julian.

62 Case C-379/87, 1989 ECR 3967, 3993, para. 20.

63 Opinion of Advocate General Darmon in *Groener*, 1989 ECR 3979, 3982, para. 20.

64 Bruno de Witte, "Surviving in Babel? Language Rights and European Integration," in *The Protection of Minorities and Human Rights* (Y. Dinstein & M. Tabory eds., 1992), 277, 295.

The ECHR does not itself address education, but its Protocol No. 1 does, which provides in Article 2 that:

> No person shall be denied the right to education. In the exercise of any functions which it assumes in relation to education and to teaching, the state shall respect the right of parents to ensure such education and teaching in conformity with their own religious and philosophical convictions.[65]

Article 2 does not mention language, and the Court of Human Rights, in one of its first opinions, interpreted this provision narrowly so as to effectively render it irrelevant to speakers of minority languages. In the Belgian Linguistics case, the Court considered challenges by French-speakers living in Flanders to the exclusive use of Dutch in the educational system in that region.[66] The Court concluded that the protocol entailed only "the right to be educated in the national language or in one of the national languages," and since Dutch is one of Belgium's national languages, there had been no abridgment of the rights protected under that article.[67] The Court also rejected a challenge under Article 14's non-discrimination clause, ruling that the difference in treatment of different language groups was justified by the objective public interest of ensuring "that all schools dependent on the State and existing in a unilingual region conduct their teaching in the language which is essentially that of the region."[68] Bruno de Witte has criticized this reasoning as circular, pointing out that the complainants were challenging the legitimacy of the very decision to divide Belgium into two language zones for educational purposes.[69] This notwithstanding, the upshot of the Belgian Linguistics case was that advocates of minority language educational rights have looked elsewhere, principally to the UN instruments, for legal support.[70]

---

65 All twenty-five Member States are parties to this Protocol, although some have lodged formal reservations.

66 *Case Relating to Certain Aspects of the Laws on the Use of Languages in Education in Belgium* (Merits), Series A (1968).

67 *Id.* at "Interpretation Adopted by the Court," para. 3.

68 *Id.*, para. 7.

69 De Witte, "Surviving in Babel? Language Rights and European Integration" at 286.

70 In a case before the UN's Human Rights Committee involving a challenge to Ontario's practice of funding Roman Catholic schools but not schools of other religious persuasions, Martin Scheinin issued a concurring opinion in which he stated that Article 27 of the ICCPR did not permit states that opt to fund minority language education to make unjustified distinctions among different minority languages. *Waldman v. Canada*, Comm. No. 694/1996, (Scheinin, concurring), para. 5, published in Report of the Human Rights Committee, GA Official Records A/55/40 (1999). Fernand de Varennes has gone even further, arguing that if a state provides support to any private schools, it must also provide such support, under the non-discrimination requirement of Article 26, to minority language private schools. De Varennes at 23.

In 2001, however, the Court of Human Rights departed from its ruling in the Belgian Linguistics case when it issued a decision concerning a number of alleged human rights violations that stemmed from Turkey's occupation of the northern portion of Cyprus.[71] Following the Turkish invasion of the island in 1974, the Turkish Republic of Northern Cyprus ("TRNC") was established there, although it has not generally received international recognition.[72] The TRNC abolished Greek-speaking secondary schools and it was alleged that this was a violation of the educational rights guaranteed under Protocol No. 1. The TRNC permitted Greek-speaking *elementary* schools to continue to operate, however, and allowed Greek-speaking children to continue beyond elementary school in Turkish or English-language secondary schools. Because students could receive an education in some language, the Court stated that "[i]n the strict sense, accordingly, there is no denial of the right to education, which is the primary obligation devolving on a Contracting Party under the first sentence of Article 2 of Protocol No. 1."[73] Citing its Belgian Linguistics judgment, the Court remarked that "this provision does not specify the language in which education must be conducted in order that the right to education be respected."[74]

Nonetheless, the Court decided that "[h]aving assumed responsibility for the provision of Greek-language primary schooling, the failure of the 'TRNC' authorities to make continuing provision for it at the secondary school level must be considered in effect to be a denial of the substance of the right at issue."[75] This ruling appears to be an overturning of Belgian Linguistics, as the Court has indicated that the right to education is no longer confined to the right to an education in a state's choice of its official languages.[76] Similarly, in the United States, the Supreme Court has held that a school system that provides instruction only in English may be in violation of the prohibition against discrimination on the grounds of race or ethnicity contained in the Civil Rights Act of 1964 if the result is that children of a particular racial or ethnic group

71 *Cyprus v. Turkey*, App. No. 25781/94 (2001).

72 In fact, Turkey is the only country that has recognized the TRNC as an independent state. Turkey has not recognized the Republic of Cyprus, but in December 2004 promised to take steps in this direction in exchange for the opening of accession negotiations.

73 *Cyprus v. Turkey*, para. 277.

74 *Id.*

75 *Id.*, para. 278. In the context of child adoption, Judge Costa of this Court has pointed to the difficulties that face children who move to an unfamiliar linguistic environment. *Pini c. Roumanie*, App. Nos. 78028/01 & 78030/01 (2004) (Costa, J., concurring).

76 The precedential impact of this case is uncertain, however, in light of the unique political complications concerning the identity of the "state" in Cyprus. The state held responsible in this case was Turkey, to which the actions of the generally unrecognized TRNC were attributed. Turkish is the sole official language of both Turkey and the TRNC. Turkey Const. Art. 3; TRNC Const. Art. 2(2). Greek and Turkish are both official languages in the Republic of Cyprus. Republic of Cyprus Const. Art. 3(1).

who speak another language are placed at a disadvantage relative to English-speaking students outside that racial or ethnic group.[77]

Educational rights are prominent in many of the more recent language rights instruments. The UN's 1992 Declaration states, in Article 4 that "States should take appropriate measures so that, wherever possible, persons belonging to minorities have adequate opportunities to learn their mother tongue or to have instruction in their mother tongue." Moreover, states' efforts in this field should not be confined only to members of minorities, but rather they should "encourage the knowledge of the history, traditions, language and culture of the minorities existing within their territory." The ECRML's list of optional protections begins with those in the educational field, and contains numerous provisions regarding state support for minority language education at the pre-school, primary, secondary, university and vocational levels.[78] Among these is a provision that, as the Explanatory Report explains, aims to ensure that non-members of minority groups are also allowed access to this component of Europe's cultural heritage.[79] The Framework Convention goes even further, as it requires, in Article 14, that in principle states *shall* provide minority language education: "In areas inhabited by persons belonging to national minorities traditionally or in substantial numbers, if there is sufficient demand, the Parties shall endeavour to ensure, as far as possible and within the framework of their education systems, that persons belonging to those minorities have adequate opportunities for being taught the minority language or for receiving instruction in this language."[80]

The various instruments of the Council of Europe and the UN, coupled with the recent liberal view of educational language rights articulated by the Court of Human Rights in *Cyprus v. Turkey*, indicates that the EU's decision to exclude minority languages from educational programs such as Lingua is inconsistent with what appears to be an emerging norm of international language law, particularly with regards to the obligation of states to take positive steps to promote minority languages. Moreover, to put the issue in the economic terms with which the EU is traditionally more comfortable, speakers of minority languages who are denied education in their native languages are not given the same educational opportunities as those who speak official or national languages (they will experience, for example, cognitive difficulties that their official language-speaking peers will not) and this will impede their future ability to find jobs.[81]

---

77 *Lau v. Nichols*, 414 U.S. 563 (1974). The case concerned Chinese-speaking students in San Francisco.

78 ECRML Art. 8.

79 ECRML Art. 8(g), as explained in ECRML Explanatory Report, para. 86.

80 Framework Convention, Art. 14(2).

81 Henrard at 258-59.

D. Human Rights, Language and the Free Movement of Goods

In Chapter III, I considered the use of language in the context of the free movement of goods in the EU, particularly with regards to language use on product labels. It will be recalled that in its decision in *Piageme I*, the Court of Justice stated that "Article 30 of the EEC Treaty [now Art. 28][82] and Article 14 of Directive 79/112 preclude a national law from requiring the exclusive use of a specific language for the labelling of foodstuffs, without allowing for the possibility of using another language easily understood by purchasers or of ensuring that the purchaser is informed by other measures."[83] As was pointed out in Chapter III, the Court's opinion had misconstrued the Belgian law at issue, as it did not require the exclusive use of a particular language. Moreover, the case did not involve a situation in which the label might have appeared in a minority language that lacked protected status in the country at issue or elsewhere in the Community.[84] Had the Court been faced with a situation in which a Member State outlawed the use of a minority language on a label, would the Court have ruled that such a measure was invalid under Community law?

It is not entirely obvious how such a case would be resolved. If such a restriction were analyzed solely under the economic terms of Article 28 of the EC Treaty, there would not necessarily be the requisite effect on the interstate movement of goods, as the minority language might not be used outside the state which had banned its use.[85] Assuming there was such an effect, however, would the Court rule that it was justifiable for a state, in the interests of forging a national identity and establishing an internally uniform market, to impose such a restriction on a language that lacked official status in the Union, perhaps invoking *Groener* as support for a state's freedom over its internal language arrangements? Such reasoning, even if valid on its own terms, would not be consistent with human rights law, however.

This issue is not simply fodder for academic rumination. Authorities in the Slovak Republic, before the country's accession to the EU in 2004, interpreted that country's labelling law as precluding the use of any language besides

---

82 Const. for Eur. III-153.

83 Case C-369/89, 1991 ECR I-2971, 2985, para. 17.

84 It will be recalled that the languages at issue were Dutch, French and German, all of which have constitutional recognition in Belgium. Belgium Const. of 1994 Art. 4.

85 In discussing the permissibility of state aid to firms that use minority languages, de Witte argues that such measures would not always have a Community dimension, giving as an example the claim that subsidies to the Catalan publishing industry would be unlikely to either improve Spain's market share elsewhere or prejudice the import of books into Spain. De Witte, "Surviving in Babel? Language Rights and European Integration" at 299.

Slovak.[86] While such a law insofar as it applied to Hungarian (which is spoken by a significant portion of the state's citizenry and was the apparent target of the law)[87] would certainly be impermissible in the EU of post-2004, would this Slovakian law be consistent with EU law if it acted to preclude the use of a language that did not have official status somewhere in the Union (the language that is spoken by Slovakia's substantial Roma population, for example)? A 1993 decision by the UN's Human Rights Committee suggests that such an application of a labelling law would violate international human rights norms. In *Ballantyne v. Canada*, the HRC considered a challenge by English-speaking residents of the province of Quebec who had been prohibited from using English on outdoor signs advertising their business under a provincial law that required the exclusive use of French on such signs.[88] The challenged québecois statute was designed to protect the historically subjugated francophone minority of Canada, but was now itself under fire by another minority – English-speakers in Quebec. The HRC ruled that the statute violated the freedom of expression protected by Article 19 of the ICCPR and rejected Canada's argument that it could be justified as a means to protect the rights of French-speakers, pointing out that less restrictive measures could have been implemented that would have furthered this goal, such as requiring signs to be in French, but allowing them to be in other languages as well.[89]

E. Human Rights, Language and the Free Movement of People

As discussed in Chapter IV, the ECJ in the *Mutsch* and *Bickel and Franz* cases considered the language rights of EU citizens who travel outside their home states and get entangled in criminal proceedings in other Member

86 Bart Driessen, "The Slovak State Language Law as a Trade Law Problem," in *Language: A Right and a Resource* (M. Kontra *et al.* eds, 1999), 147, 161-62.

87 In the 1991 census, nearly 11 per cent of Slovakia's 5.3 million inhabitants identified themselves as being of Hungarian ethnicity. Martin Votruba, "Linguistic Minorities in Slovakia," in *Linguistic Minorities in Central & Eastern Europe* (C. Paulston & D. Peckham eds., 1998), 255, 259. The authorities' construction of the labelling law is consistent with the Slovak state's general attitude towards its Hungarian-speaking population. Susan S. Nello & Karen E. Smith, *The European Union and Central and Eastern Europe: The Implications of Enlargement in Stages* (1998), 22.

88 Comm. Nos. 359/1989 & 385/1989 (1993), published in 14 HRLJ No. 5-6 (1993), 171.

89 *Id.*, para. 11.4. The HRC rejected a claim under the minority protection provisions of Article 27 of the ICCPR, however, ruling that the notion of a "minority" referred to the population of a state as a whole, and not simply one sub-part of it, and that anglophone Quebecers accordingly could not claim status as a protected "minority" due to the fact that English-speakers constitute a majority of the population of Canada. *Id.*, para. 11.2.

States.[90] In the latter case the Court expressly acknowledged that the protection of minority groups was a legitimate aim of Member States.[91] While these cases examined language rights from the standpoint of the free movement provisions of the EC Treaty, the ECHR is also relevant to such cases. As indicated above, however, the rights it accords to criminal defendants are rather limited; accused persons are only entitled to be informed of the charges against them and to have an interpreter in a language they "understand" or "speak,"[92] as opposed to the potentially more generous option that may be available under national law to have a trial conducted in the language that the accused chooses, as was the situation in *Mutsch* and *Bickel and Franz*. Indeed, those two cases indicate that the EC Treaty, by requiring that a Member State provide the same choices to foreign EU citizens as it does to its own nationals, may at times be a greater source of linguistic protection than the ECHR is. Advocate General Lenz remarked on this in *Mutsch* and declined to agree with the view that protections under Community law could be no more extensive than those which the ECHR provides.[93] This is a significant point, as it indicates that the ECHR (and perhaps other human rights instruments as well) should be regarded as establishing minimum, and not maximum, standards of protection in the EU.

Also in the context of the free movement of people, the Court examined the issue of a person's right to a name in a minority language in the case concerning the spelling of Mr. Konstantinidis's name by German authorities.[94] The Court's economically driven approach was in stark contrast to that of Advocate General Jacobs, who also looked at the ECHR and other human rights instruments in his analysis. Several human rights documents adopted since this case was decided have strengthened the Advocate General's argument that a right to a name in a preferred language form is a fundamental human right.[95] The ECRML provides, as one of its optional protections, for parties to "undertake to allow the use or adoption of family names in the regional or minority languages, at the request of those concerned."[96] The Framework Convention extends this right to both

---

[90] Case 137/84, 1985 ECR 2681; Case C-274/96, 1998 ECR I-7637.

[91] *Bickel and Franz*, 1998 ECR at 7659, para. 29.

[92] ECHR Arts. 5&6.

[93] Opinion of Advocate General Lenz in *Mutsch*, 1985 ECR 2682, 2690.

[94] Case C-168/91, 1993 ECR I-1191.

[95] Shortly after the ECJ decided *Konstantinidis*, however, the Court of Human Rights rejected a claim by a Finnish man that Finland's refusal to allow him to change his surname, which was of Swedish origin and allegedly difficult for Finns to pronounce and a source of confusion and ridicule, violated the ECHR. The Court of Human Rights agreed that the right to a name was within the scope of the right to family and private life in Article 8 of the Convention, but was of the opinion that Finland had acted within its margin of discretion in declining to allow the name change. *Stjerna v. Finland*, App. No. 18131/91 (1994).

[96] ECRML Art. 10(5).

family names and first names.[97] The Oslo Recommendations Regarding the Linguistic Rights of National Minorities issued by the Organization for Security and Co-operation in Europe in 1998 starts out by recognizing in Recommendation No. 1 that "[p]ersons belonging to national minorities have the right to use their personal names in their own language according to their own traditions and linguistic systems."[98] OSCE's accompanying explanatory notes make clear that state authorities are justified in using the script of their own official languages to record a person's name in a minority language, but points out that they must transliterate such names "in accordance with the language system and tradition of the national minority in question."[99] Disrespect of minority names is part of the complicated socio-linguistic interactions in parts of eastern Europe, and this issue may accordingly come before the ECJ in the aftermath of the accession of new states from this area. In the Slovak Republic, for example, in the late 1990's there were reports that state officials had coerced Hungarian women into adding the Slovak suffix *–ová* to their family names, and the phone company had apparently re-spelled Hungarian names pursuant to Slovak orthographic rules before publishing them in the phone book.[100]

F. Human Rights Principles and the Use of Languages by the EU

I will now come full circle and conclude this book where I began it, with a look at the EU's own internal language regime, but this time through the lens of human rights principles.

1. International Law and the Right to Use a Language with Authorities

The Council of Europe's minority language instruments encourage states to allow the use of minority languages in citizen-government interactions to the extent that it is feasible to do so.[101] The ECRML contains

---

97 Framework Convention Art. 10(2).

98 OSCE Ref. No. MC.DOC/1/98.

99 OSCE Explanatory Note to the Oslo Recommendations Regarding the Linguistic Rights of National Minorities at 2.

100 Miklós Kontra, "Don't Speak Hungarian in Public!" in *Language: A Right and a Resource* (M. Kontra *et al.* eds., 1999), 81, 82-83.

101 However, two major human rights tribunals have expressly stated that states are free to choose which languages they will accord official status: the European Court of Human Rights in *Podkolzina v. Latvia*, App. No. 46726/99 (2002), para. 34 and the UN's Human Rights Committee in *Ballantyne v. Canada*, Comm. Nos. 359/1989 & 385/1989 (1993), para. 11.4, published in 14 HRLJ No. 5-6 (1993), 171.

numerous provisions in this regard in Article 10, providing states with a range of options such as undertaking to ensure that the administrative authorities (at the national, regional, or local levels, as well as bodies that provide public services such as postal services, hospitals and transportation) use the regional or minority languages, allowing speakers of such languages to submit materials in these languages (with or without a right of reply in them), and producing various documents in minority language versions. The Explanatory Report explains that not only are such provisions important to the dignity rights of minority-language speakers, but they are crucial to the health of minority languages themselves:

> [A]llowing the use of regional or minority languages in relations with [public] authorities is fundamental to the status of these languages and their development and also from a subjective standpoint. Clearly, if a language were to be completely barred from relations with the authorities, it would in fact be negated as such, for language is a means of public communication and cannot be reduced to the sphere of private relations alone. Furthermore, if a language is not given access to the political, legal or administrative sphere, it will gradually lose all its terminological potential in that field and become a "handicapped" language, incapable of expressing every aspect of community life.[102]

The ECRML does not contemplate that states should provide minority language services where doing so is economically or administratively impracticable. Article 10, like the charter in general, is full of wording indicating that language services should be provided when the "number of residents who are users of regional or minority languages justifies the measures" and that such measures should be taken "as far as this is reasonably possible." The Explanatory Report amplifies these caveats:

> [The ECRML] does seek to take account of the fact that some of the measures provided for have significant implications in terms of finance, staffing or training. An acceptance of a particular provision with respect to a given language necessarily entails a commitment to provide the resources and make the administrative arrangements required to render it effective. Nevertheless, it is recognised that there may be some circumstances in which total and unqualified application of the provision in question is not, or not yet, realistic.[103]

The Framework Convention contains a similar provision in Article 10(2), which also implicitly provides allowance for financial and administrative constraints:

---

[102] ECRML Explanatory Report, para. 101.

[103] *Id.*, para. 104.

> In areas inhabited by persons belonging to national minorities traditionally or in substantial numbers, if those persons so request and where such a request corresponds to a real need, the Parties shall endeavour to ensure, as far as possible, the conditions which would make it possible to use the minority language in relations between those persons and the administrative authorities.[104]

A case can also be made under the non-discrimination provisions of various human rights documents (such as Article 14 of the ECHR or Article 26 of the ICCPR) that a state may not discriminate against different language groups by providing services in some languages but not in others unless there is an objective justification for doing so. Such justification may exist where a minority language is spoken by relatively few people or where the state's fisc cannot reasonably support linguistic largesse. As de Varennes has argued:

> [T]here is increasing support for the view that the operation of non-discrimination must take into account the need to balance a state's legitimate interests and goals in prescribing certain preferences with the ensuing disadvantage, denial or burden this may effect on individuals. Everything comes down to whether or not in the end the measure or conduct is "reasonable," "arbitrary" or "fair." Under this analysis, it seems clear that the prohibition of discrimination on the ground of language does not mean a state cannot favour one language over others. A state could never be obligated to conduct all of its activities in every language which is spoken by the inhabitants in its territory. Non-discrimination does not prohibit every distinction involving a language, only those that are "unreasonable" when one considers all relevant factors: those that relate to the state's interests and goals, and those that relate to the individual's interests, rights and how s/he is affected.[105]

Such principles should be extended to the EU itself, as it has repeatedly affirmed that it is based on human rights ideals, and these principles should inform the EU's decisions regarding which languages it conducts business in and which ones it will use in interacting with the public. The EU should allow speakers of a language to use their language in the EU (or a particular institution or body of it) if doing so is reasonable in light of the financial and administrative costs entailed. The Council appears to have undertaken a cost-benefit analysis in crafting its language policy for the Office for Harmonisation in the Internal Market ("OHIM") that was at issue in the *Kik* case discussed in Chapter I, but the Court of First Instance and the European Court of Justice reviewed this deci-

[104] Dunbar has observed that the phrase "where such a request corresponds to a real need" may arguably serve to dis-entitle speakers of a minority language who can also speak the state's official language. Dunbar at 114.

[105] De Varennes at 9-10.

sion in economic terms that did not allow Ms. Kik's human rights (as opposed to her purely economic rights) to be factored into the equation, at least not overtly. It may be that had it done so, the result would have been the same, but that does not make it appropriate for the Court to have failed to explicitly consider the principles of human rights that the EU is supposedly guided by.

2. The Use of Minority Languages

The same balancing approach should apply to the minority languages spoken in the Member States as well, and the EU should include Member State minority languages in Regulation No. 1 when doing so can be cost-justified by the number of speakers concerned.[106] Because changes to the linguistic systems of EU institutions require unanimous approval by the Council, a minority language could obtain status within the EU only with the support of the relevant Member State (as well as all the others).[107] The EU should encourage (or pressure even) Member States to allow the use of minority languages when it is financially reasonable to do so, as a Member State which unreasonably declines to support the inclusion of a minority language in Regulation No. 1 may be violating norms of minority language protection.

It might be contended that because the EU is a union of Member States, it is objectively appropriate for the Union's language policy to mirror that of the Member States comprising it. Such an argument would not give sufficient credit to the fact that the Union has become something more than a mere union of states, however, and that it has also become, as EU rhetoric repeatedly proclaims, and as the advent of EU citizenship suggests, a democratic union of the *people* of the Member States.[108] Indeed, the democratic nature of the Union is the

[106] In 2002 a group of academic institutions in Catalunya known as Europa Diversa submitted several proposed language rules for the EU to the Convention on the Future of the European Union, including the following: "Community documents and other actions (such as advertising campaigns) informing European citizens, or affecting their everyday lives, will be available in at least all European languages in which citizens have the legal right to correspond with their regional and/or national authorities, and preferably all European languages which have speakers literate in them. Documents presented in any of these languages by European citizens should be admissible and should receive a reply in the same language. Europa Diversa Group, "Linguistic Proposals for the Future of Europe," submission to the Convention on the Future of the European Union (2002). Available on-line at the website of the European Bureau of Lesser Used Languages, www.eblul.org.

[107] EC Treaty Art. 290; Const. for Eur. Art. III-433.

[108] The tripartite relationship among the EU, the Member States, and the citizens of Member States (who are also now citizens of the EU) has received much attention from political philosophers, but a full discussion of the various theories regarding the nature of this relationship is beyond the scope of this paper. For a review of several views on the topic, *see* Pavlos Eleftheriadis, "The European Constitution and Cosmopolitan Ideals," 7 *Columbia J. of Eur. L.* 21 (2001). With respect to historically marginalized

rationale typically invoked for having each Member State's national or official language (ignoring the full or partial exceptions of Cyprus, Ireland, Luxembourg and Malta) used as a Regulation language. One typical explanation for the EU's multilingual regime is the following:

> [It is] vital to democracy that Community legislation should be available to Europe's citizens in their own languages, as a guarantee of equality before the law. Ignorance of the law is no defence, so the law cannot be imposed on anyone in an incomprehensible foreign language. Danish farmers, German industrialists, British barristers, French wine growers, Swedish civil servants and everybody else must always have access to the European legislation which affects them. And they must each have access to it in their own language.[109]

It is difficult to justify on democratic grounds (although perhaps it could be on economic grounds) why Danish farmers and German industrialists have the right to read materials in their own language, but Breton farmers or Corsican-speaking wine growers do not. While it may be true that most speakers of minority languages also speak the official language of their state, all of them do not, and certainly not with the level of expertise necessary to process legislative requirements (to the extent that "normal people" read such things anyway). Moreover, if the citizens of the EU only have the right to the use of a language when they do not understand one of the others that is used, it should not be necessary to allow the use of all the Slavic languages that are currently in use, as speakers of these languages, in the words of a Eurobarometer study, can "converse to some extent with other Slavic speaking people with little difficulty."[110] There would likewise be no justification for even the limited rights of the reportedly entirely bilingual Irish-speaking population. Similarly, given the overwhelming penetration of English in Sweden (a Eurobarometer survey indicated over 88 per cent of the country claims to have good knowledge of it),[111] there would be little reason to allow the Swedish civil servants referenced above access to Swedish texts of Community legislation. The right to have materials in one's language is not solely based on the right to have materials in a form one can understand;[112] the right to equal treatment demands that people not be

---

sub-national groups such as the Catalans, some have seen the EU as providing the framework for a larger pan-European identity that is not based on state citizenship. A man in Girona, for example, may consider himself to be a Catalan, a European and a national of Spain – in that order. *See, e.g.*, David D. Laitin, "The Cultural Identities of a European State" 25 *Politics and Society* 3 (1997), 277.

[109] Kristina Cunningham, "Translating for a Larger Union – Can We Cope with More than 11 Languages?" *Terminologie et Traduction* 2 (2001), 22, 24.

[110] Candidate Countries Eurobarometer 2001 (March 2003), 35.

[111] Eurobarometer Report 54, "Europeans and Languages" (Executive Summary) (2001), 2.

[112] Moreover, one cannot be confident of the meaning of Community legislation simply by looking at the version in one's own language, for as the ECJ has repeatedly said in cases where the meanings of diffe-

treated differently unless there is a legitimate non-discriminatory reason for doing so.

It might alternatively be suggested that minority languages should be excluded from Regulation No. 1 in an effort to limit the overall number of languages used in EU organs and thereby promote operational efficiency. While the desire to improve efficiency is certainly legitimate, it is not acceptable to achieve that efficiency by simply weeding out languages with minority status any more than it would be acceptable for an employer to attain a necessary reduction in a workforce by eliminating all employees of a particular ethnicity or religion. Any linguistic limitation should be based on objective criteria such as the number of speakers of a language in the EU. Moreover, arguments about the inefficiency of linguistic proliferation cannot reasonably be made by those who advocated the addition of ten new languages upon the 2004 accessions. While one may plausibly argue that an organization with a small number of languages, say two to four, should not, in the interests of efficiency, add any more, it would seem rather tenuous to maintain that an organization with twenty languages could not add another couple without incurring an unacceptable decline in efficiency.

Moreover, a cost-based argument can be raised about the use of many of the Regulation languages themselves. Multilingualism is costly, but the cost is a function of the number of speakers of a language and not of the official status of that language in a given Member State. Indeed, one recent study has revealed that when the cost of translating materials into the various Regulation languages is divided by the respective numbers of speakers of these languages who thereby obtain access to those materials, these languages had widely varying price tags. Starting from a base system in which the three most commonly known EU languages of English, French and German are used, Fidrmuc and Ginsburgh calculated the marginal cost of translating EU materials into other languages.[113] Some of these languages have rather low marginal costs; Italian, Polish, Spanish and Hungarian each cost less than ten euros per person. Others seem moderately pricey; Portuguese, Greek, Czech, Slovak and Dutch each have a marginal cost between ten and twenty euros, while Lithuanian, Finnish, Latvian and Swedish are in the range of twenty to forty euros. Other languages appear to be rather expensive; Estonian and Danish each have a marginal cost around 75 euros, the figure for Slovene is 121 euros, and for Maltese it is nearly 1,000 euros. This data drives home a question that few really want to ask, let alone answer: Exactly how much money should the EU spend to ensure the ability of its citizens to fully participate in the Union in their native language?

---

rent languages diverge, an interpretation of the Community's legislation involves looking at all language versions. *See* cases referenced in Chapter I.

[113] Jan Fidrmuc & Victor Ginsburgh, "Languages in the European Union: The Quest for Equality and its Cost" (2004), 16.

Surely the amount is not unlimited, as indeed the treasury is not. The real dispute is not whether there is a maximum price the EU is prepared to pay to ensure full multilingual participation, but rather what that price is. With respect to minority languages, any claim about the cost of their inclusion should be assessed in comparison with the cost of including the various Regulation languages, and it would presumably therefore not be reasonable for a minority language to be disallowed on financial grounds if it had more speakers than one of the Regulation languages.

Absent a wholesale reform that seriously reduces the linguistic complexity of the EU's institutions, it accordingly seems appropriate to allow any language to be used in the EU as long as it has as many speakers as the least commonly spoken Regulation language (bearing in mind the difficulties in determining what it means for someone to "speak" a language). Catalan, with its eight to ten million speakers, clearly meets this threshold.[114] It is hard to defend the exclusion of Welsh and Basque, each of which is spoken by over half a million people, while simultaneously recognizing Maltese, which is spoken by less than 400,000.[115] Allowing the use of languages that are official languages of Member States, regardless of how many speakers they have, along with other languages that are spoken by significant numbers of people, would be seen as a measure that properly reflects the dual basis of the EU's legitimacy.[116]

3. The Case for Russian

In the aftermath of the 2004 enlargement, the EU should consider allowing the use of Russian, which is spoken by approximately 1.5 million ethnic Russians in the eastern European countries that have joined the EU, primarily in the Baltic states, and particularly in Latvia where it is the first language of between thirty to forty per cent of the population. The number of Russian speakers in the EU is greater than the number who speak Estonian (around 1 million), is about even with the number who speak Latvian (1.4 million), and somewhat less than the number who speak a language outside of the Baltics – Slovene (2 million).[117] A proposal to allow the use of Russian in the institutions

[114] Catalan could also gain admission to the EU's language club if the Principality of Andorra, where it is the official language, were to ever join. While the vast majority of Catalan-speakers live in Spain, there are also Catalan-speaking communities in France and Sardinia. Catalan has official status, along with Castilian Spanish, in Catalunya, where a complex language law is in effect. *See* Spain Const. Art. 3, and generally, Generalitat de Catalunya Institut d'Esutdis Autonòmics, *Estudios Jurídicos Sobre la Ley de Política Lingüística* (1999).

[115] *Encyclopedia of the Languages of Europe* at 28, 319, 488.

[116] The very first article of the Constitution for Europe states that the European Union is established as a reflection of the will of both "the citizens and States of Europe."

[117] *Encyclopedia of the Languages of Europe* at 152, 297, 446. In addition, the number of Russian speakers exceeds the one million or so who claim some ability to speak Irish. *Id.* at 250.

and bodies of the EU would undoubtedly meet stiff opposition from the new Member States whose current leaders have no particular fondness for the language of their former Soviet oppressors.[118] However, as was discussed in Chapter IV, this lack of fondness has often manifested itself in the form of human rights violations against the region's Russian-speaking population. Allowing the use of Russian in the EU would go some distance towards compensating for this mistreatment and evidence a solid commitment to human rights principles in the new Union. Moreover, a Union that wishes to represent all of its citizens cannot do so if it fails to respect the russophilic character of such a large number of them.[119] The break-up of the Soviet Union has deprived Russian-speaking Baltic residents of a political system that embraces its linguistic and cultural identity. Having found themselves ostracized and even stateless in the post-Soviet era, the new Russian-speaking citizens of the Union should not be made to feel that their new citizenship is of a second-class nature.[120]

Providing for the use of Russian would also allow for closer and more effective communication with the Russian Federation, which the EU regards as a crucial component of a post-enlargement Union that is now squarely in the backyard of the Russian state.[121] Indeed, harmonious relations with Russia are essential to the EU's stated goal "to promote peace, security, and progress in Europe and in the world."[122] The disagreements between Russia and the West

---

[118] Nello & Smith at 56.

[119] As was discussed in Chapter IV, much of the Russian-speaking population of Latvia has been denied Latvian citizenship, and since EU citizenship derives from Member State citizenship (TEU Art. 17(1)), such persons are also denied EU citizenship as well.

[120] Similar considerations apply to the long-marginalized Roma, who form the EU's largest minority group. There is no singular "Romani" language, however, and throughout Europe this diasporic population speaks some sixty different dialects/languages. This linguistic diversity, combined with the absence of a universally accepted literary standard, complicates any suggestion that the EU should use a form of this language. Nonetheless, the Vlax dialects, which claim approximately 2.5 million speakers, have become the basis of an international standard that has been adopted by some leading Roma organizations. The accession of Romania, where these dialects are centered, would strengthen the case for the addition of a Vlax-based version of Romani as a Regulation language. *See Encyclopedia of the Languages of Europe* at 378-382; Answer to Written Question E-3062/01, [2002] O.J. 115E/221; "The Situation of Roma in an Enlarged European Union," Report Prepared for the EC Directorate-General for Employment and Social Affairs by Focus Consultancy Ltd., the European Roma Rights Center, and the European Roma Information Office (Nov. 2004), available on-line at http://europa.eu.int/comm/employment_social/fundamental_rights/pdf/studies/roma04_en.pdf.

[121] Russia and the EU have shared a border since the accession of Finland in 1995. Just before the 2004 enlargement, the EU and Russia noted in a joint statement that "[t]he interdependence of the EU and Russia, stemming from our proximity and increasing political, economic and cultural ties, will reach new levels with the enlargement of the EU." Joint Statement of 27 Apr. 2004 on EU Enlargement and EU-Russia Relations (Ref IP/04/549).

[122] TEU pmbl. *See also* TEU Art. 2.

(that is, the EU and the United States) regarding the large-scale ethnic conflict in the former Yugoslavia contributed greatly to Europe's inability to adequately respond to the human catastrophe that unfolded there.[123] Furthermore, the EU has recognized, in the preamble to the Treaty of European Union, "the historic importance of the ending of the division of the European continent,"[124] and valid concerns have been expressed that a new European divide is in the making, with a behemoth and wealthy EU on one side, and poor, struggling, mafia-infested countries such as Russia, Ukraine, Belarus and Moldova on the other.[125]

Russia will also take on increased importance as an EU trading partner now that the new eastern Member States have been admitted. In particular, Russia will be a major supplier of energy.[126] Russia will be a significant player in various regional projects, such as efforts to develop the economic resources of the Baltic Sea, which the EU's Economic and Social Committee has described in a recent report as "an area of particular importance to the EU," and where, as the report stated, English and Russian are considered the two most important languages.[127] Furthermore, cooperation in Baltic issues, as well as in other matters, will also necessitate a strong working relationship with the Russian enclave of Kalingrad, which following the admission of Lithuania and Poland is now completely surrounded by the EU. The one million inhabitants of this oblast are much more intimately connected to the immediately surrounding region than to the Russian mainland, and the serious problems facing Kalingrad (it is notorious for smuggling, and sex tourism has fueled a serious AIDS epidemic) should be of concern to its neighbors.[128]

Many are of the opinion that the EU's leaders have given insufficient thought to their relationship with Moscow and believe that a failure to decide "what is to

---

[123] Jean Raux, "Towards a Pan-Euro-Mediterranean Association of Proximity," in *The EU's Enlargement and Mediterranean Strategies: A Comparative Analysis* (M. Maresceau & E. Lannon eds., 2001), 42, 56-60. As events of the past few years have demonstrated, Russia, the EU, the United States and other parts of the world face real threats from terrorist organizations that operate internationally, and multinational cooperation by intelligence and law enforcement agencies is necessary to address this problem adequately.

[124] The preamble of the European Constitution proclaims that "the peoples of Europe are determined to transcend their former divisions and, united ever more closely, to forge a common destiny."

[125] In 2002 the President of the European Council, in a statement that specifically referred to its relations with these four eastern countries, declared that it "remains determined to avoid new dividing lines in Europe and to promote stability and prosperity within and beyond the new borders of the Union." Copenhagen European Council Presidency Conclusions of 14 Dec. 2002 (DOC/02/15).

[126] Avery & Cameron at 141-47.

[127] Report of the Economic and Social Committee, "Northern Dimension: Action plan for the Northern Dimension in the external and cross-border policies of the European Union 2000-2003," paras. 1.1.7, 3.3.1, [2001] O.J. C139/42.

[128] Christopher Dickey & Michael Meyer, "Is Europe Broken?" *Newsweek*, 12 Aug. 2002, 14, 17.

be done" with Russia may, as another commentator has put it, ultimately prove to be the Achilles heel of the EU's eastern enlargement.[129] There is a serious risk that Russia may become alienated by a European club that excludes it from membership, and if isolated and left to fall into economic decay and political paralysis could pose grave danger to Europe and the rest of the world. As one commentator has stated, without stability in Moscow,

> [Russia and eastern Europe] would be not only a fertile breeding ground for organized crime, neighborhood genocide, and stampedes of terrified populations, but also a highly counterproductive environment for West European integration. It cannot be healthy to have the German government back in Berlin, with Moscow enfeebled and Eastern Europe weak. It would be hard for Germany to resist being drawn into that revisionist vortex. Germany unbalanced in Middle Europe would alarm France and Britain and undermine the foundations of the European Union. At the same time, a weak Russia, with only a feeble hold on its huge Siberian empire, would be a menace to stability in Asia as well as in Europe.[130]

Setting such apocalyptic scenarios aside, it is likely that a Russia that feels frozen out of Europe might decide to concentrate its energies in the Asia-Pacific region with which it also shares geographic and cultural connections.[131]

Of course, adding Russian to its roster of languages in Regulation No. 1 would bring to the fore the discomforting question of whether Russia itself might eventually join the EU. Although the Constitution for Europe promises that the EU is open to "all European States,"[132] the accession of Russia, assuming it could someday meet the economic and political criteria for membership, would overwhelm and utterly transform the EU, perhaps beyond recognition, as the magnitude of its population would cause the center of EU political and cultural gravity to shift far to the east. Few people speak realistically about the possibility of Russian accession. The accession of Ukraine, however, is under serious discussion,[133] and the eastern portions of this country are predominantly Russian-speaking.[134]

---

[129] Marc Maresceau, "The EU Pre-Accession Strategies: A Political and Legal Analysis," in *The EU's Enlargement and Mediterranean Strategies: A Comparative Analysis* (M. Maresceau & E. Lannon eds., 2001), 3, 24.

[130] David P. Calleo, *Rethinking Europe's Future* (2001), 345.

[131] Living in a country that stretches across two continents, Russians have long struggled with the question of whether their identity is European, Asiatic, a blend of the two, or something unique altogether. *See* James H. Billington, *Russia in Search of Itself* (2004), 73.

[132] Const. for Eur. Art. I-1(2).

[133] Ukraninan President Kuchna stated in 2002 that he would like his country to be in a position to formally submit an application by 2011, to which the EU has replied with a noncommittal response "acknowledging Ukraine's European aspirations and welcoming the country's European choice." Commission Staff Working Paper of 12 May 2004: European Neighbourhood Policy Country Report for Ukraine, SEC(2004) 566, COMM(2004) 373, p. 5.

Moreover, Russian is a language that is known by large numbers of people in the new EU Member States. It is the most widely spoken foreign language in Estonia, Latvia, Lithuania, Poland, Slovakia (if its close linguistic cousin Czech is not counted).[135] In all of these countries it is known by at least one fifth of the people; in Lithuania it is known by more than eighty per cent. It is conceivable that Russian could enjoy currency as a lingua franca among citizens of eastern Member States. It is rather unlikely, on the other hand, that significant numbers of non-native speakers will ever learn Estonian, Latvian, Lithuanian, Polish, Slovak, or any of the other relatively obscure languages that entered the EU in 2004. The use of Russian would also help to offset the potential "de-Europazination" of a European Union that has increasingly relied on a language that is deeply, perhaps even primarily, associated with the United States.[136]

G. Conclusion

The EU's approach to language use has up to now been largely an economic affair. The Court of Justice has analyzed language requirements imposed by Member States, or the EU itself, in terms of their impact on the economic freedoms guaranteed by the EC Treaty – the free movement of goods and the free movement of people engaged in economic activity. The EU's political actors have similarly been chiefly motivated by economic considerations when implementing language programs, and the Council's creation of the quintilingual policy at OHIM was fueled by financial pressures. The transformation of

[134] In November 2004 the russophonic regions threatened to secede after widespread protests from both within Ukraine and abroad (including from the EU) challenged the legitimacy of the election of a Russian-backed candidate to the country's presidency. The EU stated that it did "not believe these results reflect the will of the Ukrainian people" and actively engaged in diplomatic efforts aimed at finding a peaceful resolution of the situation, which, it maintained, required "the unity of Ukraine." Declarations by the Presidency of the European Union of 25 Nov. 2004 and 29 Nov. 2004.

[135] This information comes from a Eurobarometer report which surveyed language knowledge in thirteen candidate countries in 2001 (the ten new Member States along with Bulgaria, Romania and Turkey). Candidate Countries Eurobarometer 2001 (March 2002), 36. Taken as a whole, in these countries Russian is known by 14 per cent of the population, compared to 18 per cent of the population who know English, 10 per cent who know German and just 4 per cent who know French. The inclusion of Turkey suppresses the figure for Russian (and English), as it is not well known there.

[136] Of course, the relationship between the EU and the US is an extremely complicated matter. The EU competes with US-dominated organizations such as the North Atlantic Treaty Organization and the Organization for Security and Co-Operation in Europe as a basis for pan-European identity. A number of Member States (and/or the citizens thereof) have been deeply troubled by the unilateralist tendencies of the administration of George W. Bush, but American popular culture is widely enjoyed throughout Europe and the EU and US continue to be significant trading partners.

the EC into the EU, with its mandate now extending beyond bread-and-butter issues, requires that the EU contemplate the human rights ramifications of actions that affect language use. The EU's founding document, the Treaty on European Union, expressly endorses an ideology of human rights, and this commitment has been reiterated and intensified in the Charter of Fundamental Rights which forms an integral part of the newly propagated Constitution for Europe. In the linguistic arena, however, such pronouncements have seemed rather hollow, and though the EU may have stayed within the letter of linguistic human rights law, in so doing it has failed to embrace its true spirit, or as it would have been said in Europe's original international language: *Qui hæret in litera hæret in cortice.*[137] The recent expansion of the EU into eastern Europe, whose linguistically rich landscape has too-often in recent history been the scene of gross human rights violations, has provided the EU with a wonderful opportunity to re-conceptualize language as being something more than a medium through which commerce is conducted and to recognize that it is at the core of what it means to be a human being. We will have to wait and see whether it chooses to do so.

[137] Black's Law Dictionary translates this Latin expression as "He who considers merely the letter of an instrument goes but skin deep into its meaning." Black's Law Dictionary (6th ed. 1990), 1249.

Bibliography

Books and Articles

ABRAMS, DANIEL M. & STROGATZ, STEVEN H.
"Modelling the Dynamics of Language Death," *Nature*, 21 Aug. 2003, 900.

AHLQVIST, ANDERS
"Language Conflict and Language Planning in Ireland," in *Language Conflict and Language Planning* (E. Jahr ed., 1993), 7.

AVERY, GRAHAM & CAMERON, FRASER
The Enlargement of the European Union (1999).

BEETH, HELEN TITCHEN & FRASER, BILL
"The Hidden Life of Translators," *Terminologie et Traduction* 2 (1999), 76.

BERTELOOT, PASCALE
"Babylone à Luxembourg: Jurilinguistique à la Cour de Justice," *Vortrag vor dem Europa-Institut der Universität des Saarlandes* Nr. 136 (1988).

BILLINGTON, JAMES H.
Russia in Search of Itself (2004).

BUNNEN, LOUIS, VAN
"L'emploi des languges dans l'étiquetage et le droit communautaire," *Journal des Tribunaux 1988*, 41.

BURMEISTER, FRANK & MIERSCH, GERALD
"Gemeinschaftsrechtliche Sprachregelung und deutsches Lebensmittelrecht," 1995 *EuZW* No. 9, 273.

CAHILL, THOMAS
Sailing the Wine-Dark Sea: Why the Greeks Matter (2003).

CALLEO, DAVID P.
Rethinking Europe's Future (2001).

CALSTER, GEERT, VAN
"The EU's Tower of Babel – The Interpretation by the European Court of Justice of Equally Authentic Texts Drafted in more than one Official Language," 17 *Yearbook of European Law* (1997), 363.

CAÑAS, GABRIELA
"España Pedirá que el Catalán Sea Oficial en la UE si se Admite el Gaélico," *El Pais*, 27 July 2004.

CHRISTOPHORY, JUL
"Lëtzebuergesch and the Overall Language Situation in Luxembourg," *Terminologie et Traduction* 3 (1998), 116.

CONANT, EVE
"Saying *Nyet* to Russian," *Newsweek*, 1 July 2002, 30-31.

COPPEL, J. & O'NEILL, A.
"The European Court of Justice: Taking Rights Seriously?" 29 *CMLR* 669 (1992), 692.

CRAIG, PAUL & DE BÚRCA, GRÁINNE

EU Law: Text, Cases and Materials (2d ed. 1998).

CUNNINGHAM, KRISTINA

"Translating for a Larger Union – Can We Cope with More than 11 Languages?" *Terminologie et Traduction* 2 (2001), 22.

CURTIN, DEIRDRE & VAN OOIK, RONALD

"The Sting is Always in the Tail: The Personal Scope of Application of the EU Charter of Fundamental Rights," 8 *Maastricht J. of European and Comparative Law* 1 (2001), 102.

CURTIN, DEIRDRE & MEIJERS, HERMAN

"Access to European Union Information: An Element of Citizenship and a Neglected Constitutional Right," in *The European Union and Human Rights* (N. Neuwahl & A. Rosas eds., 1995), 77.

DAM, CAROLINE, TEN

"La Législation Linguistique Française dans le Cadre de la Libre Circulation en Europe," Doctoral Dissertation, Europa-Institut Universiteit Utrecht, 1996.

DICKEY, CHRISTOPHER & MEYER, MICHAEL

"Is Europe Broken?" *Newsweek*, 12 Aug. 2002, 14.

DRIESSEN, BART

"The Slovak State Language Law as a Trade Law Problem," in *Language: A Right and a Resource* (M. Kontra *et al.* eds, 1999), 147.

DUNBAR, ROBERT

"Minority Language Rights in International Law," 50 *International & Comp. L. Q.* 90 (2001).

ELEFTHERIADIS, PAVLOS

"The European Constitution and Cosmopolitan Ideals," 7 *Columbia J. of Eur. L.* 21 (2001).

ENCYCLOPEDIA

Encyclopedia of the Languages of Europe (Glanville Price ed., 2000).

ENGBERG, JAN

"Statutory Texts as Instances of Language(s): Consequences and Limitations on Interpretation," 29 *Brooklyn J. of Int'l Law* 3 (2004), 1135.

EUROBAROMETER REPORT 54

"Europeans and Languages" (Executive Summary) (2001).

EUROBAROMETER REPORT

Candidate Countries Eurobarometer 2001 (March 2003).

FIDRMUC, JAN & GINSBURGH, VICTOR

"Languages in the European Union: The Quest for Equality and its Cost" (2004).

FLEISCH, COLETTE

"Le Service de Traduction de la Commission Face au Défi du

Multilinguisme dans l'Union Européenne Élargie," *Terminologie et Traduction* 1 (1999), 92.

FORREST, ALAN
"The Challenge of Languages in Europe," *Terminologie et Traduction* 3 (1998), 101.

FRANGI, MARC
"Le Consommateur Français Entre Loi Toubon et Droit Communautaire," *Revue Internationale de Droit Économique* 135 (2003).

FROMKIN, VICTORIA & RODMAN, ROBERT
An Introduction to Language (3d ed. 1983).

GARRIGA, JOSEP
"Convergència Rechazará la Constitución Europea si el Catalán no es Oficial en la UE," *El Pais*, 15 Sept. 2004.

GENERALITAT DE CATALUNYA INSTITUT D'ESUTDIS AUTONÒMICS
Estudios Jurídicos Sobre la Ley de Política Lingüística (1999).

GINSBURGH, VICTOR & WEBER, SHLOMO
"Language Disenfranchisement in the European Union," Manuscript (2003).

GRILLO, R.D.
Dominant Languages: Language and Hierarchy in Britain and France (1989).

GRIN, FRANÇOIS
"Market Forces, Language Spread and Linguistic Diversity," in *Language: A Right and a Resource* (M. Kontra *et al.* eds, 1999), 169, 180.

GRIMM, DIETER
"Does Europe Need a Constitution?" 1 *European. L. J.* 282 (1995).

HABERMAS, JÜRGEN
"Why Europe Needs a Constitution," *New Left Review* (2001), 5.

HABERMAS, JÜRGEN
"Remarks on Dieter Grimm's 'Does Europe Need a Constitution?'" 1 *European L. J.* 303 (1995).

HALE, JOHN
"The Renaissance Idea of Europe," in *European Identity and the Search for Legitimacy* (Soledad García ed., 1993), 55.

HENRARD, KRISTIN
Devising an Adequate System of Minority Protection: Individual Human Rights, Minority Rights and the Right to Self-Determination (2000).

HERODOTUS
The Histories (Aubrey de Sélincourt, trans., Penguin Books edition printed 1985).

INGO, RUNE
"Translating from Finnish into French, German, or English," *Terminologie et Traduction* 2 (1998), 199.

KONTRA, MIKLÓS

"Don't Speak Hungarian in Public!" in *Language: A Right and a Resource* (M. Kontra *et al.* eds., 1999), 81.

LAITIN, DAVID D.

"The Cultural Identities of a European State" 25 *Politics and Society* 3 (1997), 277.

LAVERY, BRIAN

"Ireland: Speak Gaelic or Hit the High Road," *New York Times*, 19 Dec. 2002.

LEBORGNE, LOUIS

"Les Droits Linguistiques à l'École et dans l'Administration de l'Autriche-Hongrie entre 1867 et 1914," in *Language and Law : Proceedings of the First Conference of the International Institute of Comparative Linguistic Law* (Montreal, 1988) (P. Pupier & J. Woehrling eds., 1989), 325.

MACQUEEN, HECTOR L.

"Laws and Languages: Some Historical Notes from Scotland," presented at a meeting of the Ius Commune Research School in March 2002.

MARESCEAU, MARC

"The EU Pre-Accession Strategies: A Political and Legal Analysis," in *The EU's Enlargement and Mediterranean Strategies: A Comparative Analysis* (M. Maresceau & E. Lannon eds., 2001), 3.

MARÍ, ISIDOR & STRUBELL, MIQUEL

"The Linguistic Regime of the European Union: Prospects in the Face of Enlargement," paper presented at symposium in Barcelona 31 May – 1 June 2002.

MCCLUSKEY, BRIAN

"Respecting Multilingualism in the Enlargement of the European Union – the Organizational Challenge," *Terminologie et Traduction* 2 (2001), 7.

MCCLUSKEY, BRIAN

"A Different Kettle of Fish: The Challenge of Multilingual Translation in Specialist Fields" (1998).

NELDE, PETER HANS

"Contact or Conflict? Observations on the Dynamics and Vitality of European Languages," in *Language Conflict and Language Planning* (E. Jahr ed., 1993), 165.

NELLO, SUSAN S. & SMITH, KAREN E.

The European Union and Central and Eastern Europe: The Implications of Enlargement in Stages (1998).

NEUNREITHER, KARLHEINZ

"The European Parliament and Enlargement, 1973-2000," in *The Expanding European Union: Past, Present, Future* (J. Redmond & G. Rosenthal eds., 1998), 65.

OZOLINS, ULDIS

"Separating Language from Ethnicity: The Paradoxes of Strict Language Policies and Increasing Social Harmony in the Baltic States," in *Language: A Right and a Resource* (M. Kontra *et al.* eds., 1999), 245.

PALERMO, FRANCESCO

"The Use of Minority Languages: Recent Developments in EC Law and Judgments of the ECJ," 8 *Maastricht L.J.* 3 (2001), 299.

PARIJS, PHILIPPE, VAN

"Europe's Three Language Problems" (Provisional Draft 2003).

"The Parliament's Use of Language," The Scottish Parliament Information Centre SPICe Briefing 03/22, 31 Mar. 2003.

PAULSTON, CHRISTINA B.

Linguistic Minorities in Multilingual Settings (1994).

PEARL, STEPHEN B.

"Modified Babel: The Keepers of the Tower, A Guided Tour to Interpretation at the United Nations," in *Language as Barrier and Bridge* (Kurt Müller ed., 1992), 24.

PEPPER, TARA

"The Fall of Babel," *Newsweek*, 12 Aug. 2002, 60.

PUISSOCHET, JEAN-PIERRE

L'Élargissement des Communautés Européennes : Présentation et Commentaire du Traité et des Actes Relatifs à L'Adhésion du Royaume-Uni, du Danemark et de L'Irlande (1974).

RAUX, JEAN

"Towards a Pan-Euro-Mediterranean Association of Proximity," in *The EU's Enlargement and Mediterranean Strategies: A Comparative Analysis* (M. Maresceau & E. Lannon eds., 2001), 42.

RIEDER, IRMGARD

"Das Österreichische Deutsch aus der Sicht des Sprachmittlers," *Terminologie et Traduction* 2 (1997), 155.

RÍOS, ENRIQUE JIMÉNEZ

"Pasado, Presente y Futuro de la Traducción Automática," *Terminologie et Traduction* 1 (2001), 138.

SALMI-TOLONEN, TARJA

"Legal Linguistic Knowledge and Creating and Interpreting Law in Multilingual Environments," 29 *Brooklyn J. of Int'l Law* 3 (2004) 1167.

SARCEVIC, SUSAN

"Preserving Multilingualism in an Enlarged European Union," *Terminologie et Traduction* 2 (2001), 34.

SECRETARIAT

Secretariat of the Convention on Biological Diversity, *Handbook on the Convention on Biological Diversity* (2001).

SHAW, MALCOLM N.
"The Definition of Minorities in International Law," in *The Protection of Minorities and Human Rights* (Y. Dinstein & M. Tabory eds., 1992), 1.

SKUTNABB-KANGAS, TOVE
"Linguistic Diversity, Human Rights and the 'Free' Market," in *Language: A Right and a Resource* (M. Kontra *et al.* eds., 1999), 187.

SPARKS, BRIAN A.
Greek Civilization: An Introduction (Brian A. Sparkes ed., 1998), 65.

STAMMERJOHANN, HARRO
"La Fascination de l'Anglais," in *Les Langues Dans L'Europe de Demain* (F. Carton & J.M. Odéric Delefosse eds., 1994), 87.

STAUNTON, DENNIS
"Government to Seek Official EU Status for Irish Language," *The Irish Times*, 24 Nov. 2004.

STEINER, GEORGE
After Babel: Aspects of Language & Translation (3d. ed. 1998).

SULLIVAN, RUTH
"The Challenges of Multilingual, Multijural Legislation," 29 *Brooklyn J. of Int'l Law* 3 (2004), 986.

TABORY, MALA
"Language Rights as Minority Rights," 40 *Israel Yearbook on Human Rights* (1980), 167.

TABOURET-KELLER, ANDRÉE
"De L'Identité Européenne Comme Carrefour et Comme Réseau : La Place des Langues," in *Les Langues Dans L'Europe de Demain* (F. Carton & J.M. Odéric Delefosse eds., 1994), 129.

TONKIN, HUMPHREY
"Esperanto in Eastern Europe: An Insurmountable Opportunity?" in *Language as Barrier and Bridge* (Kurt Müller ed., 1992), 59.

DE VARENNES, FERNAND
"To Speak or Not to Speak: The Rights of Persons Belonging to Linguistic Minorities," Working Paper prepared for the UN Sub-Committee on the Rights of Minorities (1997).

VOTRUBA, MARTIN
"Linguistic Minorities in Slovakia," in *Linguistic Minorities in Central & Eastern Europe* (C. Paulston & D. Peckham eds., 1998), 255.

WAGNER, EMMA & MARTIN, TIM
"Fighting the Fog at the European Commission," *Terminologie et Traduction* 2 (1998), 131.

WEILER, J.H.H.
"Bread and Circus: The State of the European Union," 4 *Colum. J. Eur. L.* (1998), 223.

WITTE, BRUNO, DE
"Cultural Legitimation: Back to the Language Question," in *European Identity and the Search for Legitimacy* (Soledad García ed., 1993), 154.
WITTE, BRUNO, DE
"Surviving in Babel? Language Rights and European Integration," in *The Protection of Minorities and Human Rights* (Y. Dinstein & M. Tabory eds., 1992), 277.
WYZNER, EUGENIUSZ
"Languages in International Organizations: The Case of the United Nations," in *Language as Barrier and Bridge* (Kurt Müller ed., 1992), 7.
"You've Got Courriel," *International Herald Tribune,* 29 July 2003.

Websites

Court of Justice of the European Communities: www.curia.eu.int
Euromosaic Report: www.uoc.es/euromosaic
European Bureau for Lesser Used Languages: www.eblul.org
European Commission: www.europa.eu.int/comm
European Court of Human Rights: www.echr.coe.int
European Parliament: www.europarl.eu.int
European Union general website: www.europa.eu.int
Mercator Project: www.mercator-central.org

Table of Cases

European Court of Justice

European Court of Human Rights Cases

United Nations Human Rights Committee Cases

Permanent Court of International Justice Case

Cases from Domestic Legal Systems

Index